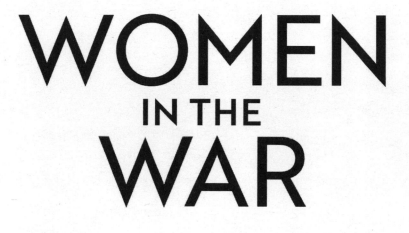

# WOMEN
## IN THE
# WAR

# WOMEN
## IN THE
# WAR

### THE LAST HEROINES OF BRITAIN'S
### GREATEST GENERATION

## LUCY FISHER

HarperCollins*Publishers*

HarperCollins*Publishers*
1 London Bridge Street
London SE1 9GF

www.harpercollins.co.uk

HarperCollins*Publishers*
1st Floor, Watermarque Building, Ringsend Road
Dublin 4, Ireland

First published by HarperCollins*Publishers* 2021

10 9 8 7 6 5 4 3 2 1

A catalogue record of this book is available from the British Library

ISBN 978-0-00-845611-5

Printed and bound in the UK using 100% renewable electricity at CPI Group (UK) Ltd

# CONTENTS

# FOREWORD

The women of the Second World War have a special place in my heart. I grew up among them in the 1940s. My mother and our neighbours worked in the factories, or on the farms, or were called up for other wartime occupations. Being too young to be drafted, I joined a group of young entertainers who sang and danced every Sunday evening for servicemen and women in their camps around Yorkshire, my home county.

My Yorkshire roots served me well when I came to London. Just as the women of the Second World War prevailed, so did I. When the women who had served at the York barracks asked me to help raise money for a monument to the women of the Second World War – no easy task as it cost in the region of £2 million – I did my best and became their patron when I was Speaker of the House of Commons.

Various sites were suggested for the monument. We went into battle, insisting its home should be the centre of White-hall, the great traditional parade route in our capital city. After many years of work, our reward was the joyous unveiling by the Queen and my dedication of the bronze master-piece sculpted by John W. Mills in July 2005. It depicts 17 of the uniforms and work clothes worn by the women whose memory we cherished that day and now.

I ended my dedication saying I hoped that future generations who passed this way would ask themselves, 'What sort of women were they?' This timely book offers answers, depicting the wartime stories of ten of the last surviving women of that era in their own words. Taken together, these oral histories illustrate the scale of the efforts and sacrifices made by women during the conflict.

At the end of the war, millions of women unceremoniously hung up their uniforms and work clothes and quietly readjusted to life in peacetime. Some returned to hearth and home to care for their loved ones and some sought fresh opportunities for employment. They showed humility about their contribution to the war in the decades afterwards, but that should not obscure its importance.

When you read the pages that follow, or pass by the monument in Westminster, I hope you will pause for a couple of minutes and pay tribute to what your mothers and grandmothers did to save their families, our democracy and our country.

*Betty Boothroyd*

The Rt Hon. Baroness Boothroyd OM
House of Lords

# INTRODUCTION

'If you have lived in a war and you've seen people dying and you've lived through bombing, you can't stay that little girl you were,' reflects 96-year-old Marjorie Clark, who was recruited as a teenager to serve with the Special Operations Executive during the Second World War. 'Of course it affected me. I always think of London and St Paul's, all the bombing. We had chaps in London ready to fight with us. We met a whole lot of individual people. It was interesting in a strange way.'

Centenarian Christian Lamb, who served as a plotter in the Battle of the Atlantic, agrees that amid the horror and tragedy of the conflict, there were positive outcomes for her sex. 'Women were spared a great deal of boredom,' she explains. 'There was a certain amount of freedom one had. It gave you choice and opportunities for doing what you wanted to do.' Catherine Drummond, now aged 99, who volunteered as a wireless operator, says her wartime experiences widened her horizons and stiffened her resolve. 'I know it changed me,' she says. 'It gave me more confidence in myself and it made me very independent. You were away from home and had to fend for yourself.'

The final years are now in sight for the remaining women of Britain's 'Greatest Generation', who displayed extraordinary fortitude and endurance on the home front and beyond in the Second World War. The women who came of age during the conflict are in their mid-nineties at the youngest, lending an urgency to the task of capturing their recollections and reflections for posterity. Ten former female recruits have related their compelling wartime experiences of triumphs and losses for this oral history.

Speaking from their homes, ranging from personal housing to assisted living accommodation, they reflect from the vantage point of later life on how they coped with danger, trauma and pressure, and tell how their spirits were fortified by friendship and romance. The aim herein has been to use first-person testimony, gathered through extensive interviews, to foreground the distinctive voice of each woman. Their words have been interwoven with other contemporary sources, including letters, diaries and newspaper reports.

Having inhabited a variety of vital wartime roles, collectively these women also represent the widest social and geographical cross-section of society. Some came from backgrounds of grinding poverty, while others enjoyed gilded childhoods before joining the war effort. They grew up in locations all across Britain and beyond the Atlantic in pre-independence Jamaica, at the time a British colony.

Their work during the conflict took place in a range of diverse environments too. Joy Hunter, who is 95, served as a secretary in Winston Churchill's subterranean Cabinet War

Rooms beneath Whitehall. For 102-year-old Jaye Edwards, an airfield in Yorkshire was the base from which she worked as a pilot delivering Spitfires to the front line. Together, these women's stories paint a rich picture that illustrates how the status and expectations of their sex evolved throughout the conflict.

The subjects of this book are also certain that the wartime contribution of women had a lasting impact on their place in society during subsequent decades. 'It became recognised that women were up to it,' declares 98-year-old Betty Webb, who assisted code breaking at Bletchley Park. Ena Colly-more-Woodstock, now 103, who travelled from the West Indies to join the British war effort in an anti-aircraft unit, agrees: 'The women held their own and showed they were strong and capable.'

Myriad female volunteers leapt at the chance to enlist from the start of the war in 1939, while conscription, introduced for women aged between 20 and 30 at the end of 1941, netted millions more. By mid-1943, 90 per cent of single women and 80 per cent of married women were employed in essential activities linked to the war effort. While they were not required to bear arms, and in all but a clutch of excep-tional units were barred from doing so, many women still took up jobs that placed them under enemy attack and the threat of death.

Several hundred thousand signed up to the female branches of the Armed Forces that were created in the year leading up to the outbreak of war. The Auxiliary Territorial Service

(ATS) was established in connection to the British Army, the Women's Royal Naval Service (WRNS) was set up to assist the Royal Navy, and the Women's Auxiliary Air Force (WAAF) was the all-female organisation linked to the Royal Air Force. Each auxiliary service had its own character and quirks. The WRNS was seen as dominated by high-born recruits, while the WAAF was widely viewed as the most meritocratic service.

The range of military roles that women were permitted to perform expanded as the war dragged on. For no service was this truer than the ATS, which at the start of the conflict allowed female enlistees to work only as cooks, clerks, orderlies, store women or drivers. Later the authorities switched tack to recruit and promote women into more than 100 specialist technical positions. This expansion of opportunities was underpinned by the early competence and dedication shown by women, but also by necessity: they were required to fill the ever-increasing vacuum left by men sent into combat.

Millions of women also took part in civilian activities to support the nation at war. The Women's Land Army (WLA), which had been set up initially in the First World War, was revived to help feed the country. Tens of thousands of female recruits volunteered to labour in the fields, many flocking from London and other urban neighbourhoods to escape the heavy German bombing campaign waged on city centres. Some enlistees were already schooled in agriculture, however, such as 98-year-old Hilda Bainbridge, who was made forewoman of her 'gang' and grew fruit and vegetables. Other Land Girls kept livestock and chopped timber.

The largest demand for female workers emanated from the new factories manufacturing armaments and ammunition. Connie Hoe, who is 99 years old, was among those who joined up to build ships, aeroplanes and tanks after she fled to Oxfordshire to escape the Blitz in London's East End, then the site of Europe's oldest Chinatown. Women were also crucial to the civil defence services, including the Air Raid Precautions, the fire service, and the Women's Voluntary Services which organised evacuations and bomb shelters.

Female experiences of the war were documented by women contemporaneously - in pictures as well as words. Artist and illustrator Evelyn Dunbar recorded women's contributions on Home Front, with a particular focus on Land Girls, and was the only full-time salaried woman on the War Artists' Advisory Committee. Dame Laura Knight was another notable war artist, who was commissioned to produce paintings to bolster the recruitment of women to factories and farms. The part played by women inspired male artists as well. Photographer Cecil Beaton captured striking images of female welders and naval volunteers on film, as well as society beauties.

The war was in some ways a great leveller between the classes, as women of all social backgrounds were drafted in to help. Even Queen Elizabeth II, then a teenage princess, enlisted in the ATS to train as a driver and mechanic in early

1945. Churchill's daughters also served their country: Diana enlisted in the WRNS, Sarah worked in the Photographic Interpretation Unit of the WAAF, and Mary operated anti-aircraft batteries with the ATS. Mary accompanied her father to the Quebec conference of 1943 to act as his aide, while Sarah travelled as his adviser to Tehran later that year and to Yalta in 1945.

Another major effect of the conflict was to propel women from the domestic sphere into a public and economic arena, overturning social conventions and affording many unprecedented levels of independence from their families and spouses. This pioneering generation built up new reserves of confidence and proved that they were 'up to it' in an array of roles, directly advancing women's equality. While the First World War paved the way for female enfranchisement, the Second World War laid the foundation for equal pay and equal opportunities campaigns, state funding for nurseries, and rights for housewives.

Despite progress, gender inequality and sex discrimination abounded throughout the war. Women were almost universally paid less than men for the same or equivalent jobs, although wage equality was achieved after intense wrangling in a handful of cases. This included the civilian Air Transport Auxiliary, where redoubtable female pilots successfully fought to be paid the same as their male counterparts. In other female auxiliary services struggles erupted over the right of women to be granted full military status. Women whose husbands died in the war also felt aggrieved at their treatment by the state, as widows' pensions were deemed unearned income and subject to the highest level of taxation.

The camaraderie between men and women was nonetheless often strong, with many delighted at the war's generation of new ways to meet the opposite sex. That is not to say that women were always welcomed into military and civilian workforces by their male counterparts, however. Some men launched savage bids to prevent the participation of female recruits, while others subjected female colleagues to derogatory comments. Male soldiers sometimes labelled female recruits in the ATS 'officers' groundsheets', a nickname that caused deep offence.

Some female campaigners also mounted objections to the Government's encouragement, and later enforcement, of women undertaking war work. Labour MP Agnes Hardie was a leading proponent of the 'maternalist position', arguing that 'war is not a woman's job' and that 'women share the bearing and rearing of children and should be exempt from war'. She also insisted that 'barrack life and camp life is not suited for women'.[1] A sizeable proportion of the female population felt a strong sense of patriotism and passionately wanted to serve their country, however.

In addition, for many women the war introduced novel and thrilling opportunities: an unexpected chance to leave home, enrol in a job, be useful, travel abroad, make new friends and embark on romances. The stories in this book chart the centrality of friendship and love during the war years, as well as sadness and loss. Some, like Christian, met their future husbands, while Ena describes forging life-long friendships, and Betty recounts developing a taste for military service that became the foundations of a proud decades-long career in the British Army. Almost all agree that their war experiences transformed their outlook on life and bolstered their belief in their abilities.

Victory in Europe was welcomed with euphoric relief, but the aftermath of the conflict was anticlimactic. 'It was almost flat. You lost the impetus. Afterwards, you just didn't quite know what to do with yourselves,' recalls 98-year-old Marguerite Turner, who served as a nurse in the Voluntary Aid Detachment. Talking about the war swiftly fell out of favour. Secrecy rules that lasted for 30 years after the conflict curbed discussion of many topics, while the persistence of a wartime culture of discretion cast a veil over others. Joy describes a tacit agreement that took root across society to focus on the brighter future ahead rather than the darker, recent past. 'It was finished,' she says of the war. 'It was over, behind us. You don't keep on about things that are behind you.'

As a result, some of the events narrated in the following chapters have not been spoken of, nor thought about, by their subjects for many decades. It is noticeable, however, how vividly the women who have contributed to this book can remember episodes that took place more than 75 years ago. Some remarked that their impressions of their war years are far clearer in their minds than events from recent decades. This phenomenon may be explained by what developmental psychologists call the 'reminiscence bump' - a significantly enhanced recollection of late adolescence and the early twenties that is observed in older adults. As a period of life infused with important milestones, it tends to form a cornerstone of an individual's identity and takes on special dominance in the memory. For those who came of age during the war, the backdrop of conflict further magnified the emotional significance of this period.

The resilience Britons exhibited on the home front in wartime continues to resonate in the modern era. 'Blitz Spirit' still underscores notions of contemporary national identity today and is the first analogy reached for in times of shared hardship. While the Second World War is a period of history that appears evergreen in the public imagination, in the past the focus has centred on the role of men. The balance has altered in recent years, however, amid rising curiosity about the unsung part played by female volunteers. This book seeks to build on that shift, offering a glimpse of the war days of ten brave women who epitomise the 'Greatest Generation', and insights into how they navigated some of the most extreme vicissitudes of life.

# Marguerite Turner

**DATE OF BIRTH:**

18 May 1923 (aged 16 at the outbreak of war)

**ROLE:**

Nurse in the Voluntary Aid Detachment (VAD)

When she thinks of the war today, it is the scent of lilacs and the roar of unseen aircraft overhead that are evoked in Marguerite Turner's mind. A single night in May 1942 has crystallised in her memory. She was stationed as a nurse at an imposing civilian house in East Sheen, southwest London, which had been converted into a medical facility. It was a role she had taken on only a year earlier, after receiving the call-up on her eighteenth birthday. She had witnessed a lot in just 12 months.

Around midnight, she seized the opportunity for a short break from the busy night shift on the ward and stepped outside. 'It was a beautiful, balmy night – quite lovely, as it can be in May,' she recalls. Standing alone, she inhaled the fragrances of the garden, but the tranquillity of that mid-war evening did not last. 'I heard a sort of engine noise from somewhere. There was no light,' she says. 'The noise grew louder and louder, then a whole lot of planes flew over. You couldn't see them; they were so high up. They went on and on. I knew they must be ours because there was no one shooting at them. I stood listening in that garden. Then they grew fainter and fainter, obviously going somewhere.'

She was captivated by the deafening din in the darkness, intuiting from the volume and duration of the cacophony that this must be a significant outbound aviation force. It was only the following morning that she learned the true significance of the mission, however. It had been the first of the controversial 'thousand-bomber raids' on German cities, masterminded by Royal Air Force marshal Sir Arthur Harris to wreak devastation and shatter Nazi morale.

The overheard bombers had joined forces with other aircraft from more than 50 bases across the UK as part of 'Operation Millennium'. Their destination that night had been Cologne. In the ensuing raid, the RAF lost 43 aircraft, while the force's aerial bombardment killed 469 Germans outright and made another 45,000 homeless by razing their neighbourhoods.

Marguerite, now aged 98, has thought often of that night in the intervening decades. The same two vivid details always accompany the memory: 'What I can remember about that afterwards was the scent of lilac and a curtain of engines.'

Born Marguerite Emily Gysin, she had joined her local Red Cross in her hometown of Wilmslow, Cheshire, after leaving school at 17. It had been a chance to gain a little experience and take some exams before she came of age and was able to join the war effort full-time. Nursing appealed because it avoided complicity in the violence raging across the Continent, she felt. The neutral stance maintained by Switzerland – the home of her father's family – had left an impression on the teenager. 'It felt rather one of those Swiss things of not wanting to be on either side,' she says. 'I thought, *I can't be on the killing side.*'

Young and energetic, she enlisted as a mobile nurse – free to deploy anywhere in Britain or abroad – with the Voluntary Aid Detachment (VAD). Established in 1909 by the British Red Cross and Order of St John, the VAD had played a crucial role in the First World War. It was the organisation in which Vera Brittain – the best-known nurse of the Great War, who had gone on to publish the 1933 bestselling wartime memoir *Testament of Youth* – had served. Crime novelist Agatha Christie also enlisted in the VAD during the earlier conflict. It was through grafting in hospitals that she had acquired an encyclopaedic knowledge of toxins and poisons, which later became key plot devices in her murder mysteries, from belladonna-laced cosmetics to cyanide-spiked champagne.

The VAD was still operating by the time the Second World War broke out, and Marguerite was one of 15,000 women who enlisted during the conflict. While its activities were closely bound up with the war effort, its nurses were civilians and did not come under military control. In theory, this distinguished the VAD nurses from those who served with Queen Alexandra's Royal Army Nursing Corps, Princess Mary's Royal Air Force Nursing Service and Queen Alexandra's Royal Naval Nursing Service. In practice, however, it meant that the VAD volunteers tended to work for the more qualified military nurses.

Marguerite's first deployment was to a big hospital outside Manchester, where she was 'thrown in at the deep end'. She was tasked straight away with changing dressings, administering medicines and ensuring her charges slept well. 'When I think of the responsibilities we had at that age, it was quite frightening,' she says. 'Ward five was the heavy medical side of the hospital. We had to do everything – literally everything. On night duty, for instance, we would have one ward which would have, say, five men on either side of the ward – about ten people.'

Hourly rounds were conducted by more qualified women from Queen Alexandra's Royal Army Nursing Corps. A significant proportion of these 'QAs', as they were known, had been dispatched abroad to treat men felled in battle. The shortage of experienced 'state-registered' nurses on the home front had precipitated the urgent enlistment of 'state-enrolled' nurses like Marguerite. She and her comrades received only the lightest of training. She recalls being instructed to practise subcutaneous injections on orange peels, but the citrus fruits were a scarce and valuable luxury during the war. 'We couldn't get them,' she explains.

The challenge for these young, newly enlisted nurses was two-fold: they had to pick up technical skills quickly, while also learning how to conduct themselves with authority around their male patients, many of whom were more than twice their age. Marguerite tried to conceal her nerves and project an air of unflappable poise. Creating the impression of composure was key to gaining the trust of the senior nurses, as well as the more domineering patients.

Reflecting now on the significant responsibility she was handed right from the start, she says unemotionally: 'That was our work. We did it.' She adds: 'You weren't asked to if you weren't competent. The QAs knew who could do it and who couldn't do it. They said, "You do this, you do that."' She acknowledges that the provisional arrangements under which she and her colleagues were drafted in to plug the shortfall in fully qualified nurses would be unthinkable in modern times. 'You would never dream of letting anyone do that work now,' without the requisite formal qualifications, she says. 'But it was a case of having to do it and there was nothing more to it.'

From the outset she dealt with grisly war wounds, which were often accompanied by the stench of rotting flesh. She developed an iron constitution and has not been squeamish since. 'Nothing would shock me now as far as illnesses go,' she says. 'I could see practically everything.' She also points out that the hygiene standards expected in clinical settings today were not considered a necessity in the 1940s. Tuberculosis was prevalent and she was instructed to care for and clean TB patients, as well as wash their sputum mugs, without any gloves or protective clothing. She admits with a grimace that she found handling the mugs – receptacles for the thick, sticky mucus coughed up from the lungs – 'rather revolting'. That aside, she and her fellow nurses did not dwell on the risk of contamination from their patients. 'We used to go in our bedrooms at night, sit down and chat in the same clothes,' she says, laughing with incredulity at the memory. 'We must have inoculated ourselves.'

Antibiotics were unavailable in the hospitals where she worked, and those patients who were in the final wasting stages of tuberculosis knew they had little time left. Death was faced with gallows humour. 'They'd say, "Night, night, nurse, I've got a date with JC [Jesus Christ] tonight." It was quite extraordinary. Everyone took living and dying as living and dying – stop. You did or you didn't.'

The high drama of nursing shifts marked a stark contrast with the happy, quiet childhood Marguerite had known, shuttling between Cheshire and her family's holiday cottage in Anglesey, north Wales, where they spent long summers sailing. It was at the latter house where she first learned that war had broken out in September 1939. 'We were sitting in my father and mother's bedroom with the wireless on,' she recalls. 'We heard Chamberlain saying, "As a consequence, this country is now at war with Germany." It was something terrible, but it didn't sink in. We went back to Wilmslow.'

She was the elder of two daughters born to Charles, a Swiss businessman who had travelled to Lancashire in the 1920s to work for his godfather, and Welshwoman Alice. Her sister Rose, who was younger by 18 months, also became a nurse during the conflict, though appeared – to Marguerite's mind, at least – to enjoy a far more glamorous war.

The girls had grown up in a 'strict but loving household' and their early years had been unblighted by upset of any kind. As a pupil Marguerite had excelled at art and enjoyed English literature. Upon leaving school in Wilmslow, she had joined a nearby repertory theatre, the Green Room. A starring role in a production of Terence Rattigan's play *French Without Tears* followed, which won her admiring write-ups in the local press. Although memorising lines proved a struggle, she was a natural on the stage and had begun to entertain ideas of a career in the theatre.

Her fledgling ambitions were extinguished, however, by the advance of war. Like many teenagers of her generation, she shelved her plans without complaint and resolved to be of use in the grave situation at hand. In the months between finishing school and turning 18, the earliest age at which she could enlist in the VAD, she volunteered at a local medical facility, known as a camp reception station, while living at home. Her mother worried deeply about her being hit by a bomb as she cycled to the unit for night shifts. Laughing, she recalls: 'My mother – I think it was a joke – said, "I'd feel safer if you'd got a colander on your head." I wouldn't have dreamed of it.'

She adds: 'It really wasn't such a silly remark. Later in the war a rocket dropped and I remember a girl was brought in. She had been walking in Croydon. The rocket hadn't hurt her, although she was very shocked, but it was the glass from the window of a shop she was passing. I spent hours sitting on her bed with a very fine pair of pincers taking slips of glass the size of the nail of your little finger out of her face. They were shallow slips. And her hair – oh, I don't know when she got rid of the glass in her hair. That would have protected you, a colander, so it might have been useful.'

Marguerite's parents were proud of their elder daughter's decision to become a nurse in the VAD and, as became customary, commissioned a photographic portrait of her in uniform, which was then displayed on the drawing-room mantelpiece for the rest of the war. At 5 foot 5 inches, with green eyes and dark-blonde hair, Marguerite was striking. She recalls now her affront at having to pay for her uniform – a blue dress, a white apron with a red cross on the bib, and a hat. 'I used to have a silk stocking round my head, to tuck my hair into it under my hat,' she says. However, for hosiery she wore lisle stockings, made from cotton. 'They were awful; they were thickish, black. Silk stockings were far too delicate for nursing work; they would ladder.' She adds: 'They were very, very much treasured. Anyone who had an American boyfriend had them.'

Leaving home earlier than might have been expected had war not broken out, Marguerite was forced to grow up quickly. Engaging with distressed families visiting their loved ones in hospital demanded emotional maturity. 'I remember an old couple coming to see their grandson,' she recalls. 'I was told, "Go and warn those two they're in for a shock." I had to prepare them – that sort of thing. There was a lot of tenderness. You had to be very tactful and understanding.'

She also sought to soothe the sharp anxieties of her patients, which ranged from battlefield trauma to broken hearts. 'One I was really upset by,' she says. 'I went into a room and there was a young officer on his bed. He was sitting down with his head in his hands. I went to him and I put my arm around him and said, "What's the matter, can I help you?" His head never moved. His batman [orderly] came up to me – a young private. He said, "He's very depressed – very depressed. Nothing will make him talk."' Pausing, she continues: 'I sat with him as long as I could, then I had to go on and do other things. But you see, we didn't have depression in those days. Or post-traumatic stress disorder. I couldn't stay there. I would have talked to his batman a lot, but I hadn't got the time to do it.'

She recalls one British soldier who arrived at her hospital after being wounded in Egypt, where British forces had been involved in the Western Desert campaign against Axis powers since 1940. He was one of scores transported home from the bitter fighting in North Africa and deposited in her hospital over several months. Gravely ill, the young soldier was nonetheless upbeat – giddy at the prospect of seeing his sweetheart again now that he was back in Britain. His enthusiasm captured the imaginations of the young nurses tending him, who rushed to ensure the best reception possible for his girlfriend. 'He'd got a photograph of her, and he was telling us all about her – so excited – saying, "She's coming to see me." So we rushed around and made him look very presentable – clean pyjamas and a bedspread; clean curtains,' she says. The reunion did not go to plan, however. 'He was on a side ward. I went off duty and I came back in the evening and I said, "Well, how did it go?" I looked at him and his face was white and drawn. She'd come back and she'd told him, ill as he was, that she'd found someone else.'

Life seemed to move faster during the war. Marguerite cycled through deployments, including stints at a variety of civilian houses on the outskirts of London that had been converted into hospitals. At one of these she witnessed for the first time the 'doodlebug' flying bombs, which were launched by the Nazis from the coast of France and the Netherlands. These unpiloted aircraft – early iterations of a cruise missile – were designed to fly until they ran out of fuel, then plunge to the ground and explode. More than 8,000 were targeted at London in a bid to cause carnage and terrorise the population. 'They asked for volunteers to go and help them when the doodle bombs started,' she recalls. 'I heard the first one going and no one could understand what it was. It made a noise, then the engine stopped, then you counted to five and there was an explosion. I saw five doodlebugs in the air at one time from my window. You could see the glow from them.'

She adds: 'We had some terrible times, but on the other hand, I was never in the Blitz at the place it was aimed for. I was always to one side of it, because all the medical stations and houses and hospitals [to which she was assigned] were out of the main bombing areas. I've driven through it in an ambulance after a raid was over, but never as a direct result of it exploding in front of me.' Fear became blunted over time and gruelling shifts afforded little time to dwell on the threat of death. 'Every night I remember going to sleep thinking, *Gosh, I wonder if I'll wake up in the morning*,' she recalls. The thought was always followed, however, by a resigned yawn, she says, laughing. '*Ah, well, I'm tired now – better get a good night's sleep.*'

Life on the wards was characterised by a strong sense of shared purpose with her fellow VADs, and lively evenings sometimes ensued. One of these took place on Christmas Eve 1942, which Marguerite recorded in the first pages of a fresh diary she received the following day.

I spent Christmas Eve until 11 p.m. on Ward 2. Well, it wasn't so bad. The only grumble I have there is that I seemed to spend the whole evening making drinks of coffee for the sisters who came to visit the ward. Our midnight meal is at 11.30, so instead of attending that, I went to a party. We had grand fun, eating mince pies and jelly, and drinking rhubarb wine and cider and blackcurrant cordial. What a mixture!

At 12.15 a.m. I was told to report to Ward 4 where I found Barrett [a fellow nurse]. Actually, I went before 12 a.m. so I could keep her company. At two minutes to 12 a.m. we were joined by Joan and another VAD, so we welcomed Christmas Day in by singing 'Auld Lang Syne' in the linen room.

At about 2.30 a.m. whilst I was resting I heard two men creeping in the ward and asking Barrett if sister was on duty. She told me afterwards that they were two young MOs [medical officers] who looked very merry and bright. However, when Barrett and I were in the office at 4.20 a.m. I heard steps again – my word, if it wasn't the same two, still up, and looking for a brighter xmas!

I really don't blame them, this place is deadly dull, and many's the time I have longed to paint it red. They were most amusing and offered to write the report for us (imagine the scandal it would have caused!). Poor dears, they just couldn't settle down … Later we hung the stockings, one on each bed. It was such a queer feeling, creeping up the ward clasping stockings, loaded with gifts. Small things such as an apple, cigarettes, matches, toothpaste and peanuts – things that always find a home with one of HM Forces.

Becoming a mobile nurse provided an opportunity to see something of England. As a child, Marguerite had enjoyed the rare privilege of having travelled abroad on annual trips to see her father Charles's relatives on the Continent. The family of four had driven to Dover, taken a ferry to Calais, then motored on to Switzerland for a fortnight's stay. The first week of the yearly trip was always spent with extended family, while the second was used to explore new areas of the Swiss countryside.

The Gysins were highly educated and formed part of an intellectual elite in Basel, the city near Switzerland's intersection with France and Germany. Charles's younger brother was the director of the Swiss National Museum. The whole family were trilingual, speaking German, French and English. Strikingly, Marguerite never heard her father speak German at home in Britain – apart from on the rare occasions he cursed. Nor did he insist his daughters learn the language, as he demanded with French.

Germany had become a taboo subject in their household long before the outbreak of the Second World War, she remembers. Her father's brothers, living on the threshold of the Third Reich, impressed on their relatives in England their concerns about Adolf Hitler from the early 1930s onwards. Charles's sister Rose, who had married German Jewish doctor Ernst Magnus and lived in Germany, confirmed the family's worst suspicions through first-hand reports. As the environment in Germany became increasingly hostile to Jews, Rose and Ernst fled to Turkey.

'The family kept saying to us, right to the very end of the war, "You do not know what they're doing in Germany now. You have no idea in England. You don't know what's happening." They knew a lot more in their country about what was going on in Germany. The whole family were horrified by it,' Marguerite says.

She was aware that her international links, and the luxury of travelling overseas as a child, were unusual for the time. While she had visited swathes of the Swiss countryside and a significant part of France, however, she had seen little of Britain before the war began. The chance to travel the length of the country to work at new stations, usually for deployments lasting between a fortnight and several months, appealed to her sense of adventure. She was also fascinated by the households in which she was billeted, captivated by the various personalities and rhythms of life at each. It was a particularly colourful family that hosted her when she was posted to the northeast. She wrote in her diary on 6 March 1943:

The army have billeted nine men here. I do hope that it doesn't mean we will have to move. We are getting to know this family a little better now. 'Nana' seems to rule the roost. She is a small, wispy woman of uncertain age, becoming a little bald on top. This slightly embarrasses her, so she is mostly to be seen wearing a large 'Carmen Miranda' turban in brown velvet, which looks rather rakish when perched over curlers. She attends to all money matters, and enters into any argument that's going, notwithstanding the fact that she's very deaf and can only hear half of what is going on.

Her daughter, runs the house. She loves to be in the limelight and succeeds. Rather a hard woman, I should say. Very kind to us, but if she didn't happen to like anyone they would be 'in for it'. Her main theme is money. 'The so-and-sos have such a lot of money, they own such and such.' 'Of course people who can afford that these days ...' Her daughter is one of the world's worst spoilt children I have ever known. She likes skating, she likes riding. Very well, [she] must ride and skate.

Later that month Marguerite wrote about the 'really tragic news' that her make-shift hospital was to be wound up. 'At the moment we are in the midst of checking all the equipment – a hopeless task,' she wrote. The permanent hospital in the town was meanwhile 'overflowing, with patients sleeping on the floor and in the linen room,' she noted. 'It really does seem false economy.'

One lengthy posting was at Shenley Hospital in Hertfordshire. Built as a psychiatric institution, it was requisitioned to become a military medical facility during the war after the primary site at Millbank in Central London became overwhelmed with patients. More than 3,000 wounded servicemen were treated at Shenley, along with high-ranking German prisoners of war. These included Field Marshal Gerd von Rundstedt, one of Hitler's most senior military leaders, who was taken there for 'diagnosis and observation' in 1945. Like many hospitals, Shenley was struck during Luftwaffe raids. It was hit by both land mines and oil bombs.

The former tore down the ceilings in three villas, while the latter sparked a fire in the laundry room, which was successfully distinguished by the hospital fire brigade.

Often Marguerite found that her expectations of a place, based on rumour and stereotype, were confounded by reality. She had been less than thrilled to learn she was destined for Nelson, a small town in Lancashire. 'I thought, *Oh, how awful! It will be sleet and rain and lots of cottages, all the same,*' she says, but concedes: 'When I got there, I was pleasantly surprised. It was the most beautiful country up in north Lancashire – absolutely lovely.' Although she was only there a fortnight in the end, the posting ranked among her favourites, due to the kindness of the elderly couple with whom she was billeted. They 'fussed about me' and lavished treats, she recalls.

Some of her new-found friends were billeted with sterner hosts. One of these was Kay, a driver in the Auxiliary Territorial Service, who was living nearby with a middle-aged medical officer and his wife. Marguerite wrote in her diary of a 'very funny incident' that erupted in her friend's house. 'It seems [Kay] was fire-watching one night and at about 12 o'clock she heard the cat meowing outside. So she went to the door and looked outside. A few minutes later the MO [medical officer] stumbled down the stairs in a terrific hurry and proceeded to search the lower rooms of the house. Then he came to Kay and demanded to know who was with her. He was gently persuaded no one was there, and returned to bed. It was not till afterwards that Kay realised what had happened. When she had coaxed the cat, she had said in a sweet tone: "Timmy, darling, come on in!"'

Marguerite's next deployment was to a medical facility in Croydon, south London, which allowed for diverting day trips into the heart of the capital. She remembers her parents travelling down to take her to lunch on her twenty-first birthday, though celebrations were cut short because her attendance was required at the hospital for a mandatory lecture on digging artesian wells, the kind that do not require a pump.

Marguerite and her new friends would often venture out on a free afternoon in their nursing uniforms, garnering significant attention from outsiders. Sometimes it even helped them secure a lift home. 'We used to catch the last train back home when we had a day off. We had to be in by a quarter to midnight,' she recalls. 'It was a very, very steep hill out of the station onto the road. There used to be crowds of people on that train and we used to walk to the top, and at the top of the hill on the main road there would be a police car waiting.' She laughs, remembering what happened next: 'These dear policemen – they were so lovely – whenever they saw anyone in nurse's uniform, they used to go up to them and look at them very sternly, take them by the shoulder and push them into the car and slam the door and drive away – taking us home. They pretended to arrest us, but it was so nice of them.'

Friends were easy to make but difficult to keep. Even today she can recite the names of the nurses with whom she was stationed for only a few weeks at a time, never to see them again after the posting ended. 'You made friends with people who were working with you at the time. One girl I made great friends with was Oriel Pakenham. Her father was a naval commander for the Western Approaches – that was a great thing,' she says.

Marguerite's parents spent the war on the Welsh coast, and she took every opportunity to visit them there during leave, even taking friends when it was possible. The family cottage was situated on a peninsula on an inland creek between Anglesey and Holy Island – 'miles away from anywhere,' she explains. It could only be reached at low tide, because the causeway on which a car could pass was flooded at high tide.

'I used to go if I was in Chester, for instance, and I had a bit of leave. I used go on the train and get off at Valley, the nearest station, and walk to the cottage and spend a couple of nights there and go back again, all through the war. I remember going with three of my friends who were nurses. We had the temerity to ring up the hospital and ask if we could have an extra day because it was a bit difficult to get off the island where we were. The answer was: "Definitely not!" After the rebuke, we had to go.'

She did her best to shield her parents from the reality of how dangerous life was on the edge of London, where she was posted to a series of the makeshift medical facilities known as camp reception stations, including the one in Croydon. 'I remember ringing my mother up from a camp reception station where we had one call a night,' she says. 'I took the call in the doctor's office, who was off duty. I was under the desk, because there were doodle bombs landing around, and my mother said, "Are you in any danger? Have you got anything happening?" and I said, "No, nothing at all." Everyone did that with their parents.' She adds that in camp reception stations where there was insufficient shelter from bombs, she and her colleagues would improvise protection. 'We used to get two mattresses on each bed,' she says. 'In a raid you used to lie on one under the bed, with another mattress on top of the bed to prevent any shrapnel coming in.'

Beyond an occasional phone call, she did not keep in regular touch with her sister during the war. 'We went our own ways. Not because of a lack of affection, but it just didn't occur to do anything different,' she says. Nonetheless, what contact they did have convinced her that her sibling was having 'a much better time' than her. Rose was a nurse attached to the Royal Navy and had been awarded the equivalent of an officer's rank, which came with enviable privileges. Marguerite, although supposed to remain independent of the Armed Forces as a VAD nurse, had been attached to the Army. At first she had also been afforded some officers' rights, but she adds: 'They soon changed that.' The Army demoted the nurses to privates and thereafter 'we had to work our way up via their exams'.

While nurses in the Navy boasted their own private mess, Marguerite and her colleagues had to share with the soldiers.

Wincing, she recalls: 'I remember the first time we had to go in for a meal with the privates. We had to hold our plates out. The [serving] man put his hand on some roast potatoes and put a handful on each of our plates. I thought, *Oh, gosh, sorry, I can't bear that.*'

After being served with bare hands and tasting the 'awful food' on offer, 'we hardly ever ate in the mess,' she says, laughing. 'But we all survived.' Instead, she and her friends 'lived off lettuce and various things we could get after rations'. She admits, however, that she missed meat – and butter, particularly slathered on hot toast. Occasionally, when she returned to Anglesey, local farmers she knew would give her illicit care packages of butter and bacon.

She was also obliged to undertake laborious cleaning duties, which her sister managed to avoid. 'We did everything, from scrubbing the beds down and cleaning them after a patient came in and out, to brushing the floors,' she says. A particularly onerous task was using tools known as 'bumpers', which were 'very heavy lead squares, like a brick with a long handle', to polish the linoleum floors. 'We had to do that. That took pounds off us,' she recalls, adding: 'Once, I remember we had two German prisoners in. We used to ask the convalescent men if they would do the "bumping" for us and the two Germans refused. I didn't know quite what to do, how to handle them.' It was rare for prisoners of war to be kept on the wards. 'A sergeant came in and said, "What's the matter?" I said, "Well, they're not inclined to help us." And he took hold of them both and said: "When I say bump, you bump." He was a tough guy.'

The workload in the VAD was heavy. Marguerite had one day off a week, which once a month was upgraded to a day and a half. 'There was very little time off. We were absolutely flat out. Everyone, not just us. We really worked hard,' she says. However, sometimes the rare opportunity to enjoy a night out arose. 'There were very few parties – we didn't get those at all,' she stresses, but adds: 'If you knew someone in the Army, they would say, "I'm on leave, will you come and have a drink?"' She spent one memorable evening in a nightclub with David Stirling, the legendary maverick who founded the Special Air Service (SAS) in July 1941. She had met him and Paddy Mayne, his infamous comrade, through a young man who had been billeted with her parents in Wilmslow during a short stint of training: Peter Warr.

Her mother and father had accommodated an array of children evacuated from heavily bombed cities such as Manchester before the young army officer turned up. They saw little of him while he was there, though occasionally her father was woken shortly before dawn as he heard the soldier leave the house for drills. Much of Peter's mysterious training at the nearby RAF Ringway – the wartime base for No. 1 Parachute Training School RAF – was conducted under the cover of night.

Marguerite eventually met him during a visit home and the pair became firm friends. Soon afterwards he was posted to Egypt, but upon his return to London he introduced her to his new comrades, David and Paddy. It was only in later years that he disclosed to her what they had been up to while overseas in North Africa. 'They used to dress up as Arabs and go out in the middle of the night and put bombs under parked aircraft and dash back again and have breakfast in Cairo,' she says.

David Stirling, who was well known even then, was charming and mischievous, she recalls. 'One night we went to a party – all of us in uniform – about eight of us. I was sitting next to him. There was a French singer and David had a plaster on his face and the continental singer – zhee talked wiv an accent like ziss, you know – said, *"Ah, le pauvre soldat, il est blessé, il est blessé!"* [Ah, the poor soldier, he is hurt, he is hurt!]' Then she turned to me and she said, "Kiss the poor man, kiss the poor man." So I kissed his little bit of sticking plaster and he put his hand over his face and said, "Don't be worried, I only cut myself shaving this morning."' The party erupted in laughter.

She says of Paddy Mayne, with a sharp intake of breath: 'He was a one.' Widely regarded as both a hero and a rogue, he was awarded the Distinguished Service Order (DSO) four times, an accolade offset by four court martials during the war. The renegades of the SAS were 'completely different' from other men, she says. 'Their characters were enormous.'

In September 1944 Peter, or Major Warr as he had become by then, parachuted into the deadly Battle of Arnhem in the Netherlands as part of 'B' Company, 10th Battalion,

Parachute Regiment. He was badly wounded in the ferocious hand-to-hand combat that ensued. 'He had his shoulder blown off,' says Marguerite. 'He was a prisoner of war and then he was brought back very quickly after that.' He, too, was given the DSO, which was awarded for distinguished service by officers of the Armed Forces during wartime, typically in actual combat and serving under fire. 'It was very good going,' she says.

His recommendation for the award, made by Brigadier John Hackett of the 4th Parachute Brigade, records an extraordinary feat of bravery. On 19 September 'he personally led the depleted Battalion in a bayonet charge through strongly held woodland to open a way for the remnants of the Brigade into the Divisional perimeter,' it notes.

With his Battalion now about 50 strong, he was then ordered to take and hold some houses in Oosterbeek on the critical North Eastern edge of the Divisional perimeter. He led the attack on each house in turn himself, and in stiff hand-to-hand fighting, in which he was wounded in the face, drove the enemy out. During these attacks he surprised and captured intact a Mk IV tank, finding the crew outside of it and killing or wounding them all with his Sten gun.

During the night 20th/21st September he encouraged and grimly drove exhausted men in defensive preparations so that on the morning of 21st September he was able to meet and drive off strong attacks by tanks, self-propelled guns and infantry, with mortar and machine gun support, during which he moved fearlessly from house to house and kept the men constantly inspired by his own magnificent example.

That afternoon a still stronger attack overran the Battalion position. Major Warr collected a handful of men and savagely counter-attacked, driving out the enemy and re-establishing the 20 men, who were now left out of the Battalion, in the same houses. With his little band of weary men, some of them wounded, he held the position against repeated attack and continuous fire at close range, with neither food nor water, often cut off and with ammunition almost exhausted, until in the rush attack during the night 21st/22nd September he was severely wounded and fell into the hands of the enemy.[2]

Warr was sent to the Luidina Hospital in Apeldoorn to convalesce. He and a comrade, Major Gordon Sherriff, planned an escape with the help of the Dutch Resistance but eventually decided it would bring suspicion upon the hospital staff and local population if enacted. Instead, they successfully requested a transfer to the German-controlled St Joseph Hospital in January 1945, with a view to conducting their escape from there. However, the pair were told shortly after that they were to be taken on to Germany, at which juncture Peter – not yet healed sufficiently to flee – urged his companion to complete his escape without him.

The city of Apeldoorn was liberated in early April and Peter returned to Britain, where he was sent to Stoke Mandeville Hospital in Buckinghamshire. Marguerite learned of his arrival back in the country from her parents, who in turn had been alerted by Peter's mother and father. She set off to see him at once, after begging an assortment of small gifts for him from friends. 'It was a hot day and I had been round the place I was at, asking, "Have you got anything you can give me that I can take?" Someone gave me an orange; someone gave me some chocolate. It was miles from the station. I had to walk and I was in uniform. All the chocolate melted,' she recalls.

When she arrived at the hospital reception, she announced the name of the patient she had come to see, which sparked a reaction from those in the room. 'All these boys crowded round me and said, "Oh, he's in an awful way – we must warn you; be prepared." I said, "Look, I'm a nurse!" I got very cross with them,' she says, laughing gently. 'He didn't look all that bad. I'd seen much worse anyway.' Peter was in the best place possible to receive care. The hospital had become a specialist facility for spinal injuries and a surgeon based there was able to rebuild his shoulder using just the remaining sinew, though his arm never functioned properly again.

Marguerite continued to visit him during his rehabilitation and they grew close. An engagement followed shortly after the war. The surgeon who had worked on Peter's shoulder became a dear friend to the couple and went on to become godfather to their eldest child, David.

Today Marguerite still has Peter's original cap badge, featuring the iconic winged dagger of the SAS – one of a bungled batch made in Egypt. Where it was supposed to say 'Who Dares Wins', they separated the words in the wrong places so it said 'Whod Are Swins' instead.

New nursing assignments arose, however, while Peter was in hospital. One of the bleaker postings was to Blackpool, where she was billeted for two months in a requisitioned hotel. 'I can remember it was cold and it smelt of seawater. I didn't like Blackpool at all,' she says. Her antipathy to the place was fuelled in part by the behaviour of a particular male soldier who was showing her unwanted attention. 'I had a small paybook with my army number, which was W515382 – see, I've never forgotten my army number! You had to hand it in to prove who you were,' she explains. 'One of the soldiers there [in Blackpool] was a particularly objectionable chap. He said, "I want you to come out with me – I want you to let me take you out." I didn't want to, but he pinched my paybook and he said, "I'll give it you back if you come and have a dance with me at the Blackpool town hall."'

She was furious but had no choice other than to attend the event in order to retrieve it. 'I had to go to the doorway. I stood right by the door until he saw me. There was a crowd there and he gave me the book, and before he could stop me, I was out like a flash, leaving him in the dust. He didn't get a dance at all. He would have been in great trouble for taking it, actually, but I didn't report him. It was too near the end of the war to bother about that.'

Eventually the Nazis surrendered and the war in Europe came to an end. Victory in Europe, declared on 8 May 1945, did not come out of the blue for Marguerite. 'You had a jolly good idea it was coming,' she says. She was in the capital on the day itself, where upon hearing the news she dashed with a friend to Piccadilly. 'It was so crowded, you couldn't move. We were really quite frightened we couldn't get out of it and get back to report for duty again,' she says. 'Then I saw a line of four sailors. Each held the back of the other one, so they made a sort of chain. The girl with me put her hands around [a sailor's] back – she had no idea who he was – and I put my arms around her waist and we just went through in the wake of these men. They were a force of nature, pushing their way through everybody.'

It was 'a real mixture' of people who took to the streets to celebrate, including all sorts of civilians, service personnel and American military police, known as 'snowdrops' due to their iconic white hats. 'I didn't once see anyone drunk or behaving badly,' she adds. 'It was just sheer exuberance. There were a lot of people together making noise and that was not something that had happened for a long time.'

After the war it was difficult to keep up with the new friends she had made in hospitals and medical facilities across the land. 'All my friends lived in very different places from me – one in the west of the country; one up in Scotland. You settled back into your home life quite quickly,' she says.

A final tragedy marred the joy she felt at the dawn of peace, however: the death of one of her closest Anglesey friends, whom she had known since childhood. 'He was a very romantic type of boy who was a poet. He was tough as nails and very good looking. He was a friend of all of ours. He had got a little peasant cottage where shepherds used to live and he'd got it converted into a little house.' She and her sister, along with other local friends, used to visit often before the war, somewhat in awe of the young man. 'He'd been to Yugoslavia and bought a donkey and written poems about it. They had been published. To our amazement, in the war he joined up and was in the Royal Engineers.'

The pair lost touch during the conflict, but she was aware he had made it through unscathed until the final juncture. 'He was dismantling a mine at the end of the war and it blew up. That was that. He was the closest friend we had who was killed …' she says, trailing off. 'That I thought particularly tragic, really.'

Marguerite was not demobbed immediately. 'You went on,' she explains. More than a year passed before she was discharged from the VAD, during which time she worked in a hospital in Epping Forest. While she was there she was forced to sign the Official Secrets Act ahead of a senior intelligence officer undergoing surgery, since the authorities feared he was at risk of blurting out state secrets as he came round from the anaesthetic.

Delirium in patients was common, she recalls. 'You had to soothe them down, because they were almost tight [drunk] when they came to, saying all sorts of nonsense.' She and a colleague were warned by their superiors that the important patient 'could say anything to you' and that his utterances were to be kept in the strictest confidence. The chance to hear classified war information from a VIP patient was a thrilling prospect, but their hopes were dashed. They 'listened avidly', but the man's burblings were unintelligible.

The period after the war was strange. 'It was almost flat,' she says, adding that the sense of purpose that had spurred people on during the conflict had finally dissipated. 'You lost the impetus. Afterwards, you just didn't quite know what to do with yourselves.'

Marguerite had little time to dwell on this, however. After taking a holiday with Peter and his parents in Devon, the pair became engaged and then swiftly married. They moved to Bisley, Surrey, where they lived in a brick and timber cottage. 'Life went on in its own way,' she says. 'I had to learn how to become a housewife. I had £5 a week for house-keeping and, my goodness me, well, I thought I was rich.'

She recognises that her wartime experiences changed her. 'It's embedded in you. You accepted it; it was a part of you. What I did in the war was what everyone did in the war. Perhaps they didn't do exactly what I did, but they went up in a plane in danger; they went in a boat and risked being drowned – you just did it.' She concludes: 'You just accepted it, but it must have enlarged one's being.

What you'd done gave you confidence. It made you more self-sufficient and independent. It was a great part of our lives.'

Marguerite and Peter went on to have four children, nine grandchildren and thirteen great-grandchildren. The couple later divorced and she went on to marry another war hero, Wing Commander Robert Turner.

# Marjorie Clark

**DATE OF BIRTH:**

14 July 1924 (aged 15 at the outbreak of war)


**ROLE:**

Wireless operator and coder in the First Aid Nursing
Yeomanry (FANY), attached to the Special Operations
Executive (SOE)

Marjorie Clark was a reserved schoolgirl from the Welsh
Valleys when the war broke out. By the end of the conflict,
she had grown into a confident and self-possessed young
woman. 'I became someone to stand on my own two feet,'
she declares. She was posted first to North Africa, then to
Italy, and was tested to an extraordinary degree throughout
her wartime service. She survived a torpedo attack on her
ocean convoy, fell in love with a Special Operations Executive agent and endured the anguish of his disappearance
behind enemy lines. She was struck down by illness and

suffered a breakdown. Her determination and good humour did not desert her, however, despite the trials she faced.

Her contribution to the war commenced in 1943, when she was singled out for a special role by the headmistress of her school. She was talented at maths, gifted on the sports pitch, discreet and dependable – in short, an ideal fit for the First Aid Nursing Yeomanry, known as the 'FANY'. She was duly invited to London for an interview.

The independent, self-funded organisation had been founded in 1907 with the aim of sending women with first aid and other skills to the front line. A volunteer cavalry force, which explains the word 'yeomanry' in their title, the women of the FANY were initially deployed on the battle-fields mounted on horseback to tend to wounded soldiers. By the middle of the Second World War the organisation had extended into intelligence and other field work, as well as nursing. Around 2,000 women – a third of the corps' strength – were deployed in the Special Operations Executive (SOE), the highly secretive organisation created by Winston Churchill to 'set Europe ablaze'. The SOE were tasked with conducting espionage, sabotage and reconnaissance against the Axis powers in occupied Europe, and bolstering local resistance movements. It was the SOE for which 17-year-old Marjorie was to be considered. 'I found out after the war why the FANYs were held in great esteem,' she says. 'It was Churchill's idea to start the SOE and he wanted women who were intelligent and could hold a secret. I tell you, I don't know about being intelligent, but I could hold a secret.'

Born Andolyn Marjorie Beynon Lewis in Ystalyfera, a small mining village near Swansea in South Wales, Marjorie never knew her mother, Andolyn, who died two months after her arrival due to complications from the birth. The tragedy saw Marjorie and her elder sister Gwenda raised by their father, Howell, and maternal grandmother, Maria.

Howell had fought on the Western Front during the First World War, where he had been injured three times. Scarred by his experiences of trench warfare, he suffered night terrors and often cried out in his sleep, waking his young daughters. A proud patriot who had played rugby for the Welsh national team before the war and captained Swansea afterwards, he ensured that both his daughters spoke Welsh as well as English.

The family owned a small coal mine, and Marjorie's abiding memory of her girlhood is the sight of male workers emerging blackened from the shafts before taking their daily bath. Her father was a kind man and she enjoyed 'a very happy childhood,' she says, adding that her generation escaped many of the pressures that young people face today. She had a dozen-odd male cousins, but spent most of her time with her sister. 'Not having a mother, she was particularly close,' she reflects.

She attended the village primary school, and afterwards a convent in Swansea, where she recalls playing hockey on the beach. Aged 13, she took part in a school trip – her first journey overseas – to Germany. Looking back now, she marvels at the timing of the visit. It was just a year before war broke out, though she was unaware of the growing geopolitical tensions at the time. 'We went from place to place and never spoke to any Germans,' she says, explaining that she observed no hostility or ill will towards the school party as they visited Cologne and a series of other towns on the Rhine. She noticed that windows were boarded up but did not realise that this was designed to shut in light that could escape and potentially aid enemy aircraft during future night raids. 'I was aware that "blackout" was being practised there,' she says. 'I just thought they wanted to keep the sun out.' She regrets that a photograph was taken of the school girls posing in front of a Nazi swastika. 'There's a picture of my group in Germany with, unfortunately, a German flag in the background,' she says.

After Marjorie had spent three years at the convent, her father decided to move her. She recalls him declaring one day: 'Enough of this. She must have a bit of discipline.' A relative had attended Cheltenham Ladies' College, so Howell decided his daughters would follow suit and he enrolled them at the well-known Gloucestershire boarding school. Marjorie had four years of education ahead of her before receiving the school certificate, while Gwenda had two. The fees were expensive and the girls' attendance was a burden on the household finances. Marjorie was painfully conscious that she hailed from a less gilded background than most of her new peers at the school. Disorientated by their strange manners and unfamiliar cultural references, she was conspicuous due to her Welsh accent and felt sorely out of place. Her classmates compounded her insecurities by mocking her for her differences.

'When I went to Cheltenham, I realised I was a different category from all these posh young English girls who went to "deb" [debutante] dances. I'd never heard of such a thing,' she says. 'It was very, very tough. I was ridiculed because I had a Welsh accent. They were horrible.' She adds: 'Cheltenham Ladies' College offered you elocution lessons. I had to go to this dreadful, dreadful woman – and I can see her now.' Marjorie was forced to practise speaking with a pencil clamped between her teeth. 'You couldn't understand a thing you were saying,' she remarks, 'but apparently that was "correct".' She felt hesitant among her self-assured classmates, but found an opportunity to prove her mettle on the sports field. 'You got up early in the morning and the hard balls were thrown at you – and these dear ladies had never seen hard balls,' she says, laughing. 'Well, I could catch them all, so that was good.' She was an enthusiastic cricketer, captaining the first XI, and lacrosse player. After a difficult start fledging friendships began to form, and, reflecting on her experiences now, she concludes that she 'really appreciated' the school. 'They found out whether you'd got anything in you. I enjoyed my years there, mostly playing cricket.'

She was taken aback when war broke out. 'I was at school, trying to pass my exams. We were not aware. I didn't realise how bad the situation was,' she says. She felt 'very strange' about her visit to Germany just a year beforehand. The War Office swiftly requisitioned the school and transformed the sports pitches into potato fields as part of a government move to boost domestic food supplies. Ms Popham, the headmistress, faced the logistical headache of finding new accommodation for several hundred pupils. Marjorie was among 100 girls sent to stay at Cowley Manor, a grand house owned by a noted children's author named Cyril Heber-Percy. She was delighted with the new digs, which boasted a lake, spa complex and chapel. The girls travelled to the school campus twice a week and continued to work towards their school certificate. They also enrolled in the Girls' Training Corps, an organisation that was set up in 1941 to prepare teenage girls aged 14 and over for service, teaching them first aid, Morse code, aircraft recognition and other skills useful to the war effort.

Marjorie opted to assist the fire brigade, harbouring the ulterior motive of wanting to meet young men, since male cadets at nearby Cheltenham College also volunteered for it. The heads of the two schools had other ideas, however, and conspired to prevent their wards from meeting. The girls were restricted to the high street, while the boys were directed to the promenade, ensuring that 'never the twain shall meet,' she wrote in the school magazine decades later.[3]

As the end of her final year at school approached, Marjorie took the entrance paper for Oxford University and won a place. After due consideration, however, she declined to take it up. She remains resolute that this was the right decision. 'I had the great sense to realise Oxford was not the place to go to, because the war had come,' she says. By this time the Blitz was wreaking devastation across the country and she was alive to the sacrifices being made by her male peers. 'I remember St Paul's burning; young men sent to countries in Europe. I thought, *No*,' she says of further study.

Another path was already opening up. She was one of two pupils selected by Ms Popham to meet government officials who visited the school in search of recruits for skilled, secretive roles. She passed the preliminary interview and was summoned to offices at Hyde Park Corner in February 1943 for assessment by the First Aid Nursing Yeomanry. 'I'd never heard of the FANYs,' she recalls, laughing.

The interview was conducted by Marian Gamwell, who had been appointed commander of the FANY after a fallout with the Auxiliary Territorial Service, the women's branch of the British Army. Having volunteered in France during the First World War, she had moved to Zambia with her sister to run a coffee farm, before being called home to help during the Second World War. She was a formidable character. Marjorie recalls: 'The queen bee said to me, "Welsh? You'll be a wireless operator." I can remember them saying, "You're musical."' Despite the Welsh enjoying a reputation for singing, Marjorie was not a keen musician. However, she did not correct the false inference.

It was only decades later that she realised 'it was quite a distinguished thing to be part of the FANYs'. She had little conception of what to expect from the organisation or her role as a wireless operator when she enlisted. 'There I was, doing this thing I'd never heard about,' she says.

She was to be part of the FANY contribution to the SOE, which had hubs across Europe, North Africa, India and the Far East. The women deployed to these hubs, and to secret units on the Home Front preparing for potential invasion, worked as coders, signallers, forgers, dispatchers and even undercover agents. There were four fields in which female SOE recruits were trained: motor transport, wireless telegraphy, codes and general skills. The women tended to be recruited from public schools. This was in alignment with the background of most of the men in the SOE, reflecting the social biases of those in charge of the organisation. Public schools were also viewed as providing stronger training in maths and sciences, underscoring the belief that their alumnae would be better equipped to deal with codes and ciphers.

Marjorie's war records show she was officially enlisted into the 'corps unit' on 13 April 1943. Howell was listed as her next of kin, while Ms Popham and a local doctor in Swansea were her referees. She started her basic training at Overthorpe Hall, a requisitioned house in Banbury, Oxfordshire, that later housed a girls' school. On her very first day she met Nancy, a volunteer from Norwich, with whom she was to serve throughout the rest of the war. The pair forged a close, sometimes stormy relationship.

Marjorie was unimpressed by the training she received at the facility. While a few basic first-aid skills were imparted, chores formed the central pillar of the recruits' daily routine. 'I cleaned taps for two weeks and I thought that was a wonderful way to win the war,' she remarks wryly.

Several weeks later she was sent to a nearby base at Henley, which was run by the SOE, where she learned the code and cipher systems used by overseas British stations to communicate with agents in the field. The pace of the course was relentless. A significant proportion of the trainee wireless telegraphy operators could not keep up and were forced to drop out. The recruits had to learn quickly and be able to deploy their skills at speed: tapping out messages in Morse at a high rate of words per minute. The aim was to reduce the amount of time it took to transmit or receive a message to a strict 15-minute window, in order to minimise the risk to agents on the ground who faced the danger of enemy forces detecting their radio sets whenever they used them.

At the end of four months of gruelling training, Marjorie was sent north to Dunbar in Scotland to put her skills to the test by sending and receiving signals to and from the Henley base. Rehearsal in real-world conditions was essential to understand how climatic and atmospheric conditions could distort the messages. Eight weeks later she discovered she was to travel overseas. It was a prospect that was terrifying and thrilling in equal measure. She relayed the news first by phone to her father, grandmother, sister and Doris – the housekeeper, who was considered a much-loved member of the family – and then wrote to them. The evolution of her response, from barely concealed shock to giddy excitement, is demonstrated in four letters she wrote home in quick succession before setting sail. They provide a unique insight into her contemporaneous thoughts and voice. In the first, an undated four-page missive on writing paper stamped with an emblem bearing a cross and the script 'F.A.N.Y. – Women's Transport Service', Marjorie wrote:

*My Darling All,*

*I expect my voice came as a shock to you over the phone this morning. I didn't quite know how to break the news to you because it wasn't a very pleasant subject. Anyway, Daddy, I knew you'd be brave about it because really there's nothing to worry about – a whole mob of us are going and everything will be in order.*

*The chief thing is that Nancy and I will be together and really we'll be very happy. In any case we'll have embarkation leave and I'll be able to see you all.*

*We'll be leaving here on Monday and going to F.A.N.Y. HQ in London and then I don't know what will happen. In any case I shall let you know of my whereabouts.*

*I know how you are feeling because I feel the same way, but when you think what a lovely experience it will be, I'm sure you'll be pleased and think of it in the right way. We'll be able to see foreign countries and there are a lot of us together. The officer says it's a really wonderful opportunity.*

*So Grandma, Gwenda and Daddy, please be brave as I am – in any case the war will soon be over and we'll be back again. I shall be seeing you all again soon. Daddy, it was very sweet of you to answer the way you did: 'Please yourself.' I knew you'd take it in the right way. That's all until we meet. Everything is in order so please don't worry. I know you'll take it in the right way.*

*All my love as ever,*

*Marjorie*

She followed it up with another letter from Dunbar shortly afterwards. In the missive dated 29 October 1943, she wrote:

*My Darling All,*

*Here's another letter because I've been thinking about you all today. I wrote to you this morning as soon as I had been on the telephone but feel that I must write again.*

*I hope you have all more or less recovered from the shock now – as I have. Here's some good news. Another girl who is coming along with me is the married woman from Swansea – Pat by name, so I will have her company when I come on leave, etc.*

*Will be leaving this place definitely on Monday and maybe tomorrow. Have to be in Henley on Monday evening, then we have to go up to HQ on Tuesday morning to get all the news. All we know so far is that we're going abroad and that very soon. Otherwise we know as little as you do.*

*For the present don't write because I haven't got a definite address to give you. In any case I'll write and give you any news there'll be to give. But then I shall be seeing you soon I hope.*

*I want you all to be very cheerful about this decision of mine because I feel I am doing the right thing. Just you be happy too – that's all I want in the world and I too will be alright. So please, when I do come home on leave, be happy and realise that I shall be as safe as anything and have got Nancy with me. She really is one of the sweetest girls I've met.*

*So I'll be spending xmas either in Cairo, India or N. Africa. It remains to be seen. Will write again when any other news turns up. Meanwhile keep cheerful and realise that everything's for the best. Have sent home all my mufti clothing.*

*As ever,*

*Marjorie*

Five days later, Marjorie updated her family on her activities in London.

*31A Wilton Place, London*
*Wednesday, 1 p.m.*

*My Darling All,*

*I rang you up last night to tell you I was safe and well. Nancy and I had been down to Henley to collect my wireless, etc., and then gave us a roaring welcome. We came back to London last night because we have to stay at HQ.*

*Today we were issued with our tropical kit and really we look a scream in it – mugs, camouflage nets, bedding, etc. Two whole kit bags full. Then tomorrow we have to see the doctor at 8.45 p.m. and then we HOPE HOPE HOPE to get a few hours' leave. It really is a waste of time here because yesterday we were free all day after lunch, today we have the afternoon and evening to ourselves and then tomorrow we'll have the morning and afternoon.*

*This afternoon I am going to see about trains to Swansea on Thursday – I may be free after seeing the doctor. In any case [I] shall wire you tomorrow.*

*Money goes so quickly here because we have to pay for our stay and food here in HQ. Someone said we were only allowed to take £15 with us.*

*We had our passports done yesterday and the photos are ghastly – but then they always are. We were also told where we were going, but that I can't tell you – until I get there.*

*Well, this is all for now. I sent a parcel of dirty washing home to Doris this morning – please return it as soon as it has been washed.*

*Going out with Nancy now to buy some marking ink.*
*All my love,*
*Marjorie*

*P.S. Travelled up with a very nice soldier and at*
*Paddington he helped get me a taxi. When saying*
*goodbye he said, 'Remember there'll always be an*
*England.'*

Finally, before leaving the country, Marjorie wrote one last letter to her family, to which she appended the leftover pages of her ration book, insisting: 'Use up the enclosed coupons because they're of no use to me.'

*F.A.N.Y. 9.11.43*
*My Darling All,*
  *Now that I am about to leave this country I feel I must*
*write to thank you for everything you've all done for me.*
*Believe me, I appreciate it very much and in turn I hope*
*to pay you back one day.*
  *Daddy, thank you for all the money you've ever given*
*me – given ungrudgingly too. Thank you for sending me*
*to Cheltenham and for giving me the best, always.*
  *Grandma, thank you for bringing me up as Mammy*
*requested and for devoting so much to me. I appreciate*
*it, believe me.*
  *Gwenda, thank you for such loving kindness and*
*devotion you've always shown me. For you I wish a*

*speedy recovery to your former state of health and all the
very best of everything this world can give you, for,
believe me, you deserve it.*

*Doris, thank you for attending on me and being
willing to do anything at any time. But do curb your
temper, old girl, and look after everyone.*

*Well, it's cheerio for the present – we must never say
goodbye. Remember, I shall be thinking of you every day
and my thoughts will often wander back to you all at
home. I shall write often and shall be glad to have your
letters too. By the way, here is Nancy's father's address in
case you ever want to get in touch with him.*

*All my love as always. God bless and keep you all safe
for my return.*

*Marjorie*

*Will write as soon as possible so expect a letter when you
see one and don't worry.*

Reflecting on that time now, Marjorie says quietly: 'I never
saw my family again till the end of the war.'

After her initial surprise at learning she was to travel overseas – only her second trip abroad – any sense of trepidation
wore off. 'It wasn't a thing in our generation,' she says. 'We
weren't scared. There was a real sense of excitement, and it
was my duty, in a way. You just went and never regretted it.'
She and Nancy were among only a dozen or so women and

several thousand men aboard the *Monarch of Bermuda*, a turbo-electric passenger steamship converted from an ocean liner into a troop transport, when it set sail from Liverpool in November 1943. Its destination was the SOE's Mediterranean headquarters: Algiers.

Marjorie's companion was popular with the male personnel on board. 'Nancy – she was a right one,' she says, laughing. 'She attracted all the good-looking men. We were never short of them.' Peter Ustinov, who went on to become an Oscar- and Bafta-winning actor, was among them. Then a private in the Army, he was appointed as batman, or orderly, to fellow actor David Niven, an officer. The pair co-wrote and starred in *The Way Ahead*, the classic Second World War film about a group of civilians conscripted into the British Army and shipped to North Africa. Nancy spent time with the actor on board the ship, Marjorie recalls. Of herself, she adds: 'I wasn't looking for romance at the time.'

She was absorbed instead by the novelty of life onboard ship. During the fortnight-long voyage, commandos passed the time by staging tug-of-war contests on deck. The prevalence of food that had been unavailable for much of the war, including tomato ketchup, was an unexpected pleasure. The vessel sailed as part of a convoy transporting 43,000 soldiers to three destinations: Algiers in Algeria, Alexandria in Egypt and onwards through the Suez Canal to Mumbai, then Bombay, in India. She acknowledges that an ocean journey to exotic, faraway ports may suggest a hint of 'glamour' but warns that the reality was grittier. Another contemporary account by a FANY named Christine Hoon recorded widespread seasickness, nicknamed 'mal de mer', and an outbreak of bronchial flu aboard the ship.

It was also highly dangerous. 'I went out on this troop ship and we were torpedoed,' Marjorie reveals. On 20 November, Allied ships to the northeast of the convoy were ambushed by German U-boats. The convoy was attacked shortly afterwards, having navigated the Strait of Gibraltar. Marjorie recalls flashes of light streaking across the sky as the first torpedo exploded into a nearby ship. The newspapers reported that 30 German heavy bombers joined the battle, which was countered by fighters of the Northwest African Coastal Air Force. Nine enemy planes were shot down in total.

Finally the *Monarch of Bermuda* neared its first destination. Christine Hoon wrote in her diary: 'At breakfast time we sighted the coast near Algiers, pine-covered slopes dotted with dazzling white villas, and as we steamed into the harbour the town looked most attractive.' The ship disgorged the 40-odd FANYs along with hundreds of troops. Marjorie's unit travelled onwards to a secret base at the Club des Pins, a resort based a few kilometres outside Algiers. Code-named 'Massingham', it served as the headquarters from which the SOE's Mediterranean operations were coordinated. Margaret Pawley, another FANY who arrived there alongside Marjorie and Nancy, later described how the women slept on camp beds on stone floors in sparsely furnished quarters, which had no heating. Letters were immediately sent home begging for pillows and dressing gowns to be sent.[4]

Allied forces had first landed in Morocco, Algeria and Tunisia a year earlier in autumn 1942 as part of 'Operation Torch'. The invasion had successfully forced the surrender of Vichy French forces in North Africa. From that point onwards the territories had provided a forward command, communications and supply base for Allied operations against Axis powers in southern Europe. Ahead of the bid to recapture Western Europe via the Normandy landings, Winston Churchill had identified the Mediterranean as the 'soft underbelly' by which to attack Hitler's Europe. After the Allies seized Sicily, the invasion of Italy began in September 1943 with landings in Salerno and Reggio in the south, cities from which the Allies pushed north.

No sooner had Marjorie arrived in Algeria than it was decided a unit of FANYs was urgently needed in Italy. The tempo of operations was increasing and wireless telegraphy officers were required. Once again, therefore, she set sail across the Mediterranean. 'Six of us were shipped to the bottom of Italy to Taranta. We came up that coast to Monopoli, where No. 1 Special Force was stationed,' she explains. This was the name given to the SOE operating in Italy, where the organisation had been helping to build partisan resistance groups in the north and the Alps following the collapse of Benito Mussolini's Fascist regime in July

1943. It was only upon her arrival that Marjorie learned she was part of a top-secret unit.

She vividly recalls stepping off the ship at the fishing port of Monopoli and discovering that she had travelled alongside captured Nazi soldiers. She recalls looking back at the ship: 'It had German prisoners of war in the hold, I remember. They were the first German prisoners I had seen. They poked their tongues out at us, and we pulled our tongues out back at them. So much for a lady from Cheltenham!'

Monopoli was a 'delightful little place' of around 30,000 inhabitants, with castles dating from the eleventh and sixteenth centuries. Today a prosperous tourist resort, it was 'very primitive' in the 1940s, Marjorie says. 'They'd never seen people in uniform, if you can imagine. There were no restaurants.'

At the local camp, code-named 'Maryland', the women were once again assigned to an austere dormitory. The camp beds were 'very uncomfortable' and those at the far end of the room were shielded from the elements by a single sheet of tarpaulin. Hot water was also in short supply. Nonetheless, the FANYs were given a warm welcome, with local cooks devising a feast of porridge and bacon to remind the young women of home. The recipients appreciated the gesture, despite the cooks serving the two items together.

Work soon began in earnest, with gruelling 12-hour shifts becoming the norm and a hard taskmaster known as 'Captain

Oddjob' overseeing their labours. The responsibility shouldered by Marjorie was considerable. One of the most important aspects of her job was learning the characteristic style, or 'fist', of the agents to which she was assigned. Monitoring any slight changes in the way each man tapped out Morse code while out in the field was the primary method of detecting if he had been captured.

She was part of a six-woman group operating wireless sets. 'You were listening for faint signals,' she says, explaining that it was an exhausting task when performed for hours on end. Sometimes this involved listening for signals from agents who had not been heard from in months. 'It was very interesting, quite hard work,' she says.

Shortly after her arrival in Italy, she met a tall, bearded officer. Sub Lieutenant Robert 'Bob' Clark was one of four officers in the para-naval unit of No. 1 Special Force posted to the camp, and there was immediate chemistry between Marjorie and this quiet, thoughtful man. The pair grew close and the fledgling relationship became a much-needed antidote to her stressful role and his dangerous work. Bob had been recruited as a field officer in the SOE after enlisting in the Royal Navy Volunteer Reserve. He, too, had sailed to Algeria in November 1943, before moving on to Monopoli the following month.[5] He was part of a unit that infiltrated and exfiltrated agents behind Nazi lines by boat and submarine and was responsible for planting bombs and blowing up a train.[6] He and a comrade were stationed in floating quarters on the *Eduardo*, a 130-tonne boat designed for Atlantic fishing and subsequently converted by the Italians into a minesweeper.

As Marjorie got to know Bob, she was only aware of the faint outline of the missions he undertook, since he was sworn to secrecy. Despite both belonging to a small group of trusted SOE personnel, information was shared only on a need-to-know basis. 'They would go off on duties up the Adriatic Coast, bombing and performing rescues – all sorts of things they never talked about,' she recalls. 'All we wanted to know is when we could see each other.' Since he was often away from the camp, he gifted her his comfortable Navy-issue bed as a token of affection. She took to heart his strict instructions to keep hold of it, recalling with laughter: 'I turned up at the end of the war, still hanging on to this camp bed.'

When he was in camp Bob wrote to her daily, scribbling romantic messages on foraged scraps of paper and slips of cardboard. He would write on 'anything he got hold of,' she says. 'We'd see each other during the day and I got a letter in the evening.' The letters, which numbered more than a hundred in total, remain cherished possessions, preserving memories of their early relationship in Monopoli. They document trips up the coast to Bari, the main town in the region, for dinner, films, concerts and plays. Sometimes he would write suggesting tea on the *Eduardo*, while other times he would offer to collect her at the end of her shift at the signals office 'armed with a bottle of gin' to devour on the harbour wall. For Bob, life ricocheted between tense military missions and relaxed, sun-soaked weeks by the sea with Marjorie. The latter proved a tonic to cope with the former. 'I think you stood between me and the madhouse,' he told her in one letter.

In lieu of restaurants in the fishing village, a farmhouse inland offered an opportunity to dine out. Trips there made for memorable evenings, with copious amounts of the local alcoholic spirit served in a bid to distract from the slow service. 'They had to catch the chicken, kill it, feather it, cook it – by which time we were under the table, I think,' recalls Marjorie. There was plenty of time to enjoy a drink 'if you're waiting three hours for a chicken,' she adds. 'They were romantic days. Then back to work.'

In Monopoli the Brits drank a local 'version of wine', similar to vermouth, which differed markedly from the wine to which they were accustomed. In addition, wherever the Navy travelled gin tended to be abundant, and this was the case in Monopoli. The same could not be said of mixers to drink it with, however. 'We had gin and water,' Marjorie says, remembering it with horror. At the time she smoked, and deliveries of her favoured Players cigarettes became a useful bargaining chip with which to obtain other goods. 'My father used to send me duty-free and I used to exchange them with a local Italian for underwear,' she says. 'The officer in charge would wonder how all these Italians were getting cigarettes. Well, I couldn't smoke them all, so I did right by the others. I got this lovely underwear.'

While romances were not uncommon, platonic relationships also took root between the female FANYs and male SOE agents. 'There were wonderful friendships – all these men, different nationalities, and then, you know, there was no hanky-panky or what do you call it now. You could trust them, you know? Well, almost all of them,' she says, adding: 'It's quite different today.' Since there were dull spells when not much seemed to be happening, the group would embark on local adventures, or else devise comic songs to entertain themselves.

The merriment and antics dovetailed with the horror and tragedy of war. 'We worked with some of the partisans, so we could differentiate their sending of the Morse code from the Germans'. They had a different touch somehow,' she says. 'But these were young boys – 17, 18 years old – who would have been shot, of course. Such lovely boys.' She was traumatised by the death of some of the young men with whom she worked. 'These Italian boys, they were friends,' she says sadly, adding: 'I think of my grandchildren – what they would feel like to fight for their country and be shot. I wonder how many people who go to Italy think of the Italians who died? Not many.'

Bob was also deployed on perilous missions. Before one sortie behind enemy lines in May 1944, he joked that he had prepared everything except his 'last will and testament'. The black humour belied his own apprehension about the task ahead. He decided to give Marjorie his watch, cloaking the significance of the gesture by insisting it was simply a loan because hers was broken.

She also enjoyed some expeditions outside the camp. On 4 June, Allied forces finally pushed as far north as Rome and seized possession of the city. It was the first capital to be liberated from Nazi occupation. Although somewhat over-shadowed by the D-Day beach landings on the Western Front two days later, it was a momentous event that marked the culmination of months of hard fighting. Several days after American forces marched into Rome unopposed, since the German 10th Army had retreated north, Marjorie was among the first female Allied personnel to enter the liberated city. 'We were wending our way up from southern Italy into the north,' she recalls. 'I tell you, I went into Rome days after it was liberated. What a party!'

Illness was an inevitability for many UK servicemen and women based in the humid climate of southern Italy. Malaises became so common that an eleventh-century house in Ravello, a scenic village on the Amalfi Coast near Naples, was transformed into a convalescence camp. Owned by British aristocrat Lord Grimthorpe, Villa Cimbrone had been a favourite pre-war retreat for the Bloomsbury set, including Virginia Woolf, Vita Sackville-West and Lytton Strachey. In 1938 it became famous as the sumptuous back-drop to the film star Greta Garbo's elopement with her lover, the conductor Leopold Stokowski. In the event, the marriage was never consummated, but the villa nonetheless took hold as a place of high romance in the public imagination.

It was here that Bob was sent to recuperate, run-down and beleaguered by an undiagnosed malady, after returning from a three-week mission. Marjorie was given leave to accompany him, so the pair set off on the four-hour journey to the villa, where they stayed in separate rooms. He later described that special period as 'seven very happy days' in a note to her.

Their contentment was punctured on their return, however, by the intrigue their budding romance had sparked among some of their comrades. The negative reaction of people they had considered their friends was a disappointment. It did not deter them from pursuing their relationship, but it did lead to unpleasant situations. Marjorie was particularly upset that Nancy and the other FANYs appeared to have taken against her, leaving her shut out and isolated from the group. Her luck worsened: she caught malaria and had to be transferred to a hospital in Bari for a week. Bob visited her and wrote to her afterwards: 'It is only a few hours since I saw you, but already it seems like a decade. For God's sake, do not be too long in that awful place.' He was swiftly redeployed on another mission, however. After Marjorie's fever broke, she began to recover, but it was not to be the end of her ailments. She was struck down yet again by illness, likely caused by an infected mosquito bite, which led to jaundice.

Her spirits plunged and she tumbled into emotional free-fall. It was only later that she realised she had suffered a breakdown, depleted by illness and overwhelmed by the mounting pressure of her work. She had tried to ignore the growing strain of her signals role, until finally it had become unmanageable. 'When you've got earphones on all day listening to noises, listening for noises, after a while it gets a bit much. Listening to these sounds on a radio when it's been blasted by the Germans all the time is difficult for your concentration,' she explains.

Bob, deployed on a mission, was unaware that she was in crisis. She was sent back to Ravello, but this time to a 'rest camp' for recuperation from nervous exhaustion. It was populated by young infantrymen suffering burn-out, who appeared haunted by the prospect of a return to the front line. When she returned to Monopoli, she told her superiors she could not continue with wireless telegraphy. They were understanding and transferred her to a coding job. She preferred the new role, encoding and decoding messages. 'I could see what these codes were – not that I could talk about it. You realised what troop movements were happening, that sort of thing. It was easier on the ear than having a muffling noise all day long, which was terrible,' she says.

She had also made up with Nancy by the end of the summer, which made life more agreeable again. She holds no lasting grudge against her friend over their fallout. 'You know what people are like,' she remarks. 'She was my best friend to the end. I had a steady boyfriend ... so she probably was a bit jealous. You get that today, don't you?'

The following month she received a letter from Bob, sent from a secret location further north, which provided testimony to the strength of his love for her. It also encapsulated his awe at the fragility of life in war.

*Darling Marjorie,*

*I started to write a letter to you almost a week ago, which has now been torn up owing to antiquity …*
*My fortunes have been fluctuating considerably – on several occasions, either alone or with Hilary [a senior comrade], there have been opportunities for our temporary return, but as yet, darling, no luck at all; and how I regret it.*

*We cannot complain about life here, for it is very lazy, comfortable and luxurious. In this house we are quite spoiled – always eggs for breakfast, which has generally been at half-past nine …*

*Yet, despite all this 'wizzo' living, I cannot say I have been content – all these new experiences are as nothing when I am missing you. It is now over a fortnight since the last time I saw you for five minutes and God knows when the next five minutes will be.*

*How many of my past, illegible epistles have you received, posted from all corners of Italy?*

*There was a Polish padre staying with us in this house and one day he went to bury some of the killed of his regiment and got blown up by a landmine. It*

*is amazing how the news of the sudden death of*
*someone you had been talking to a few hours earlier*
*affects you.*

*Without any feeling of emotion, I heard of the*
*casualties in Normandy ... But somehow this one man,*
*more than the five thousand killed on the second front,*
*made me sit up and realise how very little we control our*
*lives. How awful was the air hanging over the mess*
*where he had been living ...*

*I really must stop now, so until God knows when,*
*All my love,*
*Bob*

The couple were soon reunited and as the end of the summer loomed, Marjorie had an opportunity to watch him practise a parachute jump. She knew it was part of the build-up to his most important, and most dangerous, mission yet. He had been assigned to 'Operation Clarion', a six-man undertaking in northwest Italy. 'I knew that he was finally going to be parachuted into occupied Italy,' Marjorie says. Clearing her throat, she adds quietly: 'We said our goodbyes. Then I never saw him again till after the war.'

Shortly after midnight on 16 November 1944, just half an hour before his jump, Bob wrote to her.

*My darling Marjorie,*
*Today looks like being the big day, and so at last it*
*really seems as if we shall be parted. The waiting had*

*become so long and the false alarms so frequent that I
had given up the idea of ever saying goodbye.*

*Maybe it is just as well, in that goodbyes like ours are
too tantalising, because I should never have known how
to leave you.*

*So, it is left to a meagre letter in which to say farewell
for the time being, and my poor hand can make no
satisfactory effort …*

*By now you must know how much I have enjoyed the
last months in your company. Everything in the world
goes right when I am with you. I have never felt so happy
as when I was with you, darling, and how the intervals
between seeing you have lingered.*

*But I go away now, laden with happy memories of
things done in your company and the hopes of many
more in the not-too-distant future.*

*It is now two o'clock and we leave at half-past, so, as
there will be a good deal of flap after that, I have half an
hour of peace.*

*There is nothing very much else to say, for you
must know how much I shall miss you and how much
I love you, Marjorie. I hope we shall not be separated
too long, but, anyway, I long for the next time,
darling …*

*My words are too inarticulate, so goodbye for now,
my darling.*

*I love you.*

*Bob*

His parachute jump did not go to plan but fell short of disaster. Marjorie explains: 'He was picked up by this man called Sergio Cerutti, a partisan, because he [Bob] had landed in a tree and hurt his back. So this man shielded him while the Germans were searching through the village.'

In defiance of the strict rules that banned such moves, Bob sent a signal to let Marjorie know he was safe. 'One night on duty a girl near me got a message which said, "Bob sends love to Marjorie", which was absolutely forbidden, but at least I knew where he was – he was still alive,' she says, recalling her gratitude. 'And then I began communicating with his mother and father, telling them …' She trails off. 'Well, I couldn't tell them much, apart from not to worry. I didn't see him again.'

In December Bob and three comrades were betrayed and captured. Taken as a prisoner of war, Bob was transferred first to a jail in Cuneo, a province close to the French border, then to a prison further north in Turin. It was there he spent his twenty-first birthday in January 1945. He did not remain there long, however. The following month he was taken to Germany: first to the Stalag VIII-A prisoner-of-war camp in Bavaria, then north to Marlag und Milag Nord near Bremen, then further north to Lubeck.

His whereabouts were a mystery to Marjorie and his family. 'I didn't know he'd become a prisoner in Italy and later on in Germany,' she says, her voice trembling. If the mission had taken place earlier in the war, he might not have survived at all. A previous edict had ordered Nazi commanders to kill all Allied commandos found behind enemy lines, even those who were unarmed or attempted to surrender.

Fraught with worry, Marjorie was instructed to transfer from Monopoli to Siena, in Tuscany, which was where the headquarters of No. 1 Special Force relocated in January 1945. She also faced the painful task of writing once again to Bob's parents. Having initially informed them in November that he had arrived safely at his undisclosed destination, she was now forced to inform them that he was missing. It was not an easy letter to write, but it meant a lot to his family to hear it from her. Gladys, Bob's mother, wrote back to her: 'The news broken to us by you, Marjorie, dear, is so much softer than the official notification which we shall get and we are very thankful to you for writing.'

Bob's fate remained unknown, though not for want of him trying to contact Marjorie. In March he wrote her a postcard, addressed to her family home in Wales. 'I hope you got to hear I was safe quickly and now I must just wait patiently for the end. Until then, all my love, Bob.' As misfortune would have it, she did not receive the card until many months later. A glimmer of hope did emerge in March, however. Bob's family were alerted to the fact that, while he was not to be listed publicly as missing, he was presumed captured as a prisoner of war.

The Maryland base had received reports as early as December suggesting that a party of seven British agents had been seized, though these messages, which indicated that some men deployed on 'Operation Clarion' might still be alive, were only passed to No. 1 Special Force two and a half months later. The Naval Intelligence Division had decided against informing his family at first, however. It appeared that they had wanted to avoid raising false hope among his loved ones, given that there was no certainty he had survived, but their decision was overturned in favour of greater transparency.

In the spring of 1945 Marjorie left Siena for Naples and on 1 April she set sail for Britain alongside Nancy. She marvels that they began their training together at Banbury and spent the whole war together. 'This same girl who was there [at the beginning] also came out to Italy and we came home together,' she says. Mary, another FANY to whom she had grown close in Italy, also sailed back on the same ship. While Marjorie was caught in limbo over the destiny of her beloved, Mary had the grim satisfaction of certainty: the Royal Marine officer to whom she was engaged had been certified killed in combat. 'Her fiancé had been blown up. She was coming home with me carrying his beret. It was the only thing she had of him,' Marjorie says sadly.

Marjorie's father was there to greet her at Liverpool when the ship arrived, and shortly afterwards she took him to meet Bob's parents over lunch. She visited them again with Nancy and, eager to make a good impression, issued her friend with strict instructions to pretend that neither of them smoked or drank alcohol. 'We were paragons of virtue,' she says, laughing, adding that Bob's parents 'must have thought, *My God, they're a boring lot*'.

Although she was granted leave to return briefly to Wales, she was summoned to return to the FANY headquarters at Poundon in Buckinghamshire. She was indignant at having to pay for personal effects and equipment that she had been instructed to leave in Italy. After 15 months' service, however, she was finally demobbed.

Unbeknown to Marjorie, Bob was to be liberated from Lubeck around the same time. On the day he was freed, he was handed a dram of whisky and promptly fainted from malnourishment.

Two days before Victory in Europe was declared on 8 May, he flew from Germany to Biggin Hill, Kent, and then made his way back to his family in East Finchley in London, armed only with sufficient funds to catch the train home. As he walked up the road towards his house, his father happened to be sitting by the bay window. He glanced out and caught sight of a bearded naval officer walking to the door: the son he had not heard from in months. The reunion was 'very emotional', Marjorie says.

She and Bob were also reunited soon after. 'As soon as he got home, I had a telegram to meet him at London Paddington. I went up by train, feeling so nervous, and when we met – we shook hands,' she recalls, laughing. 'The grandchildren love that. We didn't ravage each other.'

The couple were overjoyed at the news of Victory in Europe. On VE Day itself Marjorie was in central London. 'If you've seen pictures of those crowds on VE Day outside Buckingham Palace – that was me. It was fabulous. I'm very pro the royal family. The Queen is two years younger than me. She came out into the crowd. I saw her,' she says. Princess Elizabeth, as she was then, and her sister, Princess Margaret, took to the streets to move among the crowd after waving from the balcony with the King and Queen.

However, the war was not yet over for Bob, who received instructions to travel to the Far East to fight the Japanese. Marjorie's efforts to persuade him to resist the order were unsuccessful. He explained in a letter to her: 'It is no case of mad patriotism or wish for glory – I must go. I could never live with myself if I stayed here. I have only been in the "service" for three years and have had a very lucky and easy time really.'

He travelled across the world to join an Australian special forces unit that was tasked with gathering intelligence and conducting raids on Japanese-held territories. His old boat, the *Eduardo*, was transported to join him, on loan from the Royal Navy, and he headed a crew of ten. Although the atom bombs dropped on Hiroshima and Nagasaki ended the war in the East in August 1945, he remained in the Pacific until mid-1946.

After Bob returned home to Marjorie, the couple paused and 'worked out what we wanted,' she says. 'We had to start taking exams. I had to learn typing after Morse code.' The Army paid for Marjorie to complete a London-based secretarial course that guaranteed a job afterwards. She went on to work for Rolls-Royce, earning £5 a week. 'I could live on it. I had bed and breakfast, and housing, and I could see my ever-loving when he wasn't working hard, and eventually we saved up for a flat,' she says.

Bob, meanwhile, secured a job following a chance encounter with Sir Hilary Scott, his former commanding officer in Monopoli, when walking down St James's in the West End. Sir Hilary asked him to lunch and suggested he come and work for the law firm Slaughter and May.

He and Marjorie got engaged at Kenwood House on Hampstead Heath and married in 1949. They had avoided a betrothal in Italy 'because if you became engaged they separated you,' she says. Once they were home, there seemed little reason to rush.

The sense of purposefulness that had propelled her during the war was replaced with new goals. 'I'd caught up with my husband. We were both working for a purpose. We had this little flat in London. It cost £7 a week – extravagant,' she says. After starting married life in London, they moved to a village in Surrey, and then to other towns in the county. The couple had three children: Tim, Will and Catherine.

Bob excelled as a corporate lawyer and later switched to merchant banking, earning a knighthood that was awarded by the Queen at Buckingham Palace in 1976. The honour meant that Marjorie, as his wife, was granted the right to use the title 'Lady'.

As life moved on after the war, Marjorie missed the close contact she had enjoyed with her wartime female friends. She kept up with many but has now survived them all. 'The worst thing about my age is, I don't know anyone older than me,' she remarks ruefully. The conflict was never discussed after it ended. 'After the war, you didn't say, "Well, hello, what did you do in the war? I did this." No, you didn't.'

Bob never disclosed to his family any details of his experiences in the SOE or detainment as a prisoner of war, only ever talking of his experiences to one other veteran. However, his son, Tim Clark, and family friend Nick Cook reviewed his wartime service in their wonderful book *Monopoli Blues*, which also charted many of Marjorie's highlights in the FANY.

She joined Tim and Nick on a trip to Italy some years ago to retrace Bob's footsteps. 'We went round every place. The big prison in Turin where we went is now a museum. They showed you where the partisans were, where the Gestapo were – it was too terrifying; I had to go out. It was horrible,' she says.

In time, nine grandchildren and six great-grandchildren followed. 'They are wonderful,' Marjorie says. 'They won't listen to much advice, but they've all done well.'

She and Bob also remained friends with partisans they had known during the war. Some years after the conflict ended, a letter from Sergio Cerutti reached Bob. She recalls her husband receiving it out of the blue and wondering at its contents: 'It said, "If you are Robert Clark, are you the man who descended on this night?"' Marjorie and Bob travelled to stay with Sergio and his wife in Mondovi, which was then repaid with a visit to Surrey. 'It was a tremendous friendship,' she says. 'We met all [Sergio's] friends who were partisans. What a life they lived. They were brave.'

Bob died in 2013, aged 89. 'What a very, very happy marriage it was,' Marjorie reflects. 'He was so good and kind. He was a wonderful, wonderful father. I miss him like hell.' She takes some comfort in visiting the memorial erected for him in the garden of her younger son, Will, who lives in Australia. 'I go down there and say, "I wish to God you were here too. Then I wouldn't mind staying longer and longer."' She continues to reside in Godalming, Surrey, although she was stuck in Australia for the best part of a year during the coronavirus pandemic.

She has kept her medals from the war, a collection that includes the War Medal, which was given to those who completed at least 28 days of service; the Africa Star, for those who served in North Africa; the Italy Star, awarded to those who served in the Italian Campaign; and the 1939–45 Star, for completing more than 180 days of service overseas.

Reflecting on the conflict, Marjorie says slowly: 'I think about the war all the time, but nobody is interested. I think how strange it was. How I got there, how I left Cheltenham and happened to choose the FANYs that nobody had heard of. I remember I've got the letter I wrote to my father – to think I went away for over a year and he didn't know where I was. Think of it today – people are all in touch today with their phones. They know where you are every minute. I had no contact – nothing.'

She is alive to how much the conflict, and meeting Bob, changed the course of her life. Considering what might have been, she muses: 'Well, of course I'd never have left my Welsh village. I'd have gone up to Oxford; if I'd worked hard enough, got a degree. What would I have done? I don't know – go back to the coal mines? I never went back to Wales.'

Summarising how her wartime experiences shaped her as a person, she says: 'I grew up, didn't I? If you have lived in a war and you've seen people dying and you've lived through bombing, you can't stay that little girl you were. Of course it affected me. I always think of London and St Paul's – all the bombing. We had chaps in London ready to fight with us. We met a whole lot of individual people. It was interesting in a strange way.'

Marjorie strongly believes that the conflict transformed for good the way women were able to live their lives. 'I notice now about women, how they have come forward. I always find the woman is the dominant character in the home now. Women helped win the war. They got up from the bottom, so to speak, and they were vital in industry and in the services. Now, today, they are as important as the men.'

# Hilda Bainbridge

**DATE OF BIRTH:**

12 August 1921 (aged 18 at the outbreak of war)

**ROLE:**

Land Girl in the Women's Land Army

Agriculture is in Hilda Bainbridge's blood. Her grandmother had owned a small farm and her aunt a dairy estate. After leaving school at 14, the County Durham teenager had gone straight into the family trade. By the time war broke out when she was 18, she had amassed several years of farming experience and was destined to join the Women's Land Army (WLA).

Originally set up in the First World War, the organisation was reformed in June 1939 as the government rushed to put in place a framework to draft in extra agricultural labourers before war was formally declared. Ministers knew that food imports transported by sea, on which Britain was heavily reliant, would be threatened by enemy submarines during wartime. Domestic food production needed to be urgently boosted to avoid the danger of severe shortages. An added complication was the flow of male workers out of agriculture into the Armed Forces. The Women's Land Army, a mobile force of women deployed to undertake all kinds of farm work across the country, was therefore crucial to upholding and expanding the industry.

The Land Girls, as members of the WLA became known, grew produce and picked crops, operated heavy machinery including tractors and excavators, milked cows, birthed lambs and kept pigs and poultry. They were also involved in ploughing, threshing, hay-making, hedging, ditching and weeding, as well as reclaiming unused land for arable farming. Their basic working week was 48 hours in winter and up to 56 hours in summer. By its height in 1944, the organisation boasted more than 80,000 members.

Hilda explains: 'You went out to different farms in "gangs".' Despite her relative youth, upon enlisting she was immediately appointed as a forewoman of a gang. 'I had been in agriculture before and I was so experienced in everything – you name it. I could plough a field with a pair of horses. I used to help to teach the other girls,' she says. She was a natural leader and undaunted by the prospect of directing others. Large farms tended to request multiple gangs, which meant a single task could be assigned to each woman. On smaller, private farms, however, where deployments tended to last a week at most, 'you did everything – milk cows and the rest,' she says.

While rural areas were generally safer than British cities during the conflict – a rule that underscored the evacuation of more than 1.5 million children out of urban centres – this maxim did not hold true for Hilda. Posted south from her home in the northeast to Bedfordshire, she faced danger both by day and by night. When she worked on the farm during daylight hours, Nazi aircraft would strafe the fields with machine-gun fire aimed at trains on the adjacent railway. The enemy gunners had only a narrow window to target the trains on open tracks before they disappeared into subterranean tunnels, leading to frenzied attacks. With horror, Hilda recalls: 'They used to fire on those trains nearly every day and we used to run for cover under the hay stacks or somewhere we could hide. But we used to watch the tracer bullets come all the way down, hitting the train.'

The Luftwaffe planes made a menacing throbbing noise, which helped the Land Girls detect them before they soared into view. 'If you heard that, run for cover!' she says. 'It was scary – scuttle to hay pikes and get in and hide there until it went away. During the war I used to hate it; in fact, I used to get frightened when the bombers came over. They used to drop little pieces of silver paper and you could hear them coming down. The next morning when you got up the ground used to be covered with pieces of silver.'

This aluminium foil-backed paper and chopped aluminium wire was chaff dropped from German aircraft in order to confuse RAF radar and frustrate the efforts of anti-aircraft operators attempting to shoot them out of the sky. The thin metal strips would resonate with incoming radio waves and also re-radiate the waves. This meant that radar detectors, which measured the reflection of radio waves off incoming objects, were tricked into 'seeing' an array of objects instead of a single aircraft – making that sole plane difficult to hit. The technology had first been created to protect RAF planes during raids over Germany. It was developed in part by a brilliant Welsh physicist named Joan Curran, who had studied at Cambridge University in the 1930s but was not awarded a degree due to the institution's discrimination against women at the time.

The anxiety Hilda felt at hearing the roaring blasts of machine-gun fire has never left her. Loud bangs made her jump throughout the rest of her life. 'When the raids came, they weren't very nice. I never liked it. I was always frightened. I still am; I don't like noise,' she observes. At night she also faced danger in her hostel, situated above a secret munitions factory. She was well aware that if the Nazis discovered the nature of the goods produced in the building, it would become a high-value target for destruction. Its close proximity to Bedford train station also entailed a higher risk of stray bombs or gunfire hitting the site. The location of the factory was a deliberate choice, as it facilitated the easy transport of weapons produced there to other parts of the country by rail.

The wisdom of placing a hostel above it was less certain, however. 'We were on top of an ammunition factory,' says Hilda, with an air of disbelief. 'There was a station the other side and the trains and the wagons used to come in, they used to get loaded up, then they used to go underground.' The aerial attacks aimed at the trains and their cargo carried on throughout the night as well as the daylight hours.

She followed a gruelling routine. Bells rang out at Chimney Corner in Bedford at five-thirty each morning, marking the end of the night shift for the male workers in the factory below, and the start of the working day for the women in the dormitories above. A hearty breakfast was served before transport arrived for the fields, where the Land Girls' toil began at seven-thirty. The women were spared work at the weekends, but no exceptions were made for the weather or the seasons. Labouring through storms was not uncommon, says Hilda, recalling vivid memories of getting drenched by torrents of rain. The day after a downpour was little better either. 'Can you imagine working on a fruit farm, up a ladder, when it'd been raining the night before? Your boots were full of mud and clods. You had to get up a ladder and pick apples and be very, very careful coming down the ladder, because you could have had a nasty accident. Those were the sorts of conditions we used to pick apples in.'

Digging root vegetables out of the earth in icy weather was another demanding job. 'It's not nice walking along, picking the potatoes out of the ground, [covered in] mud – not a very nice job,' she says. 'Then, when you come off the fields, you used to have to brush all the stuff off you. Come November, we would get a bit of frost, and you were pulling turnips, your finger ends used to be frozen.' Even snow was not considered an impediment to a day's work in the fields.

Hilda and her fellow Land Girls got on with the job, however, and strove to retain their good cheer. Laughing, she notes drily: 'You had a good waterproof.' In the summer months, she enjoyed cutting and stacking hay. She also helped produce silage – animal fodder made from pickled pasture grass. 'We used to take our shoes and stockings off and get inside [a silo], put treacle on and stamp and stamp and stamp, and run around and flatten it down until it got right to the top,' she explains.

The most fun to be had was riding horses, or driving vehicles and machinery. Since she had been taught how to plough with a tractor by her childhood sweetheart, Ted, Hilda was often awarded the privilege. In 1941, as government fears of a Nazi invasion of Britain spiked, she was also instructed how to disable tractors to prevent fully functioning machines falling into enemy hands.

Born in Stanley, County Durham, Edith 'Hilda' Nicholson was the seventh of nine daughters, two of whom died in infancy. In a curious coincidence, both her mother and her grandmother had each been seventh children too. Hilda was not a welcome arrival in the Nicholson family as far as her mother Kate was concerned. She had believed she was past the child-bearing phase of her life when she discovered to her shock that she was pregnant again. In fact, she was to have three more children in total. Kate never let go her resentment towards her youngest daughters, Hilda believes.

'I was very close to my father, but I was never really close to my mother,' she says. 'The simple reason was – so my elder sisters told me later on in life – that my father joined the Army in the 1914 war. He was away all that time and when he came back, my mother thought with her age, as she had turned 40, that she was finished having children. And guess what? I appeared on the scene. My mother wasn't a very happy woman. She carried that right through my life.' Her mother was fickle and capricious. Kate had originally named Hilda 'Edith' after a family friend, but several years later she insisted the name be changed after she fell out with that friend. It was at this point that the young girl adopted the nickname Hilda, and it stuck.

The family was poor, which also contributed to the difficult nature of Hilda's early years. 'It was a very hard childhood,' she recalls, adding quietly: 'I don't like to be reminded of it.' Her father, Edward, had been a military policeman, known as a 'Redcap' or 'Cherrynob', in the First World War and had joined the civilian police after leaving the Army. However, 'It didn't pay enough money, so he ended up being a miner in the coal mines. There was more money there,' she explains.

Resources nonetheless remained tight for a household of nine and, with seven children to care for, her mother was unable to work. The general strike of 1926 – a bid to force the government to legally prevent mine owners from slashing miners' wages by 13 per cent and increasing their shifts by an extra hour to eight a day – looms large in her memories of childhood. 'When the pit was on strike, nobody had any coal,' she recalls. 'There wasn't any central heating or running water in those days. You had a tap halfway up the wall. When the strike was on nobody could have a fire, so they couldn't cook; they couldn't do anything – couldn't get any hot water. That's why we had to go to the soup kitchens.'

It was a journey she undertook every weekday lunchtime while at school. Since enrolment in education was one of the criteria to qualify for the free meal, Hilda started school young. 'There were no nurseries or anything like that,' she remarks. 'We were very poor, very poor. I had to go to soup kitchens and I still remember it. It's still there [in my memory] where I went. We didn't have money,' she says. 'I never had a lot. I never had a pair of proper shoes or a proper coat till I left school and I could buy them myself.' Tattered pass-me-downs, often threadbare, had to suffice. She left education aged 14. 'I didn't want to leave school; I wanted to carry on, but my mother wouldn't let me.' Her answer to that question was, 'We've kept you long enough. Now it's your turn to help out the family budget.'

Hilda's first job was picking potatoes on a farm. She was expected to fill a bucket a day for a paltry wage. It was hard, physical labour, but the routine was not unfamiliar to the teenager. 'It was back-breaking, but I was more or less used to it, because my grandma had a farm and my aunt had a dairy farm, so I was pretty used to farming and that kind of life,' she says. For extra money she also delivered milk from a float pulled by a horse named Peggy.

She happened to be on a rare trip to London within weeks of the outbreak of war. She visited Buckingham Palace to watch the Changing of the Guard ceremony, in which soldiers, dressed in traditional red tunics and bearskin hats, exchange responsibility for protecting the palace. Having clambered onto Queen Victoria's monument for a clearer view, what she remembers now is not the guardsmen, but the wagons packed with soldiers whizzing past, with a white chalk sign attached to the back of each vehicle, reading: 'Danzig, here we come!'

She says it was common knowledge that Poland had 'suffered very badly' under Adolf Hitler and she felt a strong sense of patriotic support for Britain entering the war. None-theless, she returned home 'a bit frightened' by the prospect of conflict. Since she was 18 years old, she knew she was likely to play an active part in the war effort. Her initial desire was to enlist in the Auxiliary Territorial Service. 'I wanted to be a PTI [physical training instructor] in the Army,' she said. However, since she was already working on a farm and had experience, the authorities directed her to the Women's Land Army. She reconciled herself to the decision with good grace. 'I was quite happy to do it,' she says.

The warm and comfortable uniform she was issued was an immediate boon. Some women later admitted joining up solely for the fashionable knee breeches, since the WLA was the only service to hand out and permit such attire, but Hilda was content simply to own new, practical clothing. This included an overcoat with three linings and deep pockets, khaki wool stockings, a green pullover, white shirts, a necktie and hat. Overalls and a jumper were provided for the fields, alongside wet-weather clothing, including wellington boots and a raincoat. A Women's Land Army badge, which bore a sheaf of wheat, was also included.

Since it was a civilian organisation, the uniform was optional and its recruits could wear their own clothes if they preferred. What was not tolerated, however, were attempts to embellish the formal attire. Advice published in 1942 for the Land Girls warned: 'Uniform must be *uniform* or it loses all its point. Come out as gay or as shabby or as Bohemian as you like in civilian clothes, but don't try to express your personality in your uniform.' It added: 'A volunteer seen in the streets of a large town (this is a true story) wearing a hat cocked on one side and tied on with red ribbon in a large bow under her chin, red tie and fancy shoes, with otherwise correct uniform, makes passers-by gaze at her with a wild surmise as to whether it is she or the Land Army which has gone crackers.'

Overall, the WLA boasted a strong sense of identity, illustrated by its popular ditty:

> *Back to the land, we must all lend a hand,*
> *To the farms and the fields we must go,*
> *There's a job to be done,*

*Though we can't fire a gun,*
*We can still do our bit with the hoe.*

A monthly magazine named *The Land Girl* was also set up to boost morale with news, jokes and gossip, and to try to remould the reputation of the organisation. Its first issue, published in April 1940, acknowledged in its cover article the unkind stereotype of Land Girls that had taken root. 'There is a curious delusion that land workers are rather slower than town folk; that, like brains and brawn, cows and culture don't go together,' it said. 'Perhaps it all depends on what is meant by culture. There is certainly more cash and more comfort attached to the commercial or clerical city existence. Whether it also shows a better sense of values or proves the possession of superior brains is quite another matter.'

It continued: 'At any rate, members of the Land Army have proved *their* intelligence by joining the Land Army. Coming from every profession and calling, they have all realised what is the most important job they can do to-day.' Further bids to improve the social standing of farm work, which was seen by many as superior only to deployment in the munitions factories, were mounted by the royal family. In 1941 Queen Elizabeth, who later became the Queen Mother, became a patron of the WLA and later hosted a 'birthday party' to mark its anniversary.

Hilda's first posting was to a farm within her home county of Durham. Her time there was brief, however, because she decided to answer the call for volunteers to travel south, where there was a labour shortage. Her destination was Bedfordshire. She was excited for the adventure ahead, but regretted having to leave behind her boyfriend. A year older than Hilda, Edward 'Ted' Bainbridge had attended the boys' school affiliated with her girls' school. He, too, had left at the age of 14 and went on to join the family business by working on his grandparents' modest dairy farm. The couple were physically alike: both tall, with dark hair and brown eyes. They were opposites in personality, however. While Hilda was feisty and extroverted, Ted was quiet, gentle and calm. When war broke out, he joined the Home Guard, which obliged him to remain in County Durham. In an emotional parting, she promised to keep in touch and visit during leave.

In her new home at the hostel above the ammunition factory in Bedford, Hilda lived with 30 other young women. They were split between three dormitories, each of which was filled with ten beds. Her feelings about the arrangements were mixed: privacy was lacking, but the mattresses were comfortable. She was put in charge of a gang of six women. Occasionally, if a farmer required only one or a pair of workers rather than a gang, she would live on the farm itself. 'It was a better life in the hostel than it was on a private farm,' she says. 'I did both.' The main benefit of a hostel lay in its sociability, she explains, adding that she enjoyed being around other women her own age. Experiences of private farm billets varied, depending in large part on the personality of the farmer at the helm – or his spouse. Some Land Girls were embraced as members of the family during their stay; others were ostracised and forced to dine separately from the rest of the household.

The WLA, which fell under the auspices of the Ministry of Agriculture, had been set up by Lady Gertrude Denman, a women's rights activist who had campaigned for women's suffrage earlier in the century. She set up the headquarters of the organisation at her West Sussex home, while in each area of the country representatives were appointed to check on the welfare of the Land Girls. This was particularly important since the WLA allowed recruits to enlist from the age of 17 and a half – a younger threshold than many other services – which led to an influx of teenagers.

Today Hilda is damning about the authorities' interest in the Land Girls' wellbeing, however. 'Nobody ever came out to see me when I was in the Land Army – all the times I worked privately, not one person came out to see if I was all right,' she says. Alluding to some women suffering abuses, she admits: 'It did happen.' She adds resignedly, however: 'At the end of the day, I suppose there was a war on. Things were scarce and people were very busy doing what they should do.'

While Hilda thrived in agriculture, some of the young recruits who volunteered for, or were conscripted to, the Women's Land Army were ill-equipped to cope. Life in the countryside proved a stark culture shock for 'townies' who were unfamiliar with being outdoors in rough weather and undertaking physical labour. 'Some girls I felt very,

very sorry for because they had worked in an office, and they'd come to work outside. They had blisters on their hands.' She recalls tentatively asking two Land Girls why they had signed up when they seemed to her so poorly suited to the labour. They admitted they had bought into romantic visions of working outdoors in the fresh air, which they had found to be a far cry from the grinding reality.

The government fostered such perceptions with a series of propaganda posters urging women to join the rural workforce. One typical poster showed an illustration of a glamorous and smiling red-headed woman, standing in a field and holding a pitchfork, with the caption: 'For a happy, healthy job join the Women's Land Army'. By autumn 1941, just before conscription was introduced, 20,000 women had voluntarily enlisted in the civilian organisation. One third came from London and other large cities. While some recruits received formal training at agricultural colleges, which were turned over to the WLA, most were forced to learn on the job.

Some of the roles to which the Land Girls were assigned required a strong stomach. The threat to crops, vegetables and animal fodder posed by rats led to the creation of anti-vermin squads. Women were trained to lay bait and poison in order to kill millions of rats, foxes, rabbits and moles. Other jobs were unpleasant and painful for different reasons. Reports emerged of women being forced to clear fields of weeds and thistles with their bare hands.

One of the women who joined Hilda's gang left the WLA soon after her arrival. 'It was just as well; I don't think she would have survived,' she says, laughing. Exiting the organisation was not straightforward, but loopholes existed. 'You had to have a good reason to come out of the Land Army, like the Army or the Navy,' she says.

Despite the struggles experienced by some, camaraderie prevailed among the 30-odd women living at the Chimney Corner hostel, where the Land Girls consciously strove to lift each other's spirits. Morale was not improved by the standard of the cuisine served, however. 'I wouldn't give them any Union Jacks for the food that they provided,' Hilda snorts. 'It left an awful lot to be desired. I think they should have had a better cook, but then again, everything was rationed.' She adds with a laugh: 'We didn't have very many fat people during the Second World War. You have a hell of a lot now.'

Rationing had been introduced four months after the war started, in a bid to ensure the fair distribution of food amid shortages. A series of complementary schemes was introduced to prolong the lifespan of food items and avoid waste. One of these initiatives involved Lady Denman, who, as well as being director of the WLA, was president of the National Federation of Women's Institutes. She helped organise the manufacture of vast quantities of preserves by the WI movement. The Ministry of Food awarded additional rations of sugar to local WI groups to help them make jam, which is estimated to have saved around 450 tonnes of fruit that would otherwise have rotted.

Hilda worked from seven-thirty in the morning to four-thirty in the afternoon, with a short break for lunch in the fields. She and the other members of her gang returned to the hostel around five-thirty, where a meal was waiting. 'It was already in pans – potatoes and veg,' she says. Sometimes the food had been cooked hours earlier and was blackened from sitting in the open air, she recalls with distaste. Turnips, carrots and cabbage were staples on the menu, which could be supplemented by sprouts and other vegetables from the farms at which the women worked. The farmers tended to be generous in allowing them to fill their pockets with produce at the end of the day. Sometimes even highly sought-after eggs were gifted. Hilda recalls sausages and mince being offered on occasion at the hostel, but never the Sunday roast that was her favourite meal. She dreamed of Yorkshire puddings throughout the war.

The most exciting diversion from the weekly routine was provided by weekend dances. Blanket invitations were sent to hostels, marking another reason why they were favoured above residence on a private farm. The young women checked daily to see if new dates had been announced: 'There used to be a big board in the hostel and whenever there was a dinner dance on, or just a dance, it was put on there and you had to put your names on.' Hilda loved dancing, especially 'a nice waltz, foxtrot, rumba – modern ballroom dancing,' she says, adding: 'You don't see much of it around these days.' The dances remain some of her highlights of the war. 'We had some good times, you know. We used to get invitations to visit the GIs – the Americans – up at Kimbolton and Little Staughton, to dances there. They were very nice, we enjoyed it.'

Not all dances were equal, however; they were distinguished by their hosts. The Americans were the epitome of chivalry, she says, while the local airmen exemplified diffident rudeness. The latter hosted a dance at RAF Cardington, which the Land Girls judged a resounding flop. 'Half of them didn't bother with us. The officers stood in one corner, the sergeants with the three stripes on stood in another corner and we were left,' she says. 'They were so stuck up. They were so bored; they just couldn't be bothered to have any conversation with us. We just felt we shouldn't be there.'

It was a stark contrast to the events hosted by US personnel. 'When we used to go to the GI dances, they used to come [out from inside the venue] to the trucks and carry us through the mud so we didn't get our things dirty. When we got inside there was a terrific bowl of punch and an officer standing there filling a glass for you and shaking hands. The officers came and made themselves known to us. The Liberty trucks [American military vehicles] would come and pick us up and the Liberty trucks would take us back. They were very good. But the RAF at Cardington just didn't bother with us, so we didn't go back any more. None of the girls would go back to the dances!' When the hostel warden asked why the lists thereafter were always full for the American dances, but empty for the RAF events, the girls replied stiffly of the latter: 'I don't think the boys like us.'

Over the course of a number of events, Hilda developed a close platonic friendship with an American engineer called Arthur. A steeplejack from New York City, who boasted the distinction of having cleaned the Statue of Liberty, he was only two years older than her and had also left a sweetheart behind at home. 'When I first met him, I asked him if he had a girlfriend in America and he said, "Yes, I have." And I said, "Well, I have a boyfriend here as well. Can we be good friends? If you want more than good friends, sorry." But we were friends all the time,' she says. The pair visited the picture house together and occasionally took a boat out on the river. 'They treated a woman the way she wanted to be treated,' she says approvingly of the GIs. Some of her friends in the Women's Land Army fell into romantic relationships with Americans stationed nearby and after the war emigrated to the United States.

The Land Girls took a harsher view of the Germans held in a prisoner-of-war camp situated near the hostel. Between 1939 and 1948, some 400,000 men from Germany, Ukraine, Italy and other nations became Britain's prisoners of war. Often they were based in temporary camps that were pulled down after the conflict and official records are patchy. However, it is estimated that by 1946 up to a fifth of all farm work in the country was being performed by prisoners of war, who were also dispatched to build roads and labour on other construction projects.

Prisoners who were considered benign were allowed to work alongside British civilians and in some locations earn real money, rather than the paper currency used in most camps. Many male prisoners were also deployed to fell, saw and lift trees alongside the 6,000 members of the Women's Timber Corps, who became known as 'Lumber Jills' and lived in huts in the forest. Extra stocks of wood were required by the government for pit props and telegraph poles.

Friendly relations between prisoners of war and local Britons grew in some communities, which may explain why 24,000 former PoWs decided to settle in the UK after the conflict ended. However, the atmosphere between the two parties in Bedford was unequivocally hostile. 'We used to throw stones at the windows,' Hilda recalls unapologetically. 'They put the bus stop right opposite the prisoner-of-war camp, of all places to put it. We Land Army girls used to get off there. Their ablutions were a hole in the ground with some canvas around the sides. So when we girls used to see that, these prisoners going in there, we used to throw stones at them. Yes, we did. We got pulled over the coals oh so many times. But they were prisoners; we weren't.'

She remains unrepentant about her conduct towards the young men, many of whom were only teenagers like herself. 'We thought it was a laugh at the time,' she says, adding: 'It was better than throwing a bomb over, wasn't it?' The warden of the hostel firmly disapproved of the young women's behaviour, however. She would severely castigate them when she caught them. 'We were put in our place. She didn't like us doing that sort of thing,' Hilda recalls.

Frequent lectures and reprimands from the warden, who also enforced a strict nightly curfew, contributed to a general sense among the Land Girls at Chimney Corner that they were poorly treated. Their wages were low, the work was tough, and initially – like all recruits of the Women's Land Army – they were banned from taking holiday, even unpaid. Conditions began to improve for the organisation's members from 1943, after a 'Land Girls Charter' was agreed, which raised the minimum wage and introduced a week's holiday per year.

Hilda and her colleagues were also aggrieved by their suspicion that they were paid less than their male counterparts. 'I've never been able to find out. Sixteen shillings a week, that's what we got. It wasn't a lot of money,' she says. It would not have been unusual if they were on a lower wage than male workers; most Land Girls were. They were directly employed by the farmers for whom they worked, who were supposed to pay a minimum wage of 48 shillings a week by the end of the war, or 18 shillings if bed and board were provided on site. In some areas farmers refused to hire WLA recruits altogether, believing that female workers were not worth paying for. Some of these farms would have benefited from free labour in the summer in any case, when city dwellers descended on the countryside in pursuit of a cheap holiday. They were accommodated in makeshift camps in return for their help performing tasks such as fruit picking.

Wider society was also dismissive of the Women's Land Army and held the civilian organisation in lower esteem than female branches of the Armed Forces, Hilda feels. An incident in a train station was representative of the Land Girls' treatment, she says. She and two other recruits had been on leave and were returning to Bedford. It was two o'clock in the morning when their train pulled in to Leeds Station, where they were to change. There was a fierce wind blowing and no fire had been lit in the waiting room. Desperate for warmth, they dashed to the all-night kiosk for a cup of tea but were turned away as they were 'not service' – that is, not members of the armed services. 'They wouldn't serve us,' she recalls with frustration. In the event, a soldier standing nearby intervened and brought each of the women a hot drink.

From time to time unusual and exotic jobs arose. Hilda was one of a six-member gang drafted in to assist at Whipsnade Zoo, although she was not immediately excited by the deployment. 'To tell you the truth, I'd never been to a zoo,' she says, laughing. She was mesmerised by the big cats. 'I saw some tigers – they were absolutely lovely – and some lions,' she says. A 'spitting camel' was less delightful. 'I had to muck him out and he spat at me. They're horrible things, those camels,' she says.

The zoo, which first opened to the public in 1931, had run into problems at the outbreak of war. The institution had to deal with the departure of its staff, who were called up to fight, as well as grapple with the challenge of how to feed the animals at a time when food was at a premium. The solution to the latter problem was to become self-sufficient, by turning over swathes of the 200-acre site to farming. The zoo grew wheat, grains and vegetables, and kept sheep, pigs and cattle alongside its exhibited fauna. Enough produce was harvested to sustain both Whipsnade and its sister establishment, London Zoo, which had evacuated some of its animals to the Bedfordshire site, which was at lower risk from Luftwaffe raids. Five pandas, two orangutans, four chimpanzees, three Asian elephants and an ostrich were transferred to the safer zoo.

Whipsnade Zoo did not escape the Blitz, however. In autumn 1940 it was the target of more than 40 explosive and incendiary bombs, which killed an old spur-winged goose and a young giraffe that ran itself to death, distressed by the noise of the raids. Some of the resulting bomb craters were filled with water and remain today as ponds in the paddock.

Life in the WLA enforced sociability, but the ever-changing cast of workers in each gang made long-term friendships difficult to sustain. 'When you dispersed from a hostel and went elsewhere you lost that friendship,' says Hilda. 'So you had to keep on making new friendships all the time. It was easy, to a point. Certain people – when you get a lot of girls together like that – can be a bit unruly, but you ignore that sort of thing.'

Sometimes the source of unruliness was external. Erupting into laughter, she recalls one summer's day when she and her gang heard a ruckus ringing out across the fields from the River Great Ouse nearby. 'We couldn't think what it was,' she explains. 'One of the girls decided to try and find out where the noise was coming from. So she goes to the end of the field, turns around, gives us all a wave: "Come on, come here, come here, girls!" Guess what? There were seven Italian prisoners – that was after they came on our side [Italy surrendered to the Allies in September 1943] – in the river, swimming bare buff! Yes, I always remember that. Then they had the flaming cheek to ask us to go in. Oh, we laughed, we did. You'd never see anything like that again.' Joining them was unthinkable, she adds. 'Good God, no. These Italians, no, they were sex mad. Can you imagine, looking over a bridge and seeing seven naked men? But there they were. And they hadn't got an ounce of shame in them. They stood there and we saw everything.'

From time to time she would use leave to visit her sisters, two of whom were based in London. Beatrice, her eldest sister, worked as a waitress in a pub. She had lost her husband at the Siege of Tobruk in Libya in 1941, during the Western Desert campaign. Another sister, Alice, was a dance-hall assistant at a hotel near Hyde Park. Her husband had also died in the war, fighting in France. Between them, the Nicholson sisters performed a variety of roles: Susan and Lily worked in factories, Katherine-Ann was a nun and lived in a convent, while the youngest sibling, Gwynny, suffered poor health and lived at home with her parents.

After four years in Bedfordshire, Hilda eventually asked to be transferred back to County Durham to be nearer Ted. 'I'm a northern girl at heart,' she says. By this time she had worked in every kind of farm, including dairy, arable and fruit. Her last job in Bedfordshire had been working as a lone farmhand at smallholdings run by 'a lovely family'. The placement held such fond memories that at the age of 96 she decided to visit with her son but found that none of the family was still living there.

While Hilda had been working in the east of England, she and Ted had exchanged correspondence. In lengthy letters they would share 'what I was doing and what he was doing, our friends, when was I coming home,' she recalls. 'We just kept on writing. To tell you the truth – it's a bit personal now – I always used to have an envelope and I used to fill it with kisses. Every time. And I said, "I'll collect them when I'm back."' Laughing, she adds: 'I did – I married him.' The couple wed in summer 1943.

Prior to their marriage Hilda had visited whenever she was able. A spell of rehabilitation following an operation to remove bunions caused by the stiff WLA-issued boots allowed them to spend six happy weeks together. She adds that she still winces today, however, thinking of the painful boots.

She did not see the end of the war coming. 'I don't think any of us did. I think it was a bit of a surprise,' she reflects. 'I think the big nobs did, but the ordinary man in the street didn't.' Her sense of relief was overwhelming, and one thought dominated, which has stayed with her since: 'I don't want to live through another one.' When Victory in Europe was declared on 8 May 1945, she and Ted celebrated with her family. 'We went over to my mother's. There was a party in the street with the usual things – the flags flying. So we had ourselves a little place at the end of the table and had some sandwiches and quite enjoyed it.'

She was affronted that, upon discharge, the authorities demanded the return of her uniform, which she had paid for in clothing coupons. 'They wrote to me and asked for my uniform back – would you believe it? So I wrote back: "Yes, you can have it, provided you will return my coupons." I'm still waiting for them. I'm still waiting for them to answer my letter. They never came and collected the uniform, so I just kept on wearing it,' she says. 'I thought all the years that I've worked, they could have let me keep it. Because that was a good uniform – it was lovely and warm, I can tell you.' After the war she secured a job with the Milk Marketing Board and continued to wear the uniform in that role.

The Women's Land Army is often referred to as the 'Cinderella Service', a pillar of the war effort that was taken for granted and insufficiently recognised – both during the conflict and afterwards. It is an appraisal with which Hilda vehemently agrees. 'As far as I'm concerned, the Land Army is the forgotten army. Quite frankly, I feel very, very strongly about this,' she says. 'We Land Army girls, we kept the food chain going all through that war. We picked potatoes in the pouring rain, and we did filthy, stinking jobs – and I have yet to hear one of those girls ever grumble about what they had to do.' When the trucks came to collect produce from their farms, the Land Girls would often ask about its destination and felt proud to know they were feeding other parts of the country, she adds.

Towards the end of the conflict the government excluded the Women's Land Army from post-war financial benefits, a decision that prompted Lady Denman to resign in protest. 'The Land Army fights in the fields. It is in the fields of Britain that the most critical battle of the present war may well be fought and won,' she had declared earlier in the conflict. It seemed few in power valued its importance so highly.

Around the same time, Land Girls in Herefordshire put forward a case for a Women's Land Army National Charter, in which they sought to 'remind the people of these Islands that we are their daughters'. Their manifesto stated:

During the critical days of this struggle we pledged ourselves to play – and have played – our part in achieving Victory. Voluntarily we renounced the possibilities of high wages in Industry, and accepted cheerfully Service upon the Land, bearing its hardships, the roughness of heavy manual work, the exposure to the vagaries of the British Seasons, the solitude of remote country districts, the low rate of pay, and the lack of social amenities to which we were accustomed, with fortitude and enthusiasm, believing that by doing so we were giving a vital service, combatting the U-boat Menace, releasing Vital Shipping and feeding our people through critical days, providing the vital materials to effect the miracle of production which alone could banish the dark days of defeat and usher in the dawn of Victory.

They asked the government to grant Land Girls a gratuity upon discharge in recognition of their financial sacrifice, compensation for those who had suffered agricultural accidents, opportunities to retain and enter the civilian workforce and rights to return to their former employment. It was an uphill battle. The treatment of WLA members in the years after the war may be one reason why former Land Girl Joan Quennell decided to run for Parliament. She served as a Conservative MP for 14 years from 1960, standing up for women's rights by pressuring the government to help make it easier for married women to return to work and calling for the switch from joint to individual taxation for married couples.

Hilda remarks of her own experiences: 'When I finished the Land Army I got a new badge, but not a medal – it wasn't a medal. And I got a citation from Number 10 Downing Street. But to me, that's not enough.' There has been too little discussion and recognition of their contribution ever since, she says. 'We Land Army girls have had nothing; nobody seems to mention us. People have short memories. I could never understand why they called it the Land Army if we weren't classed as "Army".'

She felt bruised by the reception from a series of other organisations too. 'When the war was over, I applied to join the British Legion,' she says. 'I was refused. They said you're not service. We poor Land Army have got that all our lives. That's what happened. I'm sure other girls suffered just the same.' It was an inevitability 'we learned to live with,' she adds. She is confident that female workers in contemporary times would not stand for such treatment. 'I think the women of today are a lot wiser than we were.'

It was only in 2000 that the Women's Land Army were finally invited to march past the Cenotaph on Remembrance Day. In 2014 a national monument to the Women's Land Army was erected at the National Memorial Arboretum in Staffordshire, while a sculptural tribute was unveiled by the Prince of Wales in Moray, Scotland, two years earlier.

Hilda and Ted, who remained in agriculture, went on to have a daughter and two sons, five grandchildren and five great-grandchildren. They lived most of their lives in County Durham, before moving south to Fareham in Hampshire after their retirement. Ted died in 2000 at the age of 80.

On a personal level, Hilda's experiences in the Land Army during the conflict taught her how to fend for herself and stand on her own two feet. It also gave her a phlegmatic view of life: 'You've just got to live from day to day.' She is unsure whether the cause of women more generally was advanced by the war. 'I don't know how to answer that, because I'm a great believer: if a woman wants to do something, go ahead and do it,' she says. 'But I do think we have a little bit more of a say now than we used to have. Not a great lot, but we'll get it eventually, I hope.'

*Hilda died on 24 July 2020, aged 98.*

# Jaye Edwards

**DATE OF BIRTH:**

12 October 1918 (aged 21 at the outbreak of war)

**ROLE:**

Pilot in the Air Transport Auxiliary

'I had no fears. I don't know why exactly,' muses Jaye Edwards, who performed one of the most perilous wartime roles to which women were admitted. Despite boasting only two hours' experience of solo flying before the conflict erupted, she was accepted as a civilian pilot into the Air Transport Auxiliary (ATA) and entrusted to fly Spitfires and Hurricanes. Demonstrating admirable pluck in the face of danger, she suffered plane crashes, a series of chastening near misses and the deaths of comrades. Now aged 102 years old, she is the last surviving British woman to have flown military aircraft in the Second World War, in which she piloted more than 20 types of plane and amassed 500 flying hours.

The ATA was, in effect, a ferrying service that was set up to transport newly manufactured and repaired military planes to the front line. It employed 1,250 pilots, the vast majority of whom were men, hailing from 25 different nations. They flew 147 different types of aircraft, criss-crossing the British countryside to deliver them from production lines and repair units to the Royal Air Force's operational hubs. Whenever the RAF lost or damaged a plane, the ATA would be tasked with delivering a replacement. Their unofficial motto was 'Anything to anywhere' and they were esteemed as a shadow air force. Their delivery of 300,000 aircraft to the RAF during the war enabled the nation's decisive victory in the Battle of Britain. Lord Beaverbrook, the Minister of Aircraft Production, paid tribute to the auxiliary service as 'soldiers fighting in the struggle just as completely as if they had been on the battlefront'.

Speaking from her armchair in her room within an assisted-living complex in North Vancouver, Canada, Jaye is eager to make one thing clear from the start. The Air Transport Auxiliary must only be referred to by its official title or initials. 'Don't make it "Attagirls",' she warns sternly, objecting to its best-known nickname. '"Attagirls" is right out! It's American.' While female volunteers from the United States were involved in the ATA for a brief period, they were soon absorbed into a new American civilian unit named the Women Airforce Service Pilots (WASP). The ATA was a British unit, albeit one that welcomed recruits from around the world, and they were not inclined towards the 'Attagirls' nickname.

A range of other monikers were also applied to the organisation throughout the war. The newspapers called its women pilots the 'Glamour Girls', while founding female member Pauline Gower quipped that its acronym had a more down-to-earth meaning: 'Always Terrified Airwomen'. Meanwhile, the ragtag assortment of men in the organisation who were recruited on the specific grounds of being able to fly but ineligible for the RAF referred to themselves as 'Ancient and Tattered Airmen'. They ranged from wounded veterans to bank managers, and disabilities were no bar to entry: one-legged, one-armed and one-eyed men were said to have been among the proud members of the organisation. A correspondent for *The Times* captured well the spirit of the service, describing it in 1941 as 'one of those curious, almost romantic improvisations which the special demands of war sometimes call into existence'.[7]

While ATA pilots did not participate in the terrifying dogfights of their military counterparts, they nonetheless faced stark dangers. Of the 168 female pilots in the ATA, 15 were killed during the conflict. These included feted aviatrix Amy Johnson, who in January 1941 bailed out of her twin-engine monoplane aircraft, an Airspeed Oxford, over the Thames Estuary. Her body was never recovered. Pilot Dora Lang and flight engineer Janice Harrington, who had been too short to qualify as a pilot, were another pair of ATA recruits killed in 1944 when their de Havilland Mosquito, a twin-engine multirole combat aircraft, stalled and crashed.

Jaye is matter-of-fact about her own record: 'I had two crashes.' She adds: 'We had no communication with the ground, no radio, nothing.' She suffered the only 'prang' of her service career when descending to land on a runway, damaging her aircraft by knocking off its wheels. 'They said I landed with drift, so the wheels collapsed. People who don't drive well drift across the street. It's the same in a plane,' she says. 'I broke the plane up, but I was okay. That happened at Sherburn [her local airbase in Yorkshire]; I was going back to my home.' Fortunately she faced no recriminations over the incident. Other colleagues involved in accidents that damaged planes had to engage with inquiries, which sometimes resulted in their expulsion from the unit.

Jaye's more serious accident almost halted her aviation career before it began. It occurred while she was learning to fly. She recalls with graphic clarity the horrifying moment of impact: 'Crunch!' Her two-seater Miles Magister monoplane – a British-made basic trainer aircraft known as the 'Maggie' – had slammed into a tree. Her teeth were smashed out of her jaw into the crash pad, but she remained conscious. Scrambling to check the engine was off, lest the plane should erupt into a fireball, she awaited help. It came swiftly. Men stationed at a nearby factory had witnessed the spectacular crash and raced over to the wreckage. Chuckling now at the memory of the disaster, she recalls how they opened with a joke, telling her approvingly: 'We don't have to cannibalise the plane – you've done it for us.'

She explains that she had been closing in to land on a runway and had just cleared a fence when the accident happened. 'I was learning to fly,' she stresses. 'I looked over my left shoulder and thought everything was fine, and forgot I had a right shoulder. That right shoulder hit a tree.' In the aftermath she was rushed to the operating room: 'I was taken to Abbotsford Hospital where my sister was a senior nurse.' She begged the paramedics to forewarn her sibling of her imminent arrival to avoid inflicting an unpleasant surprise. A dental plate was needed to replace her lost teeth. 'I was a mess,' she concedes, but adds: 'I could have done much more harm. I was lucky.' While she felt shocked and upset for a few days, her confidence did not desert her and she was soon back in the cockpit, striving to gain her licence.

Aircraft had first captured Jaye's imagination when she was an adventurous tomboy with perennially 'grazed knees' who enjoyed climbing trees. She recalls almost crashing her bicycle while cycling along a country lane when she spotted a stunt pilot, known as a 'barnstormer', performing tricks above the fields. It was the 'fascination of getting off the ground' that stimulated her, she has said previously. 'You ride a bike; you climb a tree – you're off the ground. I would say that's mostly it. A new outlook; a new life.'[8]

Later, aged eight, she was mesmerised watching her mother Stella take off on a flight to Paris for the weekend. 'It was a Moth [aircraft]. There were eight passengers in a tube and above them was the pilot,' she says. While her parents were wealthy enough to afford the luxury of air travel, planes did not become a feature of their lives. 'Father said he was not going to fly anywhere. He was adamant about that,' she says, laughing. 'Maybe he just didn't fancy something new.' Her father, John, who had been born in Sydney, had built up a successful business exporting car parts to Australia, while Stella raised the couple's four children. Stella Joyce 'Jaye' Petersen was the third, four years younger than her sister Lorna and 18 months junior to Olive, while four years older than her brother Richard. The family lived in Beckenham, Kent, and the children were sent to boarding school.

Mulling over her younger self, Jaye says: 'I wasn't an introvert, but I wasn't pushy. You went to boarding school – you were pushed around there.' Dark blonde with blue eyes, she shot up to 5 foot 11 inches before reaching her teens and felt deeply awkward about her height. 'I was taller than the 13-year-olds and I was 11, so I was never very popular,' she says. In the past she has described herself as wild and a 'bit of a renegade', remarking of her childhood: 'I never fit in, so I had to find something else to do. I don't want to say I'm wonderful, but I was a little different.'

Sent away to school, she developed a mischievous streak and was always on the lookout for new ways to subvert the strict rules. 'If you were very careful, you could sneak into the garden and pull a piece of rhubarb that was young and coming up, then tiptoe to the kitchen window. They'd give you a little sugar to put on it,' she says. 'You were doing something naughty. It can be fun to be naughty, even though you get spanked at the end of it. Oh, and we were spanked, no doubt.' She was also dispatched abroad several times – trips that she remembers fondly. 'I spent a lot of time in other places. I was sent to Germany for the summer holidays a couple of times when I was about 14, 15,' she says. There she stayed with the teenage daughter of a wealthy family. The two girls delighted in using the telephone to make nuisance calls to unsuspecting targets.

It was after leaving school, when she was 20 years old, that Jaye seized upon an opportunity to fulfil what she had considered a fanciful childhood dream of learning to fly. The year was 1939 and she had caught sight of a newspaper advert for the National Women's Air Reserve (NWAR), which was offering cheap lessons. Funded in large part by the government, it had been set up to produce legions of new pilots in anticipation of the looming conflict. The subsidised lessons cost 5 shillings an hour on weekdays and double at weekends.

Pondering the best way to raise the subject of aviation with her parents, she delicately asked her mother: 'What would you think about me learning to fly?' Stella took a dim view of such a dangerous hobby and attempted to defer the conversation, replying that she would have to think about it. Jaye countered that she could instead wait six months until her twenty-first birthday, at which point she would no longer need parental permission to enrol. Stella recognised the strength of her daughter's desire to fly and relented, agreeing to pay for the lessons, too.

On Sunday mornings Jaye joined droves of female office and shop workers to take lessons at a base in Luton, Bedfordshire. There they learned about the basic mechanics of aircraft, as well as how to pilot them. Similar in one sense to driving a vehicle – a skill Jaye had already mastered – the challenge was learning to manoeuvre in three dimensions rather than two. Despite her violent crash during this period, Jaye successfully gained her qualification as a licensed pilot. The outbreak of war, however, curtailed her hobby in the short-term. 'I sent away for my licence. You only had to do two hours solo to get it,' she recollects. 'After the war started – the day after it started – I received my actual certificate [saying] that I could fly. We had a laugh: here was the thing I'd been waiting for, and now I couldn't use it, because civilians basically couldn't fly in the war.' The irony that the NWAR had been set up to produce pilots for this very eventuality – the onset of war – was not lost on Jaye.

She was nonetheless determined to help the war effort and since flying was not an option, she turned in another direction. 'I looked after children for six months and I did nursing training for two years,' she says. 'I started looking after infirm children in Guildford. We had twelve little boys and eight little girls. The woman in charge decided to take the little girls, so I got the little boys.' While Jaye worked with children, her eldest sister Lorna served as a doctor, moving to India to practise medicine part way through the war, while Olive was a nurse. Their brother Richard suffered from chronic short-sightedness and was rejected by the Armed Forces for a front-line role. Instead, he carried documents between London and Bristol for the Royal Navy, but was plagued with guilt at escaping combat.

After half a year spent caring for children Jaye transferred to a small hospital with 200 beds near Hyde Park in Central London. It was an area heavily targeted by the Luftwaffe in the Blitz. 'If there was a raid, we'd go down to the basement,' she says. One night the hospital suffered a direct hit. Surfacing from the bowels of the building the next morning, the nurses were agog to find doors blown out of their frames on the floor. 'We had a chapel on the second floor and that got hit,' she adds. 'We'd been pretty lucky.' Across the road an apartment block had also been struck by a bomb, which had shattered the glass-lined foyer of the building. She says: 'They had a bit of trouble getting people out, but everybody was safe.'

On some occasions Jaye and her colleagues could not resist watching the bombs fall across the capital from the top of the building. 'We often went up to the roof to see what was happening. We watched St Paul's when it had a fire. We could see it from the hospital. You know it's happening – you don't know what to say,' she recalls. Dealing with wounds inflicted by the Nazi bombing campaign was a common feature of her daily work. 'We did get patients or people coming in who had been hit by bombs or by the residue of bombs – this piece of rock falling and that kind of thing – so that we were quite busy working.'

She followed press reports of the Battle of Britain – the aerial military campaign in which the RAF and Fleet Air Arm of the Royal Navy defended the nation against heavy attack by the Luftwaffe – closely during this period. 'That was the very early part of the war. We really crossed our fingers for the RAF. We knew they were having a terrible time. That was about all you could say,' she recalls.

Several years into the war nursing began to grate and Jaye realised it was not a suitable profession for her in the long run. 'When it got to the third year I thought, *Urgh*, and I had a contretemps,' she mutters. The argument erupted with the matron of the institution, who was angered by the state of one of her shoes. 'She made me turn around so she could look at it and see what I had done. I had put an Elastoplast on the heel and it had slipped a bit. Terrible!' Fed up with her duties and the heavy-handed approach of her superiors, she decided to request a transfer from the labour exchange. Wrangling ensued, but eventually she was permitted to join the Women's Auxiliary Air Force. There, she enrolled as a motor transport, or 'MT', driver. It was a short-lived spell, however, and she joined the ranks of the ATA. 'In '43 they were needing more pilots, so we got invited in. I was thrilled to think I was going to be flying again,' she says.

There was a spectrum of flying experience in the civilian service. 'There were some people in the ATA that had flown for 30-odd years. Some women owned planes pre-war. They used to have what they called "derbies". They would have set a course, and the women would in turn fly the course, being timed. Then the person who had flown it the fastest became the winner,' she says. The most experienced female pilots were a marvel. 'There were people in the ATA who could fly. One, I believe, even flew a flying boat, a Short Sunderland, out over the Atlantic looking for submarines.' Laughing, she adds: 'That wasn't me! That was someone with a lot of flying experience, who had taken flying courses and worked her way up, so that she was given the opportunity to do it.'

The service gradually grew, bolstered by recruits trained at the ATA flying school in Thame, Oxfordshire. Tuition was provided to the would-be pilots on how to navigate using only a map, compass and watch, since they were to fly without instruments or radio communication with the ground. To gain their wings at the end of the course, the recruits were required to fly circuits across the country in the most basic single-engine planes. 'As it was needed, people were added,' Jaye says of the early phase of the ATA women's section. 'Then some time in '42, I guess, a number of WAAFs had been asked if they would be interested in flying. Some agreed. They were taken in and told, "You have to solo in ten hours, or you're out."'

Jaye insists it was not an unreasonable demand. 'If you're any good it isn't difficult, to be honest, to learn to fly,' she says, quipping: 'When you're lucky, you take off.' However, she adds: 'Sometimes people were forced to leave [the service] again. One unfortunately left. Her mother was sick and she had to go and look after her.' Since Jaye had already achieved her licence, she took only a short course at Thame before being approved to take on assignments. Upon enlisting, she was sent to Austin Reed, the London-based tailor that manufactured uniforms during the war. A wool outfit similar in design to a naval officer's garb was issued. To fly, however, Jaye and her female comrades wore grey boiler suits and goggles.

Looking back with a hint of pride, she exclaims: 'I could fly any single-engine plane. I flew 20 different types. Some I only ever flew once – the Typhoon [a single-seat fighter-bomber] was one.' Her favourite was the Hawker Hurricane, a British single-seat fighter aircraft. 'It was friendly,' she says coyly. 'That sounds silly. It wasn't speedy, but it was the first plane in which you ever flew [solo] without a second. It was you, the only person in the plane, and you hadn't had a teacher there. You had taken the plane, just you. It was a funny feeling, the difference between flying with two of you and alone. You would be shown your plane, do all the checks of the parts, make sure everything is in good shape. Then you climb in, you nod to the guy, he starts the plane. Then you're on your way. You're much more independent.' She says she felt 'at home' in the bomber.

The Supermarine Spitfire could manoeuvre more quickly and efficiently than other aircraft, but it has elicited too much acclaim, she thinks. Stressing that she is 'not being derogatory', she says: 'As far as I was concerned, the "Spit" was just another plane.' Many of her colleagues took a different view of the Spitfire, however, describing its responsiveness as the closest thing to having wings. One ATA pilot named Joy Lofthouse remarked in the past that 'you practically breathed on the controls and it did what you wanted ... You could just hear the noise of the machine; it felt a part of you somehow, and you were in complete unison with it – it did what you wanted. Nobody to interfere, no voice to override you.'[9]

The Boulton Paul Defiant, a British interceptor aircraft operated by the RAF, was another of Jaye's favourites to ferry across the country. Like the Hurricane and the Spitfire, it was fitted with a Rolls-Royce Merlin engine. Despite Jaye's esteem for the aircraft, it suffered mixed fortunes in the Battle of Britain. Crewed by a pilot and a rear gunner, the position of its machine gun reduced its top speed, and its lack of forward-facing guns proved a deadly weakness in day-time dogfights with German Messerschmitt Bf 109 fighters. The 'Daffy', as it was known, nonetheless found its use as a night-time fighter and later in the war as an air-sea rescue plane and a tug for aerial targets.

Jaye also ferried the Supermarine Seafire, a naval version of the Spitfire, and the Fairey Barracuda, a British carrier-borne torpedo and dive bomber that was flown in combat by the Royal Navy's Fleet Air Arm. The latter aircraft was made entirely from metal. Her assignments were not restricted to transporting UK-made planes. She also flew Allied aircraft, including the Grumman F6F Hellcat, an American carrier-based fighter that was mass-produced at high speed and deployed to greatest effect in the Pacific theatre where it outmanoeuvred and outgunned its Japanese rival, the Mitsubishi A6M Zero.

Today, Jaye enjoys flicking through a photo album of all the aircraft she flew, which she created as a souvenir of her war days. The most unusual plane she piloted was the de Havilland Dominie, a light transport biplane that could carry eight passengers. She also piloted two other twin-engine aircraft: the Avro Anson and the Airspeed Oxford. The ATA sorted all aircraft into six categories. The simplest to fly, such as the de Havilland Tiger Moth, were labelled Class One, while the trickiest, such as the Short Sunderland flying boat, were Class Six. The Spitfire was in Class Two. Pilots progressed through the classes as they gained experience, but it was not until several years into the war that women in the ATA were allowed to fly planes in Class Two and above.

Fine weather made for sublime flights. 'You'd take off and it was a beautiful blue sky. It was just lovely to be flying,' recalls Jaye with a nostalgic sigh. She experienced a sense of peace while at the controls of a plane; the past melted away and she lived in the present. 'I was happy and content,' she

The Monument to the Women of World War II on
Whitehall being unveiled by the Queen and dedicated by
Baroness Betty Boothroyd, 2005.

Marguerite Turner in her nurse's uniform,
while serving in the Voluntary Aid Detachment (VAD)
during the war.

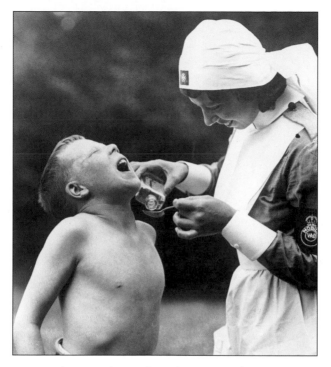

A nurse from the VAD gives a boy a
dose of medicine, 1939.

Marguerite today, at home.

Marjorie Clark in her First Aid Nursing Yeomanry (FANY) uniform, while attached to the Special Operations Executive (SOE) during the war.

Enlisted women learning Morse code in a classroom, 1942.

Marjorie (second left) with two female friends in the FANY and a US serviceman in Siena while serving overseas.

Hilda Bainbridge in her Women's Land Army (WLA)
uniform during the war.

Hilda at home, 2020.

Land Girls in the WLA operating a tractor, 1942.

A collage created for the one-hundredth birthday of former Air Transport Auxiliary pilot Jaye Edwards. It includes her aviator's certificate, a group shot in which she appears (second left on the wing, in the bottom left-hand photo) and a picture of a friend in the ATA (bottom right).

An Auxiliary Territorial Service (ATS) section arriving in Lüneberg, Germany, 1945.

Joy Hunter at 17 years old in her
Girls' Training Corps uniform.

Joy celebrating her ninety-fifth
birthday.

A code and cypher officer hard at work, 1943.

says. On these occasions her war work felt more like a hobby than a job.

She lived in Leeds while working in the ATA, residing with a relation by marriage. 'I started out in my sister's mother-in-law's place,' she explains. 'We hardly met, because I'd go out early. She had a very nice maid. She slept out, but she came in every morning early and she always gave me a good breakfast. Then I came home and dinner was served. I saw my sister's mother-in-law once in a while. She was an older woman.'

Each morning Jaye would travel to the airfield at Sherburn in Elmet, North Yorkshire, to learn which aircraft needed delivering. Often it was a newly manufactured plane made at the site. 'Close by was a factory that made Barracudas,' she says. 'I don't know how many or how often they pushed them out, but every time a Barracuda was ready, it would be flown away to an airfield. The plane would come out, down to our station, and someone would be given it to fly it to where it had to go.' At the other end, 'You go to the office and you hand in the chit that says you've done it – you had to have it signed – then you go home to supper.' Sometimes an airfield would put on lunch for her if she arrived at a suitable hour, but there was 'little fuss'. Her return journey to Sherburn was usually made by train, but from time to time another aircraft with a spare seat might be travelling in the right direction to transport her.

The premise of her job was 'very simple', although 'the doing of it was perhaps a little tougher,' she says, laughing. 'But in a way it wasn't a difficult job. Once you were content flying, you knew you could take over and you knew you could land. You always could go to Met [the Meteorological Society outpost at every airfield]. They had pamphlets on every plane,' she explains. 'So when you got a plane, if you'd never seen it before, you would go and get a pamphlet, and read it and digest it. Added to that, we had a "knee pad" [booklet]. It was about an inch and a half thick. Every page was about a different aeroplane. What the aeroplane would do was written on those cards.'

This abbreviated manual, officially called 'Ferry Pilot notes', gained its nickname from being strapped to one knee with elastic. It was 250 pages, with brief instructions on take-off, stall and landing for each aircraft model – American as well as British. Other Allied nations used different units for the fuel gauge and speed dial, so the 'bible' was essential to explain which metrics were relevant. 'Everyone had a whole pack. So if you had a plane and you just wanted to review it, because you'd flown one two days earlier and wanted to make sure you had it ready in your mind, you would just turn it to that page and put it on your knee when you sat in the plane. There was all the information you needed on take-off, landing, getting up to 2,000 feet, flying straight and level. We were supposed to fly at 2,000 feet and with 800 yards visibility.'

The duration of trips varied, according to destination and aircraft type. The Tiger Moth training biplanes were famously slow, she recalls. Some ATA pilots recorded fitting six short flights into a single day. Navigation was conducted by reference to natural features of the landscape, such as rivers and woods, as well as man-made roads and railways. Maps were provided – and often strapped to the other knee – but did not contain any place names as a precaution, lest they fell into enemy hands. Long, straight Roman roads were particularly useful and Jaye most commonly used the Fosse Way, which stretches between Exeter and Lincoln, to orientate herself when she flew south.

'We navigated by the seat of [our] pants. You had the map – that was it,' she has said in the past.[10] She was not daunted, however. 'You could always find your way home. When you took off you knew what route you were taking. There was one place in England where the water flowed upside down. Somebody saw it and this information got passed around. So if you were in that side of the country, the West, you looked for this spot. I don't know if it really did, but it looked from a plane as though the water flowed upside down.'

Peering down on the earth below, people and animals appeared only as specks. 'We would see something; you couldn't necessarily name it,' she says. Flying over the sea or estuaries, where landing was impossible, carried a greater risk. The women of the ATA were made to practise over 'a very narrow strip of water between Scotland and Northern Ireland. That was where we had to go and cross. Then we landed in Belfast,' Jaye recalls.

Visual symbols, including Morse code messages flashed from a signal lamp and flares, were used by ground crew to guide incoming aircraft. A green light indicated all-clear for take-off, while a red light signalled a warning. The fire brigade and ambulances were often called if ground crew suspected an aircraft was in trouble and at risk of crash-landing near a base.

Flying in poor conditions was the most dangerous threat to a pilot's safety. There was never any pressure to do so, however. 'We never had to fly if the weather was bad. You were allowed to choose; you weren't told you've got to do it. You were given a chit and told, "This has to be delivered. Here it is – talk to Met." We had one on every airfield. You would go to Met to find out what the weather was like, where you were, where you were going, how the trip would be and how the landing would be. You could make up your mind if it was suitable, or you felt it was not. After all, some of us had only done two hours solo. So you had to be a little cautious sometimes.'

On occasion a pilot would set off, only to return to their home base within the hour if the weather turned quickly. Since the pilots flew without radio communication and relied on sight to identify nearby obstacles, such as other aircraft, fog presented a particular problem. The low height at which they flew also meant that climbing 'above' storms and heavy rain was not always possible. Looking back now, Jaye acknowledges that many flights were fraught with danger. Recalling one perilous episode, she says: 'I do know one girl who was at the same level as I was. Her engine gave out and she had to get out and parachute down, because her plane stalled. If she hadn't got out, she would have crash-landed – and the plane did crash-land. You flew at 2,000 feet and at that height you could get out – you count to ten and then pull your parachute.'

On one of her own missions, she was alarmed to find on arrival that part of the plane was missing. 'On part of the fuselage was a door, which opened out and there was room to put something. On a plane you have it at the side, because you've got a tail at the back. On this occasion, someone hadn't closed the doorway properly, so it fell off. It wasn't there at the end. When I got there they said, "Where's the door?" There was nothing they could do about it. Somewhere on my trip it had gone. I hoped it hadn't hurt anybody, or any animal, but there was nothing you could do about it. Nobody ever complained. I covered a lot of open territory.'

She stresses that the aircraft she flew tended to be in good working order. 'Mostly the planes we flew were to replace planes that had been flown over Germany, damaged or destroyed, and they wanted replacements. We replaced planes.' However, if malfunctions did occur, airfields were dotted all over the country. In emergencies, Jaye would scour the horizon for the nearest one in which to land.

'I had one occasion in which they told me there was a snowstorm, but it was way behind and I'd be long gone before it got there,' she says, before pausing for dramatic effect. 'Except it got there before me. I found myself out on the North Sea, not that far away from the land, but I wasn't over land.' It was too late to turn back, she realised; to do so would have meant flying into the face of the storm she was trying to escape. Visibility became increasingly poor and she could not see well what lay below – whether land or water.

After several nerve-wracking minutes she finally caught a glimpse of the topography below and realised that she was over the Firth of Forth, the estuary of several Scottish rivers that flow into the North Sea. She held her nerve. 'A little power and a little turn, and hands off and feet off. Planes were built to fly, so take your hands and feet off – they'll fly,' she says. 'I could not see over the water, but I put a little power on, and made a turn and climbed up. I climbed up to 2,000 feet and then levelled off. I knew exactly where I was.' Emerging into sunshine above the storm, she felt relief and a stronger sense of confidence in her own abilities.

On another occasion ice began to spread across her aircraft, a dangerous phenomenon that distorts the smooth flow of air, increases drag and causes a loss of lift. 'I turned my head and I could see ice on the wings,' she says with a shudder. 'Well, it happens. I'd been up to 2,000 feet, and I needed to stop. I thought, *Uh-oh.*' She was able to abort the mission before disaster ensued. 'I found a field and I landed. I got down. I stayed the night, and took the plane on in the morning. You didn't always have trouble with the weather, but sometimes you did. You could always, if you felt it was bad weather and you wanted to put down, find an airfield and land.'

Barrage balloons, which were vast inflatables used to defend ground targets by rendering them more difficult for enemy aircraft to approach, presented another obstacle. They flew at around 5,000 feet, anchored to the ground with steel cables, and were often operated by female recruits in the Women's Auxiliary Air Force. Jaye's assignments did not require her to fly into areas where the balloons were used, however. 'In Southampton they had them up and down – and if you weren't ready to go when they took them down, you probably wouldn't get out, because by the time you were ready, they had probably been put back up. They went down and up, very frequently in Southampton, but not where I was up north.'

Without live weapons to defend themselves, the ATA pilots also faced the threat of enemy attack. For Jaye it was a danger that did not materialise. 'We flew all over England. We did not – at least as far as I'm concerned – meet any enemies.' She insists she did not fret about the prospect either, trusting the RAF to deter the Luftwaffe: 'The Germans were kept busy. So they didn't have time to come and hit the mainland of England.' Hers was not a uniform experience. Other female pilots did experience incoming attack, including friendly fire.

Despite her love for flying, Jaye was not interested in performing aerial tricks. An early incident while learning to fly deterred her. 'My instructor tried to teach me how to do what's called a stall turn.' The manoeuvre involved a vertical climb and sharp turn sideways. 'My stomach said, "No way!" I threw up and guess where it went: right in the instructor's face – poor girl! And she had to clean up. I didn't. It put me off aerobatics. I never, ever attempted them. They were not for my stomach.' She suspects some of her friends did practise such things, although tricks and 'joy rides' – taking a plane up just for amusement – were seldom openly discussed. 'I never asked. It was sort of illegal,' she says. 'We were meant to drive from A to B, to take a plane – usually from a factory where it had been built – to an airfield, from where it would go out to Germany, over Germany. So there was no excuse for aerobatics. Some people, I guess, when they had Spitfires just liked them so much they flew them [that way].'

On wash-out days, when poor weather prohibited flying, Jaye and her comrades convened in the common room at their Sherburn base. There they would chat and play cards. 'There was usually a bridge game going on,' she says. Other ATA women used the free time to cut dress patterns and make their own clothes. Jaye forged a number of friendships among the other female pilots, who called her 'Pete' – a nickname based on her surname, Petersen.

Her closest friend was Kay. 'She and I were good buddies,' she recalls. 'We started around the same time.' Kay's background also interested Jaye. She had lived in South America before the war, where her father had relocated from Britain after the death of her mother. Jaye wonders now what happened to her. 'She got married and I got married and we lost touch. I really regretted it, but we both changed our names.' Another friend in the organisation was Mary Ellis, a pilot based at an ATA pool in Hamble, Hampshire, who survived a crash-landing when the engine of her Spitfire over-heated due to a jam in its undercarriage.

There were fewer opportunities to get to know any of the male pilots in the force well, but Jaye was curious about the opposite sex. 'I was a very naughty girl often,' she says, laughing. 'Sometimes I'd be sitting on a couch reading, then some boys came in and started talking, and I became a good listener. A girl of 21 listening in on a bunch of boys who just didn't realise I was there, and were just chatting away to themselves. You can imagine the conversation – people they could use, which girls did they fancy ...'

While there had been early recognition in government that women could provide a useful non-combat function in the aviation sector during the war, there was robust opposi-tion from some male quarters. At first female pilots were permitted to fly only military trainer and communications aircraft, but as aircraft production escalated and the death toll of servicemen rose, the rules were eased. Women were handed fighters to deliver from July 1941. The following year the most experienced women broke through a new barrier and flew four-engine bombers for the first time.

In 1940 the editor of *Aeroplane* magazine declared: 'The menace is the woman who thinks that she ought to be flying in a high-speed bomber when she really has not the intelligence to scrub the floor of a hospital properly.'[11] Incredulity was another common reaction to the skills of the ATA's female pilots. When Mary Ellis landed a Wellington bomber at one

RAF base, the ground crew struggled to believe she had piloted it. 'They actually went inside the aeroplane and searched it,' she recalled in a later interview.[12] 'Everybody was flabbergasted that a little girl like me could fly these big aeroplanes all by oneself.'

At the ATA's inception, its women were paid a fifth less than the men. By 1943, when Jaye joined, the organisation had agreed to equal pay. It was the first of the auxiliary organisations to do so. 'I didn't really think about it, because by the time I got in, Gower had organised it so we were all paid the same,' she says. Pauline Gower, a founding member of the ATA who had been a circus pilot in the interwar years and flown her own air-taxi service, was a major influence on Jaye. Pauline was 'brilliant – a very smart girl', and as the daughter of a prominent Conservative MP she was also well connected. Having banked hundreds of hours of flying experience, she proposed the creation of the women's section of the ATA at the start of the war and was one of eight women entrusted to establish it on New Year's Day 1940.

She had successfully lobbied Gerard d'Erlanger, a pre-war director of British Airways who was the brains behind the auxiliary force, although he had initially envisaged it as an aerial courier service for VIPs, medicines and the wounded, rather than an organisation to ferry military aircraft.[13] Pauline also campaigned for equal pay, arguing that women had the same qualifications as men and ran the same risks. She declared: 'Some people believe women pilots to be a race apart, and born "fully fledged". Women are not born with wings, neither are men for that matter. Wings are won by hard work, just as proficiency is won in any profession.' Jaye says: 'She was so strong during the war. Very sadly, she married after the war, got pregnant, had twin boys and died. It was really very tragic.'

Jaye does not recall encountering any sexism herself while serving in the women's section of the ATA. She felt her male counterparts 'were more interested in what we were doing' than criticising the female pilots. 'I would say they respected me,' she asserts. Nor did she rail against the sex discrimination that prevented women from being allowed to fly aircraft in battle. 'I never thought about it at all,' she admits. 'I was so busy. You hadn't time to think about it. You were busy with the job you had.'

Romances within the ATA were rare at her airbase. 'There was one couple. One of the girls, one of our men. They were the only couple that got together and, I believe, married. Nobody else did,' she says. 'Mostly there weren't that many men that had time for anything. They were all so busy.' She says of herself: 'I don't think I thought about it much.' Her own first attraction came soon after the war when she was living in the Far East, but it was dashed by a miscommunication. 'I lived in the YMCA in Singapore and I met up with a chap. He lived in the YMCA in Singapore. What we didn't know was, I was in the civilian one and he was in the Army one. We had agreed to meet on the grass outside the YMCA – not saying which one it was, though, because we didn't know there were two. So I sat there for half an hour, got bored and went away. And I assume the same thing happened to him. Maybe it was meant to be, maybe it wasn't. That was the only time I associated with someone [of the opposite sex] and that wasn't really an association,' she says shyly.

Jaye can remember clearly her movements on 8 May 1945, when Victory in Europe was declared. 'I was on a train coming home from a flight that landed on the Isle of Man. I managed to get transportation: I flew in a plane to get onto the mainland, I was dropped off, then I walked quite a distance. I had a bed for the night, before I went on the train to get home,' she says. It was while on the train that she heard the news. While relieved that the conflict had ended, part of her was filled with deep sadness. 'I knew that was the end of flying,' she says.

After the war, she recalls: 'We were discharged – juniors like myself, who had been there since '43.' Nonetheless, some of her colleagues refused to give up aviation. When the ATA was disbanded in 1945, Jaye's friend Mary Ellis was seconded to the RAF, where she became one of the first women to fly Britain's earliest jet fighter, the Gloster Meteor.

Jaye was flummoxed, initially, about what to do next, so she decided to go abroad. 'We had a very good time [in the ATA]. I travelled quite a lot and I was sent to a lot of places. After the war, I sat back and thought, *What can I do? I haven't learned anything except flying.*' She decided to return to childcare and moved to the South Pacific with a friend and her family, helping out with the children. For a time she worked as a secretary in Singapore, then she moved to Australia, before finally settling in Canada in 1948.

She was drawn to the North American country by memories of a favourite aunt who had moved to Montreal. 'I was wanting to go and I liked her. I had looked after her when she'd been sick one time, and I made sure she had things to do. She had always been kind to me. So I thought I'd like to get there.' Jaye moved to British Columbia, the country's westernmost province, which borders the Pacific Ocean. There she became a teacher and later met William Edwards, known as Bill, who became her husband. 'I didn't marry until I was 40,' she says. The couple had one son, Neil.

Reflecting now on her years as a pilot, she says slowly: 'It was special, because I enjoyed the flying. Whether it was special for the war, I don't know – if you understand the difference.' She is keen to stress that it was a group effort. 'I was not alone. You have to realise, there were 150 women at least who participated in the Air Transport Auxiliary. It makes me mad when people want to say, "Oh, you're wonderful."' In recent years she has remarked: 'You have to have a laugh in life. The opportunity was there. I took it. There weren't so many chances in my generation to do things that were unusual.'[14]

After the war she was handed the performance reports written by her superiors and was quietly pleased that 'they said I was a better pilot than I realised,' she remarks. 'That was very nice, because that wasn't said to me then. It was written down on my service sheet.' Once the conflict ended, half a century passed before Jaye took a seat in a cockpit again. Her son Neil organised a flight in a biplane to mark her eightieth birthday. 'I went up and I was so pleased,' she recalls. 'I could remember how to turn a corner, because I wanted to go down the way, out from a grass field on the highway going towards the ocean. I made the turn, and it turned out I kept it straight and level and I went on, and then turned it again to come back in.' Neil went up too. 'His attitude is very different to mine, because he'd like to know how fast he could go.'

Today, Jaye enjoys flipping through her photo album of iconic Second World War aircraft and reminiscing about the war from time to time. On her one-hundredth birthday, which she celebrated at a local pub in North Vancouver, she was delighted to receive a video message from the Canadian astronaut Chris Hadfield. Sending his best wishes, he informed her that as 'one of the newest Spitfire pilots in the world', he was joining her club.

# Joy Hunter

**DATE OF BIRTH:**

15 September 1925 (aged 14 at the outbreak of war)

**ROLE:**

Secretary in the Cabinet War Rooms

'It was quite a terrifying situation,' admits Joy Hunter of her arrival on Whitehall as an 18-year-old shorthand typist. 'I made loads of mistakes.' Drafted into a secretarial pool staffed by permanent female civil servants at least a decade older than her, she felt a callow addition to a grave and important world. She worked hard and impressed her superiors, however, and was soon promoted to the Joint Planning Committee secretariat in the subterranean War Rooms beneath Downing Street. Tasked with typing up highly classified blueprints for crucial military operations, including D-Day, Joy was brought face to face with Winston Churchill on countless occasions through her role. She was even part of a group invited to join him for a midnight cinema session in a rare break from her duties. Today she is one of the last surviving women who worked at close quarters with Britain's wartime prime minister during the conflict. Her adventures did not end in Westminster, however. She was selected to attend the historic Potsdam Conference in Germany, at which Britain, America and the Soviet Union carved up the territorial spoils of war in July 1945, and later travelled on to negotiations linked to the Bretton Woods talks, which established a new international system of monetary management.

The daughter of a Church of England vicar, Margaret Joy Milward's earliest years were spent in Brockmoor, an industrial village in the West Midlands. She was the eldest of three sisters – two years older than Rosemary and six years older than Anne. Their father Kenneth and mother Joyce were 'very strict' and family life revolved around the church. Each Sunday entailed attendance at multiple services, which demanded hats, gloves and smart dress. Joy was mischievous, a trait she shared with Rosemary, and they could not resist wisecracks about the attire of visiting ecclesiastical figures. Once her sister exclaimed that the Bishop of Lichfield appeared to be 'wearing purple knickers!' while Joy was often in trouble for misdemeanours, including breaking window panes and taking scissors to her sister's hair.

The Milward girls occupied an uncomfortable position in the village, set apart from the other children on account of their father's vocation. 'We didn't go out to play in the street at all,' Joy recalls. 'As the vicar, you ranked with the local doctor. We did not go to the local school; we had a governess to start with. It was a very poor little urban village – it had shops and a church and a chapel. It had a big steel factory just behind us. We just had this kind of haven, really.'

When she was 11 the family moved to Staffordshire, while she was sent south to boarding school in Worcestershire, following in the footsteps of her mother. She cannot fathom now how her parents afforded the fees at Lawnside, even with a bursary for the daughters of alumnae. While the family enjoyed the grace-and-favour houses that came with Kenneth's role, they were far from affluent. At first she missed her parents sorely. 'I hated leaving them,' she says. 'I found it quite difficult to settle, really. It was very strict again, of course. I always seemed to be getting into trouble, so it was kind of a love-hate relationship. When I was younger and first went, I seemed to get bullied quite a lot. I must have been rather pathetic, really. But afterwards, I had friends and some I've kept through the years, including one who came to my ninetieth birthday.'

Joy was 14 years old when the war broke out. Although pupils at her school were instructed to read a newspaper each morning and to give regular presentations on current affairs, the development came as a sharp shock to her. She recalls with vivid clarity how the formal announcement reached her on Sunday, 3 September 1939. While millions of Britons were at home, tuning in to the wireless at quarter past eleven to hear Prime Minister Neville Chamberlain's address to the nation, she was in church where her father was leading a service. 'Somebody came in and told my father, and he gave it out,' she says. 'As we came out of church at half past eleven, the sirens went, and that was a bit scary to me. We were thinking just, *What the hell's that?* We were terrified. I gather it was a practice to ensure that everybody knew what the [air-raid] siren sounded like.' The cellar of the church was subsequently converted into a bomb shelter.

In the event, neither her hometown of Leek, nor Malvern where her school was located, were attacked by the Luftwaffe. 'We were not on the target route at all,' she says, explaining her relief. 'The only time we had air-raid warnings at school, I remember, was when bombers were returning from London to Coventry, but they weren't bombing us. It was very scary the first time. I woke up to find the whole of the room I was sleeping in – eight people – they were all getting their dressing gowns on at the sound of the siren. So I did have a shock then, as I hadn't heard the siren. But I got used to that later on when I lived in London. We had bombs and you just carry on.'

At home the most obvious sign that a war was raging in Europe was the scarcity of food. The butcher became the most powerful person in the village, she says, laughing. Strictly speaking, rations allowed for one medium-sized chop a week for each person, but the butcher could also sell meats not covered by the restrictions, including rabbit and offal. She also remembers fresh vegetables becoming difficult to source – an issue that could be remedied by families growing their own.

Joy's graduation from school in December 1941 was followed by a severe bout of influenza, which forced her to remain in bed for several months. As she regained her health, the 17-year-old's thoughts turned to the war effort. 'I'd always wanted to be a nurse and had, in fact, been very keen,' she says. 'I had done some first-aid things while I was at boarding school: I arranged for four of us to go to a full Red Cross first-aid and home-nursing course. My parents were quite surprised I had made some inquiries about entry.'

However, they were deeply opposed to the idea and soon unveiled their own plans for their daughter's future. 'My mother came upstairs. She said, "Your father and I think it really would be much better if you went to a really good secretarial college." I was not pleased at all – very grumpy!' However, Joy felt unable to resist their proposal. 'In those days, you did as your parents told you, unless you were very strong-minded. I was furious, because it wasn't at all what I wanted to do,' she says.

Brooking no argument, her mother enrolled her at Mrs Hoster's, a smart London-based secretarial college that had been evacuated to Lincolnshire during the conflict. 'It was rather funny, really. It was like a wartime finishing school,' she says with an arch laugh. 'Although they didn't promise you a rich husband, they did offer you a good job, because they had an agency in London, where you did some practical work. At the end of the course, then you had a pink slip telling you to go to various places that wanted people. And obviously the government offices were very, very high class.' She learned shorthand, typing and bookkeeping, and also took classes in contemporary history, parliamentary debate and committee procedure. She shared a bedroom with General Jumbo Wilson's daughter, Pamela, who later went on to work at Conservative Central Office, where she met and subsequently married the controversial Tory MP Enoch Powell.

Joy's popularity was assured by her mother's regular parcels of home-baked cakes, which were made with valuable dried-egg powder. She had only been at the college for three months, however, when a pink form arrived from London requesting her presence at Number 10 Downing Street for an interview. The assessment precipitated her first visit to the capital. Looking back, she notes: 'Nobody went to London unless you'd got a lot of money, I suppose, or for some important reason or for some particular job.' She travelled down by train, then navigated the city by bus, eventually arriving on Whitehall. At the entrance to Downing Street was 'one bobby, unarmed', who pointed her to the right door for her meeting.

Led down into the garden basement of Number 10, Joy was interviewed by Margaret Stenhouse, the head of the office staff. To her surprise, she passed the test and was offered a job on the spot. However, she felt compelled to respond: 'Couldn't you wait till Christmas? I haven't quite finished my course yet.' Laughing as she reflects on the episode now, she adds: 'Of course, you were so much in fear of your parents, who had paid £90 for that six-month course. That probably sounds nothing today. But then, at that time, my father was probably earning £300 a year. There were five of us. He had a house provided, but everything else had to be paid for. I thought, *I can't let them down.* You had to have your training in order to get a job. So I said, "Thank you, but no, I really can't."'

Joy returned to Mrs Hoster's and finished her course, at the end of which another pink slip arrived for her. This time she was summoned to the offices of the War Cabinet for an interview. 'Then I was 18, and I'd got no choice. You couldn't sort of say, "I'll hang about and see if I get a better offer," because at 18 you were conscripted,' she explains. It was the end of 1943, by which time conscription had been in place for women for two years.

She started work in a secretarial pool of 60 women, who worked in three columns in an office of the War Cabinet on Great George Street. The pay was £2 and 10 shillings a week and the working pattern alternated between two shifts: eight in the morning until four in the afternoon, and two in the afternoon until nine in the evening. The work was laborious. Six carbon copies of every document were required and Joy often made errors, which were then a nuisance to correct on each of the six versions. She felt under severe pressure. 'It had to be right, of course,' she says, but she feared that she was falling short of expectations. 'I suppose because I'd been to this very good college, they thought I was going to be brilliant. I was absolutely hopeless when I started.'

Within several weeks she was seconded to nearby Richmond Terrace to work as a private secretary to Major General

West, an army commander who was making arrangements for 'our occupation of Germany – hopefully' she remembers. Working alongside his aide-de-camp, she recalls setting up top-secret meetings and phone calls. It was a calmer environment, for which she felt better prepared by her secretarial training. She started work at nine in the morning and continued until the day's tasks were complete, which was often not until late. The shifts were therefore longer than in the typing pool, but she preferred a small team. The General rated her highly and sought a transfer for her to the Auxiliary Territorial Service, which would have allowed her to stay on, but the request was blocked. Her presence was required once again in the secretarial pool at Great George Street.

Upon her return, however, Joy was among a clutch of ten women asked to 'come downstairs'. The request was baffling to the group. 'We'd no idea – we didn't know where "downstairs" was. We didn't even know who was in the next-door offices,' she says. After seeking directions, the women eventually found a staircase leading down into the bowels of the building. Gingerly they descended and met with an imposing-looking door, which was bolted firmly shut. They paused. 'There was a button on it, so one of us bravely pushed it,' she recalls. 'It opened and there were two marines in full uniform and I thought, *What on earth is going on here? What is happening?* We were actually in the Churchill War Rooms, as they're now called.'

From that time onwards she worked alongside ministers, military strategists and Churchill himself in the warren of offices under Whitehall known at the time as the Cabinet War Rooms. 'We were all down there in this converted cellar, it turns out, because I remember there was a very cross letter from Churchill [when he discovered its lack of protection from air raids]. He had thought we were bomb-proof. Hitler, if you remember, had a bunker 30 feet below ground. Ours was just a cellar – a storeroom that was converted – hence the staircase down into it.' She had joined the Joint Planning Committee secretariat. She and her female colleagues were assigned to senior commanders in the Royal Navy, Army and Royal Air Force who coordinated directly with Churchill. Connie, their kindly supervisor, accompanied them downstairs so they 'didn't feel quite so lost,' Joy recalls.

A third shift was added to the women's usual rota: a 25-hour marathon that was to be undertaken three times a fortnight. 'We did usually get to bed for a couple of hours,' she says of the long shift. 'We had to wait until the work was finished, of course. And there was no overtime, no time off in lieu.' The environment below stairs, in the engine rooms of Britain's military strategy, was more exciting than above stairs, however. The work was more interesting for Joy and her female colleagues, too. Instead of dealing with extensive committee summaries, lengthy letters and long-winded communiqués, the women typed up and managed flash reports arriving hourly from all over the world, detailing British battle orders, attacks and casualties. Secrecy was all-important and she remembers the dismissal of one of her colleagues after she was overheard being indiscreet in conversation with a friend in a nearby Westminster café.

Recalling one of the most gripping tasks she undertook, Joy says: 'Two or three of us were given D-Day landing instructions to type and check. We knew they were pretty important, obviously, and it's a good thing we did check it. It would have been really stupid if we sent them to Spain instead of France – that wouldn't have been funny. I don't know if they used those in the end, or whether they were revised and revised, but that's what we did.' The period leading up to D-Day in June 1944 was tense, she remembers. The military commanders were deeply worried about the plan to launch the Normandy landings, which remain the biggest seaborne invasion in history. The stakes were high: the perilous mission involved 156,000 British, American and Canadian troops arriving by land and sea in a bid to liberate France and then Western Europe.

The operation, code-named 'Overlord', paved the way for the Allied victory on the Western Front, but it entailed the death of more than 4,400 men. 'In a way, when D-Day came, it was a bit like the cork coming out of a bottle; it was a huge relief of tension,' says Joy. 'But then, of course, the horror struck about the casualties, the mistakes that were made, the awful things that happened. So it was a mixture, really, and then we had to wait.' It would be another year before the war in Europe ended.

Working in the War Rooms beneath Whitehall, she often ran into the Prime Minister. 'We were all using the same corridors. Most of the senior people just walked past us, but he always stopped. I don't say that he had long conversations, but he'd always say, "Good morning" or "Good afternoon". And if there'd been a raid, he always said, "Are you all right? Was your home hit? Are your family safe?" I think he liked having civilians working down there. There were lots of us – dispatch writers, telephone operators, Morse operators and all sorts of people. You never saw them, of course. I never knew at the time who was down there.' Conditions were cramped. In the committee room in which Churchill presided, 'you'd see that the three heads of staff sat almost knee-to-knee with him'. She suspects that he must have 'felt very threatened' by the close proximity of such experienced military men.

Churchill was usually seen in his self-designed 'siren suit', a special boiler suit, and occasionally could be glimpsed in the evening with a glass of brandy or whisky in hand. 'He'd smoke in bed when he was reading his papers in the morning – very odd,' she recalls disapprovingly. Smoking was ubiquitous and the poor ventilation in the subterranean complex created an unpleasant, close atmosphere. She retains enormous respect for Churchill today. 'Everybody said how difficult he was, but he needed to be,' she says, pointing out his obstinate refusal to support Chamberlain's policy of appeasement towards Hitler and Fascism in the Third Reich. Great swathes of the country, from powerful politicians to workers in factories, needed robust encouragement to back the country's entry into the conflict following the devastation of the Great War.

'It wasn't just Halifax and co. at the beginning of the war,' Joy stresses, referring to Lord Halifax, the pre-war foreign secretary who was a staunch proponent of appeasement until a late stage. 'The country wasn't prepared for war. We were still suffering from the First World War. It was still the Great Depression,' she says. Many families endured unemployment and poverty, she adds, pointing to the Jarrow March that took place in County Durham in 1936 to protest against widespread hardship.

In London, homeless First World War veterans were a commonplace sight. 'I used to see injured soldiers in that little place where I lived [in Paddington], begging in the streets. There were no pensions, no aftercare. Most of the soldiers were just ordinary people; they were not trained soldiers. They were men with shock,' she says. Her own father had served in the Great War in the Royal Army Medical Corps, although he never spoke to her about his experiences. He had paid a high price physically for his involvement. 'He'd got very bad legs because he'd put his puttees [bandages worn around the ankle for support and protection] on too tightly and then gone for a route march for God knows how long. He was just an ordinary Potteries boy who'd left school at 12, training to go into the Church,' she says.

Explaining how the horrors of the conflict still haunted society in the 1930s, she adds: 'They all volunteered for the First World War until about 1916–17. Then so many people had been killed they had to conscript them. As you know, whole streets joined. So some streets had no men in them at all, because all the men had left to join the war.' In some communities the men never returned; they could be wiped out in a single, devastating battle. The thought of British soldiers buried in 'these enormous graves, all through France, just bodies filled from the bottom' also disturbed society, she says.

Public support for the war wavered during its early stages, but Churchill's leadership bolstered the nation's morale and sense of fortitude, Joy says. His series of famous speeches to the House of Commons in 1940, including the addresses typically known as 'Blood, toil, tears and sweat', 'We shall fight on the beaches' and 'This was their finest hour', were pivotal in marshalling the public's sentiments, she adds. 'I think now, looking back after all this time, and the books I've read and historians I've read, I think the speeches were as much to the civilians as to the politicians, because he had to convince the country that we wouldn't surrender. It wasn't just for politicians; it was for the people. It makes sense, because nobody wanted war.'

Since Churchill spent so much time working underground in the Cabinet War Rooms, a plan was devised to help him unwind during periods of exacting intensity. 'While we were there, he had one of the rooms turned into a very makeshift cinema,' Joy says. 'Just ordinary chairs and a cinegraphic camera. He loved films.' A short time elapsed before she and her friends were invited to join him, although their enthusiasm on that occasion was muted. 'One night we were on the late shift. It must have been about midnight, because I know we would rather have got a few hours in bed,' she says, explaining that she and her colleagues were on duty the next day too. 'The message came saying he was going to watch a film; would any of us like to join him? He'd be delighted. So a few of us thought we would – a bit grudgingly, really. We were terribly tired. Anyway, off we went to this room. I know I was sitting next to the dispatch writer and talking to him, and we waited and waited. I shuffled a bit and began to think, *Oh, goodness.* Then all of a sudden, the door burst open and in he comes in his pyjamas, dressing gown, cigar in one hand and glass in the other – shouts out something like, "Winnie's here – let it roll!" He sat at the back and we sat at the front. I can't remember anything about the film, of course. That was the only time he did it.'

Churchill did not appear to find it easy to relax. 'He loved being up in the action; after all, he stayed a man of action all his life,' she remarks. She remembers the ruses he deployed to throw off his senior advisers, recalling one particular instance: 'His aide was seeing him to bed, because of course he had a bedroom downstairs. He said, "Goodnight, Mr Churchill." And he said, "Be sure to tell Mrs Churchill that I've gone to bed down here." But he hated sleeping down there and the minute the aide had gone, he'd be out of bed, bang upstairs, up on the roof. Especially if there was an air raid. He liked to see where the bombs were falling and seeing if, hopefully, his beloved House of Commons was all right.'

She adds that after the war she met a former policeman who had been assigned to guard and protect the prime minister. 'He said [Churchill] was a devil of a man to be a detective for. Wherever he went, Churchill always managed to escape him. He'd get up on the roof, and when they were at the Potsdam Conference, he went all over the place looking for him.'

Today she marvels at having worked in such close proximity to Churchill, but admits that at the time she did not compute the significance. 'It was just wartime and work. I didn't think there was much glamour about it. You just had to get on and do it,' she says, laughing. Nor could she regale friends or family with tales of bumping into the prime minister, because the secrecy rules forbade her from disclosing any details of her role. 'Nobody knew. You don't tell anybody anything in wartime. My parents didn't know,' she says. 'You couldn't. We never spoke about it.'

Her duties in the Joint Planning Committee secretariat were draining and dominated her life. 'It was just work, work, work,' she says, adding that there was little spare time for any other activities. When she was not at the office, she tended to be at her hostel near Paddington Station, which the secretarial college had found for her. In later years she recorded in *Joy's Journey*, a memoir, how she would take part in the defence of the building. 'On returning from work some of us would take it in turns to assist the hostel's appointed air-raid warden on the roof, ready to kick off incendiaries into the garden below,' she said. 'Blackout was strictly enforced. If a warden saw even the smallest chink of light, they would bang on the door and there would be trouble.'

She continued: 'The underground stations were eerie places, with rows of metal bunks lining the platforms for people to spend the night there. We had to pick our way over sleeping bodies of all ages seeking safety from air raids, who presumably became used to the roar of tube trains arriving until well after midnight. There people were equipped with bedding and food, often with babes in arms being bottle fed, jealously guarding their "own" pitch but with a tremendous sense of camaraderie while commuters made their way home.'

Money was scarce, Joy recalls. After paying for bed and board at the hostel, lunch at work, and travel there and back each day, there was little of her wage left over. A meal out at a restaurant was a luxury that was rarely affordable. Even the gaslight in her hostel bedroom, to which a top-up meter was attached, had to be used judiciously. She swiftly became accustomed to feeling her way around in the dark.

Later in the war she moved in with her mother's cousin, Violet, who lived in northwest London, near Northolt airfield. 'We did hear a lot of bombing,' she recalls. 'We slept in a Morrison shelter – the one that goes in the house. It's rather like an iron table with netting all round it. [Violet] and I and my cousin, Tricia, we slept inside and my other cousin slept across our feet and was ready to pounce in if bombs were falling.' She reflects: 'I don't know how much it would have saved us, but it did save people. It was strong enough to hold a house.'

When she visited her parents at home in Leek, she found that they, too, had taken in an evacuee. The girl spent her evenings with Gladys, the family's domestic servant, and dined separately from the rest of the household. 'Looking back, I feel she must have been one of the miserable children who were not treated well. I presume she went to school during the day, but we never had anything to do with her,' she wrote previously.[15]

Eventually another of Violet's children returned home from the war and required a room, so Joy was obliged to move out again. 'Some of my friends managed to get flats and share with friends, but I think the rent for that was £5 a week. Having to pay my share, I couldn't afford to join them,' she says. Instead, she moved into a Young Women's Christian Association hostel in West Hampstead. It was a sociable environment and one in which, having been to boarding school, she found it easy to live. Social participation in its various clubs was encouraged and she occasionally sang with its choir in fundraising concerts.

She did not make lasting friends there, however. 'I knew one person, I think. I mean, we'd say hello at breakfast. You didn't go out, you see. You just got home, had your meal, [slept], got up and went to work.' At first she shared a room with two other women, but when an individual room became available, she seized the chance for more privacy. On one occasion she got talking to a friendly Russian girl who lived nearby, but feared an ulterior motive. 'I remember wondering, because she was Russian, whether she was trying to get secrets out of me,' she says.

It was not much easier to make friends at work. 'You hardly knew anybody's name. I didn't know if they were married or not. I didn't know how old they were,' she explains. 'I realise now they were all permanent civil servants, so they must have been much older than I was. In fact, Joan Bright, who was General Ismay's secretary, she was in her thirties and I was only 19,' she says. Joan Bright had organised the Special Information Centre in the Cabinet War Rooms, supplying confidential information to the commanders-in-chief. As a young woman she had dated Ian Fleming, the author of the James Bond novels, and is believed to be one of a handful of women upon whom his character Miss Moneypenny was based. She, too, had attended Mrs Hoster's in the past, but the opportunity did not arise to compare experiences with Joy. 'She wouldn't speak to me,' says Joy, laughing, recalling that many of the older, permanent female civil servants seemed reserved and aloof.

She was not beset by loneliness, however. 'We were so busy,' she explains. 'You didn't get any days off.' She admits that at the beginning she was daunted to be alone in London, but her fascination with the city soon took over. 'I was interested, you see. I've always loved travelling. So when I had an afternoon start, I'd take a bus into the city [in the morning], and wander all round the Old Billingsgate Market and the forum and old churches, most of which were locked up, of course, because they'd been bombed. So I did see some of the Blitz damage even though I wasn't hit.'

One raid, which took place during her first week in the capital, landed terrifyingly close, though. 'They had a proper bombing on Paddington Station and my window looked out onto it, so that was quite close. They were terribly strict at night, of course – no street lights; you weren't allowed to show a light, ever,' she explains. 'Latterly, when I was on a late shift, I sometimes had sandwiches in St James's park beforehand and then I could see the 'buzz bombs' going over. So long as you could hear them, you were safe.' These winged bombs, officially called V1 rockets, were powered by jet engines and gained their nickname from the distinctive sound they made while in flight.

'Then the V2s came; they were less frightening because you never heard them [if they were falling on you]. If you did hear them, you were alive; if you never heard them, you were dead. They were rockets, just without any buzz or noise – silent,' she adds. Explosions became so commonplace that after a while they failed to faze her. 'I don't remember being terrified,' she says. 'I was only caught three times, I think, by buzz bombs. One time I was going home [by train] to West Ealing to stay with my aunt. We got out into the open, the train came to a stop and everything fell on the floor. The driver luckily had kept his eyes about him and could see this buzz bomb coming down. So he'd stopped. Actually it fell a long way from us, so we carried on to West Ealing Station.'

The second incident took place while she was on a bus, about to reach the office in Whitehall. 'The conductor suddenly shouted, "Everybody out!" so we all leapt out and threw ourselves on the pavement and you could hear the most enormous bang, but luckily we did get up. That was a buzz bomb. The driver had seen the bomb coming down and stopped the bus. The only place you were ever safe was on the ground, flat down. Or safer.' She felt no terror, she says, because she had by this time become so accustomed to bombing raids. 'I wasn't thinking, *Help, help!*'

When Victory in Europe was declared on 8 May 1945, Joy's parents were in London visiting her. The trio headed to Buckingham Palace and 'cheered for King and Queen', joining the crowds to watch George VI and Queen Elizabeth, later known as the Queen Mother, come out onto the balcony with Churchill. They were flanked by Princess Elizabeth, then 19, and her sister Princess Margaret, then 14. Unbeknown to the public, the two royal teenagers slipped out of the palace after their appearance and joined the festivities incognito. That day there was 'laughter, tears, dancing, cheers,' Joy recalls. She and her parents walked with the throng towards Trafalgar Square, where there was a sense of 'exuberance', with people starting conga lines and leaping into the fountain. The crowd was so dense that at one point her father lost his footing and they feared he would be trampled, before two sailors swooped in to put him back on his feet.

The next day Joy returned to her desk as usual, as attention turned to preparations for the British delegation at the Potsdam Conference. It was to be the last meeting of the 'Big Three' Allied leaders in the war. The new American president Harry Truman, Soviet dictator Josef Stalin and Churchill were to convene in Potsdam, a suburb of Berlin, to discuss the borders of post-war Europe, among other serious affairs. To her shock, Joy was told she, too, would be attending as part of the administrative support. 'I was delighted and terribly surprised and quite nervous about it,' she says. She was one of six women from the Joint Planning Committee secretariat chosen for the trip.

After receiving her vaccinations and procuring her first passport, she joined the delegation set to depart from Northolt airfield. It was to be her first time aboard an aircraft. 'We as individuals would be weighed before we got on the plane,' she recalls. 'I don't think that would be very popular these days. The Dakota could only take so much weight. Everyone who flew in those days had to be weighed. I thought it was the thing you always did. I didn't know anything about flying.'

The interior of the plane contained some makeshift furniture. 'Of course, they'd been using them for trooping, so they'd hastily put in some chairs for us to sit on. There was a box with oranges and biscuits in the middle and we took off,' she recalls. 'I wrote in my diary we flew at 7,600 feet, which seemed terribly high to me. Now I sit in my garden and watch them going over at 38,000 feet.' She was one of a party of 30 people, who were split between two aircraft.

It was an exhilarating adventure and Joy remembers it vividly. 'When we were over the Channel we had to put on life jackets in case we ditched into the water,' she says. 'The pilot in our plane invited the ladies to come up by two if they wanted to and see the cockpit, so we did. I don't know why he didn't ask the men! That was really quite fun.' She continues: 'We flew to Gattau, which was then in the Russian zone, although I didn't realise that at the time. We didn't know anything about the differences, or the ups and downs. Then we were driven in a number of cars to the Potsdam Conference. On the way we followed or passed large groups of people wandering about with trucks and babies and things, and it never occurred to me at the time, but I have thought since – they were escaping from the Russian zone and hoping to get into the American or the British zones.'

She also recalls Russian check posts every quarter of a mile, at which Soviet police saluted the passing cars. 'They'd clearly been told that very important people were coming,' she says. 'So in the end I thought we can't just sit here and pretend we haven't noticed them, so I did a queenly wave of my hand each time, which I felt was appropriate. I'd never been saluted by all these people before.' Reflecting on the journey, she adds: 'The Russians were very much in charge. I didn't realise at the time, but the whole thing was in the Russian sector.'

The conference was held at a 'vast, very expensive estate' with 'super houses with lovely gardens, birds and swimming pools,' she says. 'We were in one house – all the [British] civilian women. Everything was there. The beds were made up, our names were on the doors – the amount of preparation must have been vast.' A second house was provided to serve as an office for the women, while they ate in a third. 'Would you believe, we had French menus for lunch and dinner at night? They were in French and ready-printed and dated.' She has kept the menus as mementoes.

Detailing her routine at the conference, she says: 'We didn't have shifts; we worked a proper full day. I think we started about 8.30 a.m. and finished whenever the work was finished. I spent a lot of my time taking messages between the house we were working in and various other houses.' On one occasion she visited the Cecilienhof Palace, the mock-Tudor English manor house where the high-level meetings between the Allied leaders were taking place.

Cocktail parties were hosted each evening by senior figures from the different national delegations, where musical entertainment was provided by the RAF Symphony Orchestra and other Allied musicians. At one senior commander's soirée Joy was excited to meet General Hastings Ismay, Churchill's high-profile chief military assistant. At another grand event hosted at Sanssouci Palace – a German rival to Versailles – she says: 'We actually met Churchill, Stalin and Truman. Churchill obviously I'd seen a lot of, but not the other two.'

Coy about her reaction to the Soviet leader at the time, she admits: 'I shook Stalin's hand and for years and years I kept quiet about it, because it sounded as though I was a "commie" [communist]. It sounds silly, really, but when you're young you have all these silly ideas.' The war fostered a strong sense of discretion in society, which lasted throughout the decades afterwards, she says. 'Having been through a war where you told nobody anything, and you were only told yourself that which you needed to know – I didn't even know people's names or where they worked or what they did.'

At the conference she also spotted other high-ranking delegates from across the Allied coalition, including American military chiefs General George Marshall and Fleet Admiral William Leahy, the British Admiral of the Fleet Sir Andrew Cunningham and Field Marshal Sir Alan Brooke, and Soviet General Georgy Zhukov. 'I saw them all,' she says, not without a hint of pride. 'One night I remember there was a concert. I know they played all three national anthems and in the row just across from me were sitting people like Zhukov and a whole lot of American and Russian officers.'

Halfway through the summit, the final results of the British general election that had been held on 5 July were announced. The count had been extended so that votes cast by personnel still serving abroad could be sent back to Britain. Labour Party leader Clement Attlee was declared the new prime minister, replacing Churchill. The handover precipitated a two-day hiatus at the conference to allow Attlee and his new foreign minister, Ernest Bevin, to travel to join the talks. The election result sparked intrigue at the conference, Joy recalls. The Soviets were said to be delighted by the Labour Party's victory. 'I think when Clement Attlee became prime minister, I don't know what [the Russians] thought, really, but the rumour went round they thought they could take us over because it was going to be a Labour government that was really pro-Russia. That was just a rumour,' she says.

In her diary she wrote at the time: 'As the PM had gone home for the general election results, we more or less had the day off. I was put down for the 4 p.m. trip to Cecilienhof. However, when we reached the Palace (it was built in 1916 by the Kaiser in-imitation of an English Tudor house), the Russians were so overjoyed at the Labour victory that they were holding a pow-wow for the invasion of England!'

Joy and her female colleagues picked up most of their gossip from British soldiers in the delegation. Once the UK troops attending the conference 'got hold of the idea or the knowledge that there were a lot of English women who'd come over, we got masses of invitations to dances after work,' she says. The dances were hosted mostly by soldiers rather than officers, and were kept separate from dances hosted by other national delegations. She recalls her evenings being full. 'The trouble was, you had to get your dinner first, which might not be until 8 p.m., so it was a scramble at the end of the day,' she explains. 'I went to a lot of the dances. Apparently, in my diary, another girl and I were responsible for getting the girls together. We seemed to go around finding who was going to go, and then the signals people would send their transport. Some-times we were very late back – one or two in the morning. You still had to start work at 7.45 a.m. I suppose you can do that for a short period of time.'

The success of these events was mixed, depending largely on the liveliness of the male company at each. It was one of the first times Joy – who was slim, with brunette waves, deep-brown eyes and a wide, disarming smile – had encountered attractive young men in social situations. 'Some of the dances were fine, with very pleasant men, but some were quite boring,' she says. 'Remember, I was only 19 and we didn't have loads of boyfriends or go out a lot in wartime, so I really wasn't used to talking all the evening with "adults" – making polite conversation. It was quite difficult at my age, I found. But some were better than others.' At one of the parties, held in the sergeants' mess, Joy tasted her first dram of whisky. 'I found it absolutely revolting. Now it's my favourite drink,' she says, laughing.

In the diary she kept during the trip, she wrote on 16 July: 'Today the first of the Signals Corps dances was to be held and there was great scheming so that those of us on early shift might get off in time to eat and catch the transport ... The standard of dancing was very good and 12.30 a.m. came far too quickly. Our hosts jumped at the opportunity of partners and said they would hold a dance every night if we could get enough girls together. A challenge we weren't going to disregard. Going back, we were stopped several times for passes – at night they were much stricter.'

She has thought a lot about her time at Potsdam in the decades since and has reflected previously on why it felt such an important episode in her life. 'For me, the new experiences were daring and exciting and liberating from the strictures of a rather circumscribed upbringing and the restrictions of work in London in wartime,' she wrote in her memoir.[16] Summarising her exploits and the intense emotions she felt throughout the trip, she added: 'Very chaste flirtations, unrecognised as such at the time; feelings of intense pleasure at being sought after by all these men; self-consciousness at not knowing how to make adult conversation on a social level; finding myself kissing the "boys in the band" and the lonely American soldiers guarding the perimeter of Truman's residence.'

On one of the quieter days of talks, an officer in the British delegation suggested an expedition. 'Colonel Norman arrived at the office house and said he'd got one place left in the staff car. He was going to Berlin to see if he could find the flat he lived in before the war,' she says. She was eager to see something of Germany, so leapt at the chance to join the party. 'It was very dangerous, really, because the Russians wouldn't let us use the main roads, so we drove down a lane by the side of the river – terrified in case we went over a land bomb,' she says, adding: 'We didn't, luckily.'

They drove into the heart of Berlin and walked around the city on foot. In her diary that day, 17 July, she wrote:

Every single building was in ruins. I could never have believed it if I hadn't seen it all. There was not one building which I thought looked habitable and yet there must be people living in the cellars because the streets were full of queues for the one and only bus or for newspapers.

Everywhere there were pathetic groups trudging wearily along in search of wood for fuel, willing to give us anything for cigarettes or better still a bar of chocolate or an ounce of fat. It all seemed utterly unbelievable yet somehow familiar, but never before did the pathos and hopeless frustration of it all hit me so hard.

She continued: 'Faces, while not particularly sad, looked stunned and expressionless. I had to pull myself together and realise that, but for the grace of God and the stubborn determination and sacrifice of our people, it would have happened to us. The hardest thing of all was the sight of little children, beautiful little children, fair and brown, such as you would expect to see at the seaside in England, walking along the streets without shoes, their legs and arms thin as poles, their eyes sunken and expressions old beyond their years.'

Near the River Spree, she recorded 'the ghastly stench of decaying corpses', adding: 'In one place alone a house had been hit under which 2,000 people had been sheltering. The bomb brought the house down on top of the shelter and not one of the bodies had been brought out.' She left Berlin 'full of vivid impressions and mixed feelings'.

Recalling the day trip today, she explains: 'Before we found Colonel Norman's flat, we went into the Chancellery, which had been bombed very severely.' The Soviet troops guarding the building were unaccommodating towards the party, but stopped short of physically obstructing their entry. 'I sensed they didn't really want us to go, but we managed to get in – quite closely followed wherever we went,' she says. 'In one of the rooms was where Hitler had a huge desk, made utterly of marble. It had all been bombed, but I did get a few pieces of Hitler's desk, which I have still got. You wouldn't know they were Hitler's desk unless I told you. Everybody did [the same and took a piece]; I shouldn't think there was anything left at the end of it.' Reflecting on the Nazi dictator's oak-panelled office later that evening, she wrote in her diary: 'In the Chancellery I had the feeling that I would love to have seen Berlin before the war. Here was a building designed to give the most dignified and impressive entrance possible.'

The chunks of salvaged marble were not the only German souvenirs that Joy took home with her from Potsdam. In the house where she slept, she found something else that caught her eye. It occurred to her several days after arriving that the house had likely belonged to a German family forced to flee at short notice following the Soviet invasion. 'I looked in a cupboard and saw a pile of toys in the corner, and some half-finished knitting on a coffee table, and realised that people had been made to move out with very little time,' she says. 'So I looked in the cupboard and there found the empty album, which is the one I wrote in [as a diary] and I also found two medals – not very high-class ones. I stole those, which was naughty on the one hand. On the other, I don't know what happened to the family. The fact that all those things were in there suggests they might have been Nazis anyway, not a private family. The medals – there must have been some connection with the Army, but we didn't know anything; we weren't told anything.'

Victory celebrations were hosted that weekend. Joy wrote in her diary on 21 July: 'Saturday! Everyone up at 6.30 a.m. and very excited, for today was to be the British Victory Parade in Berlin. We were 13 in our lorry with a marine responsible for us. It was a huge convoy. As we rolled along the autobahn there were 17 cars and eight lorries behind us with two buses, dispatch riders and the leader in front; it was thrilling! … We passed all the tanks, armoury and infantry drawn up awaiting Churchill's inspection … We came into contact with German police and onlookers. Several asked in perfect English, "Are you English?" or "You are English, aren't you?" I felt very uncomfortable, embarrassed even, and not at all victorious.' However, her reticence dissipated and, listening to Richard Dimbleby describe the parade in detail on the BBC, she concluded it was 'marvellous'.

Only 27 July she discovered that her entitlement to leave had arrived and she was to be sent home, despite being halfway through the conference. Miss Brown, the superintendent in charge of the women despatched by the War Cabinet to Potsdam, called her in to give her the news. 'I was sorry to leave. We weren't quite finished, but people were going home,' she says. 'Whether she thought I'd not been well behaved or overzealous, I don't know. She suggested I go, and she came with me to the airport at 8.30 a.m., I remember, and saw me off to Gattau.' By 10 p.m. that night, after transport by plane, train and ferry, Joy arrived in Sea

View on the Isle of Wight, where she joined her family, who were on holiday on the island. She could not definitively work out the reason for her early departure from Potsdam. 'On reflection, I still wonder whether Miss Brown sent me home for my leave out of kindness or because of my behaviour, or, indeed, whether she felt responsible that my tender years were being exposed in any unsuitable way,' she wrote in her diary. 'One of life's mysteries.'

However, it was not to be the end of Joy's adventures overseas. When she returned to London after leave, she was appointed as a private secretary in the Government Economics Department. She worked for a Cambridge University professor and shared an office with another secretary named Florrie, who worked for Professor Lionel Robbins, an academic attached to the London School of Economics.

Shortly after her twentieth birthday in September 1945, Joy recalls: 'I was called one day into the pay office and told not to tell anybody that Professor Robbins was going as an advisor for John Maynard Keynes to the States.' The occasion for the visit was a series of high-level negotiations in the wake of the successful Bretton Woods Conference, which had established new rules for the international monetary system. Joy was informed that she was to travel with the academic. She was astonished: 'I don't think I even knew what the Bretton Woods talks were – and he'd chosen me to go with him.' The development presented a dreadful dilemma, however, as Joy knew she would be taking the place of Florrie, by then a friend and trusted confidante. Despite the instruction to keep the trip a secret, she felt forced to warn her colleague. 'I felt terrible, because Florrie was his secretary. So as soon as I got out in the road, I went to a call box and rang her and said, "I'm really sorry." How could I possibly go into work the next day and not say anything? I shared an office [with her]; it was just the two of us,' she says. 'Of course, she was at first absolutely devastated and very upset, because she was his secretary. In the end I was given the reason later – he'd asked for me because she had already been once [to the US for economic talks]. He was trying to be kind, really. She was very good in the end – she helped me with what I needed to take, and helped me in every way she could. But it was a nasty moment, I have to say.'

Joy travelled with her mother and Professor Robbins to Southampton, where she and the economist boarded a ship bound for the US. 'I paired up with another girl called Doreen, whose father was a docker, and he and my mother stood on the platform. There were only two other women [on the ship] and they were both from the Board of Trade,' she recalls. 'We got down to Southampton and found we were actually going over on the *Queen Mary*, the old *QM*. We were in first-class cabins, but in the first-class cabins there were ten others, ten bunks.'

She says: 'There were something like 15,000 American troops on board with us, being sent home. Half of them slept on the deck, half of them slept below, and every night they'd change over.' She adds that American GIs could be found snatching naps on the corridor floors and in the dining rooms, as well as crammed into cabins and luggage hatches. Joy was one of 50 civilians on the ship, which had a crew of 800. Despite the many thousands of people on board, there were only sufficient lifeboats for 3,800. The journey took six days and the weather was poor 'so we all felt a bit queasy,' she recalls. When the ship arrived at port in New York, she was bowled over by the reception, which included a band in a hot-air balloon.

'There were all sorts of banners and flags and hoots going on and there was a message on the lifeboats on deck – nobody was to enter. Apparently, on one of these journeys previously, the Americans were so keen they jumped into one of these boats, to be able to wave more closely to their families, and the boats gave way and they all fell in the water and were killed,' she says. Once on dry land, she was astonished by the rich abundance of food and other items that were available. 'The stores were overflowing with goods – there was no rationing, no coupons.' She bought a pair of black sandals and a lipstick, as well as Mars Bars and peppermint creams.

The delegation travelled on to Washington DC, where the talks were to take place over almost three months. They resulted in the Anglo-American Financial Agreement that saw the US lend Britain, which was on the precipice of bankruptcy, $3.75 billion over 50 years. The final payments were made in 2006. Joy recalls of that time: 'Some days were hard work, but other days we walked miles and miles and miles. We met a lot of Canadian girls who were working in the embassy – very pleasant and very kind. They invited us to parties. One of them got married and invited us to their wedding.'

She was taken aback by the attitude of men on the streets in Washington. 'Walking back late at night, we were quite often accosted, which wasn't very nice. There were men walking round, stopping women,' she says. During her days off, she did a lot of shopping. 'I couldn't believe it – no ruins, no bomb damage, no blackout. Shops full of things I'd never seen before ever,' she says. 'I bought cheap dresses. I sent loads of food parcels home – tins of fruit and tins of Spam and all the sorts of things they had difficulty getting. There was no war then, but there was still nothing much at home. There was still rationing – it went on until 1954.' Transport by bus was cheap, which also made day trips possible.

The signing of the agreement took place on 6 December 1945, after which Joy returned home swiftly. To her delight she was offered a job as private secretary to the Archbishop of Canterbury. It took fierce lobbying from Miss Brown, her superintendent, to persuade the authorities to recognise that it was a significant opportunity for her and to approve her discharge, however. She adds now that her boss likely thought she was not cut out for Whitehall in the long run. 'I think Miss Brown didn't think I was civil service material,' she says. 'I was different to the other ones.'

It was after the war, in 1948, and while involved with the Girl Guides that Joy met Noel, a tall, fair, hazel-eyed student architect who had served in the Royal Naval Volunteer Reserve. The couple became engaged within months and married the following year in Manley, a village in Cheshire. Their first daughter was born ten months later, followed by a son in 1953 and a second daughter in 1955.

Tragedy struck the young family while Joy was pregnant with the couple's fourth child, however. She caught polio and was rushed to hospital. Noel contracted the serious viral infection too and, to the family's profound shock, died from it. The illness also led Joy to lose her baby. In the wake of this deep trauma, she was left with three children under the age of six to care for and support. She was forced to go out to work to provide for her family and embarked on a career that spanned teaching and roles in the healthcare and charity sectors. She retired in 2013 at the age of 88 after almost 70 years in employment. That year she was awarded an MBE for her services to Age UK and other charities. She has gone on to have eight grandchildren and 11 great-grandchildren.

It only dawned on Joy after the war had ended how unusual her experiences had been. 'There was a piece in one of the church newspapers when I became secretary to the Archbishop of Canterbury,' she recalls. 'There was a piece there that said, "Ms Milward, at the age of 19, has had the most amazing life" ... First of all working in the War Cabinet and then going to the Archbishop of Canterbury. It was quite surprising, really, for somebody of 19, and I had a very strict and very simple upbringing. We'd never been to London, of course – we didn't really know where London was.'

After the article, her service in the Second World War was not discussed publicly again for another six decades. 'Nobody's ever, ever asked me until about ten years ago,' she says. 'Nobody mentioned anything about the war to me. That was when the Churchill War Rooms were putting on an exhibition and somehow got hold of my name. Of course, not everybody wanted to travel to London – not everybody was able to. So they kindly sent cars for me so I could get there quite easily.' The 2009 exhibition gave her a 'new lease of life,' she says, and encouraged her to give talks about her wartime experiences.

Prior to that, she had not discussed her service privately, even with her children, or with her husband before his early death. Personal reminiscences were not encouraged by society after the conflict ended. 'Not the war; it was finished, you know? It was over, behind us. You don't keep on about things that are behind you,' she says. As the decades advanced, she took the view: 'It was a long, long time ago and I never look backwards.'

Today, Joy is circumspect about whether her wartime experience changed her. 'I suppose it might have done, when I went to other jobs,' she says slowly. 'In a way, I think sometimes nervous people do turn out to be rather bossy. I was very bossy, and I still am. I'm not nervous any more. I found it quite difficult in the adult world. I'd been to a girls' boarding school and then a women's college and, of course, [had] no social life in my home during the war. I did find it quite difficult, but it got easier as time went on.'

# Ena Collymore-Woodstock

### DATE OF BIRTH:

10 September 1917 (aged 21 at the outbreak of war)

### ROLE:

Wireless operator in the Auxiliary Territorial Service

Ena Collymore-Woodstock, who has reached the grand age of 103, is believed to be the oldest surviving female veteran of the British Army. She was one of the first women from Jamaica to serve in the Auxiliary Territorial Service during the Second World War, jumping at the chance when the War Office finally allowed West Indian women to volunteer from the mid-1940s. She travelled more than 7,500 kilometres to London to play her part and became the first Caribbean woman to train as a radar operator, eventually ending up serving near the front line in Belgium.

After the war she read law in London, becoming the first black woman to study at Gray's Inn, before returning home to Jamaica, where she went on to secure another record as the first woman to hold judicial office on the island. Today she is considered a Caribbean icon and, always adorned in pearls and still active in her eleventh decade, enjoys taking exercise classes. She is clear: the war was a springboard to empowerment for her sex. 'I think the war helped women, because everyone had wanted men to do the jobs in society, but the women held their own and showed they were strong and capable,' she says.

Born in Spanish Town, Jamaica, in the midst of the First World War, Ena Joyce St Clare Collymore was in her early twenties when World War Two erupted. Both her parents had passed away. Frank, a stationmaster who had lost an arm in an accident falling from a train, died when she and her two older sisters and younger brother were young. Their mother, Madeline, a postmistress, passed away when Ena was in her early twenties. She then lived for a period with her married sister, before moving into accommodation run by the Young Women's Christian Association, after her relatives observed that it would make more sense. 'They said I might as well live there, [as] I spent half my life there. They had a lot of clubs and things, dancing classes,' she has remarked.

She was ambitious as well as sociable, and her iron will propelled her into a profession previously closed to women. In 1940, at the age of 23, an advert recruiting for clerks at a courthouse caught her eye. To her chagrin it specified that only male applicants need apply, but she was not accustomed to giving up in the face of obstacles. She fought for the right to an interview and went on to impress the panel, forcing the court to relent and hand her the job. 'I never felt that women should stay where they were,' she says. 'I didn't want to do the things they said women should do.' She enjoyed the administrative role, which involved a lot of typing and was considered a high-status job for an unmarried woman. At that stage of her life, she harboured no inkling that she would later join the legal profession itself and demolish even more formidable barriers facing women trying to enter the sector.

During this period of her youth she recalls being acutely aware of the war, although she notes that the conflict did not inflict 'terror' on Jamaica on a daily basis. Nonetheless, it was a cause for concern and the island practised blackout procedures. Anxiety abounded that the Nazis viewed Jamaica as a springboard to the coast of America, and therefore considered it a direct target.

In addition, the Caribbean was strategically important geographically for the transit of oil and bauxite, which was shipped through the region from Venezuela and the Panama Canal to the US and UK. Between 1941 and 1945, German U-boats and Italian submarines waged a naval campaign in the Caribbean Sea and Gulf of Mexico, hunting for oil tankers and cargo ships. The Battle of the Caribbean, which was an extension of the Battle of the Atlantic, saw Jamaica face grave shortages of essential supplies as cargo ships were torpedoed while sailing to its ports. Fuel had to be severely rationed, which hit rural communities without electricity the hardest.

In the first years of the conflict, a modest number of young, middle-class Jamaicans had decided to travel, self-funded, to Canada and England to enlist. The men had joined the forces, while at that point the main war profession open to women was nursing. It was not an option that Ena, or the vast majority of islanders, entertained, however, as travel was expensive and unaffordable to most. Instead she volunteered as an orderly at a local camp where soldiers were based, after training with the first-aid charity St John Ambulance. The courthouse where she worked recognised the importance of the war effort and allowed her time off in the afternoons to perform the duty.

Ever open to new opportunities, however, another advert caught Ena's attention in 1943, when she was in her mid-twenties. It was a formal recruitment programme for women to join the forces and help the British war effort overseas. 'I was quite intrigued. I wanted to be involved in the war. I'm sure people thought we were crazy,' she has said previously. In part, she was inspired by her uncle, who had fought in the First World War and afterwards emigrated to the United States.

The flyer was published by the all-female Auxiliary Territorial Service (ATS), which had been created for women in 1938 as the spectre of war loomed. The force was open to women aged 18 to 43 years old, who were recruited for a variety of positions, although not front-line combat roles. At first ATS personnel tended to take on traditionally 'female' jobs, working as cooks, storekeepers and shorthand typists.

As the war dragged on and more men were called up to fight, however, the ATS were prevailed upon to backfill many 'male' roles that had been left empty. This saw women drafted in as drivers, car mechanics, military police officers and ammunition inspectors.

The recruitment drive to enlist female personnel in Jamaica, led by Junior Commander Barbara Oakley, was narrow and specific. The advert Ena spotted stressed that only a 'limited number of recruits' would be accepted. It made clear that 'only girls with good clerical experience or those with an educational standard school certificate would be considered'. It was to be the first time in Jamaican history that women were formally trained for military service.

The British Government had been on a tortuous journey before finally deciding in 1943 to allow black women from the West Indies to enlist and travel to the UK. A series of dubious arguments had been advanced by the War Office up to that point, initially based on race, then on the claim that these foreign women would struggle to carry out their duties because they would be so overwhelmed by the British climate and culture.

Figures in the War Office even resorted to invoking the Unites States' racist 'colour bar' as a fig leaf to disguise their own prejudice. British officials highlighted the need to avoid causing offence to American allies as a pretext for the UK imposing its own 'colour bars' in a variety of instances.

Contemporary accounts suggest that a de facto 'colour bar' had already existed in many parts of the British economy long before American GIs set foot in the UK, however. As well as being blocked from many jobs, black people suffered the 'refusal of lodgings, refusal of service in cafés, refusal of admittance to dance halls', as well as 'shrugs, nods, whispers, comments' while out in public, according to an English anthropologist in 1943.[17]

One motivation behind the government's reversal of its policy on recruiting women of colour living in the British colonies by the early 1940s appears obvious: new reserves of manpower were needed as the war deepened. The Colonial Office had also argued for a non-discriminatory recruitment policy in order to bolster relations between Britain and the West Indies. The tension within government was exposed in a terse memo from Sir James Grigg, Secretary of State for War, to Oliver Stanley, Secretary of State for the Colonies, in spring 1943, which read: 'I don't at all like your West Indian ATS ideas.'[18]

In the end, though, the Colonial Office triumphed in that battle, and both the ATS and the Women's Auxiliary Air Force were opened up to women from the British colonies, although the Women's Royal Naval Service was not.

By the end of the war in 1945, around 200,000 women had been recruited to the ATS from across Britain and the British Empire, serving on the Home Front and overseas. This included personnel from the dominions and India, as well as the West Indies. Around 5,000 women in the ATS served in the Middle East, 80 per cent of whom had been recruited locally.

The urge to help the war effort was strong among Ena and her friends, despite the conflict originating more than 4,500 miles away in Europe. The ties of Empire were powerful and Britain was characterised as the 'Mother Country' in the school curriculum, at church and in wider society. Children were brought up to respect the royal family, and collecting pictures of the young princesses Elizabeth and Margaret was a popular pastime among Jamaican girls. Once war erupted, placards sprung up across the island, declaring: 'Do you want to help the war cause? England needs you!'

A sense of loyalty to the UK persisted, despite simmering tensions. The British Caribbean colonies had been through a period of turmoil in the 1930s, during which strikes and riots had erupted as workers demanded better wages, fairer terms of employment and a greater degree of autonomy.

In addition, the treatment of Caribbean personnel by Britain during the First World War had been dismal in some instances. Jamaica had provided around two thirds of the 15,000 volunteers who had formed the British West Indies Regiment, which saw heavy action in Jordan and Palestine. A mutiny had erupted after the Armistice in December 1918, when Caribbean soldiers were forced to carry out laborious duties, including cleaning the latrines, for white British soldiers in Italy.

The threat of Fascism served as a unifying force between Britain and the West Indies in the Second World War, however. Keen attention was paid in the Caribbean to Fascist ideology and how it had been applied in Abyssinia, now Ethiopia, when Mussolini had invaded in the 1930s. The

Italians had imposed segregation on racial lines and banned mixed marriage. Meanwhile, Hitler's Aryan obsession and focus on racial purity also compounded fears of a Nazi victory. Beyond the desire to fight a common enemy, some West Indians viewed their contribution to the war effort as part of the wider march towards greater independence for the region.

Ena firmly regarded herself as British – even 'defiantly British', as she has remarked in the past[19] – and felt no contradiction between that and her Jamaican identity. The prospect of an overseas adventure naturally held an appeal of its own, but allegiance to King and Country was likely another factor influencing her decision to enlist. She and her friends had already waved off male peers and relatives earlier in the war who had departed to join the Armed Forces in Britain and Canada. Families of personnel would regularly check the noticeboard at the Parade in Kingston, where lists of men killed and reported missing were published.

Ena has reflected in the past on her motivation to enlist and travel abroad: 'We felt that we were British. I think you would describe me as a person who was loyal – not the person to go and shout [about it], but it was definitely the type of person I was. I was a young person, a single person, I had no responsibility, so why not go and fight?'[20] Today she explains: 'I was adventurous, but I was anxious to help the war effort. Everybody felt like that: they wanted to do something. There had been an ad in the paper for recruits – in many instances the British were after us, encouraging us to join. We had to go to the camp and then we were selected.

I was 26 years old; some of the others were a bit younger, around 22.' She was naturally athletic and enjoyed sports, having played in the netball team at school, and also boasted a suite of practical skills that she had picked up in the Girl Guides, a movement with which she developed a life-long connection. Combined with her intelligence and tenacity, she was a strong all-round candidate.

Ena flourished at the interview and in the tests that followed, which resulted in her becoming one of 600 West Indian women admitted to the ATS. It was a modest tally compared with the number of men recruited from the Caribbean, some of whom were attracted by the promise of a steady wage following the disruption to trade and employment sparked by the war. In total, between 10,000 and 16,000 men out of a population of 14 million in the British Caribbean colonies enlisted for service.

Half of the 600 female recruits remained deployed at home in the Caribbean. A further 200 were dispatched to the United States, all of whom were white Jamaicans, owing to the American 'colour bar' that discriminated against black people. Ena was among the 100-odd women sent to Britain. While she was from a modest background, the group selected were mostly middle-class, either drawn from or destined for high-status jobs in teaching and clerical professions.

The elevated social background of the ATS's black recruits from the West Indies contrasted with the wide sweep of its white British volunteers and conscripts, who hailed from deprived as well as wealthy communities. In some quarters the force gained an unfair reputation for accepting prostitutes and vagrants, which led some women to eschew it in favour of the other women's auxiliary services. This notoriety may have dampened its domestic recruitment effort. Although at its height it successfully enlisted 1,600 recruits weekly, this total fell far short of the War Office target of 5,000 a week. The trouble it faced in staffing its ranks is also likely to have heaped pressure on the government to look further afield to the colonies.

Ena was thrilled to learn that she would be heading abroad. 'It was my first trip overseas. We hadn't been anywhere abroad,' she says. She and her fellow recruits were not told their destination, however, or even their departure date or what to expect from the voyage, on security grounds. 'We were told if we were selected, but we were never told when we would leave the West Indies,' she remembers. It had been a competitive process. 'There were other young women who wanted to go to England. There were quite a few people who tried to join,' she adds. 'They selected around 24 of us in total. My sister had wanted to go, but was put off with all the different things that had to be done.'

Her documents were completed in a rush and she soon set sail along with four women who would become life-long friends: Norma, Nellie, Olga and Winnie. They wore civilian clothes aboard the ship provided by the British Government and sailed initially to the US. 'The boat stopped at New York first, then another boat went across to England,' she explains. 'Communication was difficult at that time; you weren't allowed to communicate. I had relatives in New York, but I was not allowed to say where I was going or how I was arriving. My letters were redacted, so I just arrived in New York.'

Armed with the address of her relatives, she navigated her way to the right neighbourhood and bumped into her Aunt Winnie on the street, who burst into tears of joy at the unexpected reunion. Ena was able to spend a few days in the city with her family before boarding the next ship bound for Britain, which the West Indian passengers shared with a group of New Zealanders.

It was only weeks later that she discovered there had been heavy fighting in the Atlantic during her journey across, which had given her family back home a fright. 'There was some torpedoing, and those in Jamaica heard that some [ships] were torpedoed,' she has said previously. 'They didn't know if we were alive or dead, but we weren't aware that there was torpedoing going on.' While Ena recalls seeing warships on the horizon from her transport ship, the ATS recruits escaped the heat of battle during their Atlantic crossing.

Their overriding emotion during the trip was excitement about the opportunities that they believed awaited them. The young women were alive to their status as the first black female personnel to enlist in the British services. 'I felt special. We all knew we were doing things for the first time,' Ena says. 'I thought everything would be okay, but I was aware that I had to be conscientious. I had confidence in the people I was with, though, and their friendship meant a lot.'

When the ship finally docked in England, the group was interviewed live by the BBC, which had set up a broadcast to welcome them. Nellie later recalled of that first night in Britain: 'While we reported through the BBC that we were fine, we were not fine at all. The bombs were going off over our heads and we were very nervous.'[21]

Ena recalls being less fazed by bombing raids during her time in England. 'I remember hearing the bombs going off, but it didn't bother me too much,' she says now. 'I didn't feel afraid. Somehow I knew I would be safe. As long as I was not alone, I was okay.'

The group travelled onwards to Guildford in Surrey for their initial training, followed by a spell at a base in Bicester in Oxfordshire. The cold autumn weather was a shock to the system. A memo written by Lieutenant Colonel Williams, Deputy Adjutant General, described the setbacks faced by the first two dozen West Indian recruits to arrive at the training facility. 'The women are reported to be very keen, beginning to be a bit home-sick, but have very little stamina,' he said. 'Seventy-five per cent of them have reported sick at different times, some with very small ailments, but a few have been in bed almost ever since they arrived in this country and some have got chronic coughs ... It is doubtful whether these women can stand the climate here.'[22]

This downbeat assessment did not accurately describe Ena's experience, however. She insists she was not blighted by a longing for home. 'I knew a lot of people. I had a lot of friends with me from Jamaica – we were a group,' she says.

She tried her best to ignore the cold, too, although the arrival of snow and the periodic lack of running water in the camp presented a challenge. Within a couple of weeks she had become used to bathing in only a cupful water – a feat she can still manage today. It has since become a running joke in her family, who tease her about her 'war baths'.

Norma also described the privations faced by the group in an account given after the war. 'We went to Bicester in Oxfordshire. It is now a famous camp, but in those days the camp was just being built so we were really pioneers, and we had to live under primitive service conditions,' she said. 'Some of the girls got quite ill with meningitis. The whole camp was under very bad conditions. But we did quite good work in all our different spheres.'

Ena says of the roles they were assigned: 'They gave us all safe, sedentary jobs. I think this was for safety reasons – it didn't just apply to me [due to her experience in clerking].' She was disappointed by the idea of spending the war behind a desk, however. 'My thinking was that I hadn't come all this way to go and type in an office!' she recalls, laughing. 'I thought I was going to actually do something. That's when I went up and was trained to be a radar operator.'

The lifestyle jarred too. Stirred by teenage memories of Girl Guides expeditions, Ena had nursed expectations of an austere camping-style set-up, rather than four meals a day and comfortable surroundings. She did not keep her misgivings to herself. With characteristic boldness, she wrote to the War Office and requested a transfer. She wanted to be closer to the fighting and entrusted with greater responsibility. Her plea was answered and she was summoned to an evaluation unit. There the authorities found her capable of any of the roles open to women in the ATS, so they allowed her to choose. She decided to join an anti-aircraft unit and operate the radios.

Her Jamaican comrades did not share her restlessness and appetite for more risk. 'Many of the others who spoke to me said they were okay with staying there typing, but I wanted some action,' she says. The move, which saw her leave behind her West Indian friends to work solely with white Britons, did not daunt her. 'I was confident. I got a good reception. I was not afraid,' she says, before pausing and admitting: 'I was a little bit timid at first, but when I saw how things were to be done, then I gained confidence.'

She worked in a unit with three others, based in a stationary vehicle, which focused on aircraft. She would message incoming planes using Morse code to ascertain whether they were friend or foe, then pass the answer to an operator. The order was then given to a gunner, who would attempt to shoot down enemy aircraft. Ena observed in the past: 'This was the first time they were attacking planes that couldn't be seen. You see, this radar allowed us to "see".'

Her role took her to Belgium for a short period, where she served near the front line. It was dangerous, but she does not recall feeling afraid. She has in the past made reference to working alongside a 'trigger happy' male comrade, but otherwise has rarely spoken of her time on the Continent. Her memories of this part of her war service have since faded compared with her time in Britain.

While some West Indians suffered discrimination and racism, Ena recalls a positive reception from everyone with whom she interacted and warns that not all experiences were uniform. Her skin colour and accent were unusual in 1940s Britain, but she found that people seemed friendly and interested, rather than hostile or aggressive. They recognised her as a fellow British citizen, living in the British Commonwealth. 'We were considered British,' she stresses, adding: 'I would tell people about Jamaica, but everybody in England knew at least one person with a connection. You would make a lot of it.' She noticed the differences with home, including the cuisine, but did not dwell on them.

She says: 'I had a good time in England. I had very good friends. I didn't notice the cold unless it was a particularly bad day. I am an optimist and was always positive. People were always willing to help. I had no issues. I didn't meet with any great prejudice.' In particular she was delighted to meet Mary, the Princess Royal, at a reception thrown for West Indian female personnel. The sister of King George VI, Mary was Controller Commandant of the ATS during the war. Ena has kept a photograph of the occasion, in which she appears, grinning, with her arm outstretched ready to shake the princess's hand.

The reception was part of a wider effort to encourage support for the war effort at home and overseas, which included a poster series called 'Empire War Work in Britain' published by the Ministry of Information. One of these posters, entitled 'A Volunteer from British Guiana', depicted black worker Private Diana Williams. Wearing green overalls, she was pictured retreading an army vehicle tyre in a repair depot in the Midlands. The caption stated: 'Many girls from the West Indies have volunteered for service with the Auxiliary Territorial Service. Some, volunteering for service abroad, have come to Britain; more are on their way. Every girl in the ATS has an equal chance of promotion or of taking a commission.'

While the poster stressed the idea of 'equal' opportunities within the service, it was not the experience of Connie Mark (née MacDonald), another Jamaican recruit of colour who worked in the ATS as a medical secretary at the British Military Hospital in Kingston during the war. She spoke out about the prejudice faced in the colonies after her promotion to full corporal was not accompanied by the pay rise given to British personnel who rose through the ranks. She moved to England in the 1950s and, after being denied her British Empire Medal, campaigned for the contribution of West Indian ex-servicewomen to be recognised.

Attitudes towards personnel of colour in Britain varied. Black soldiers in the US military, who were forced to remain in racially segregated units while in the UK, were said to have been welcomed by some, while also suffering prejudice from others. White American soldiers were often the worst culprits behind physical and verbal abuse, according to reports. America's 'colour bar' became a source of awkwardness for the British Government, which avoided engaging with the issue.

It was eventually raised in the House of Commons by independent MP Tom Driberg, who urged Winston Churchill to make 'friendly representations' to the US to inform them that 'the colour bar is not a custom in this country'. The Prime Minister branded the question 'unfortunate', however, and attempted to evade it. 'I am hopeful that without any action on my part the points of view of all concerned will be mutually understood and respected,' he said.

Racism was tackled more stridently in other instances. A vicar's wife named Mrs May faced a backlash when she attempted to lay down rules for white women to avoid interaction with black male personnel during a talk in Weston-super-Mare. Her speech was picked up by the newspapers and widely condemned. The *Sunday Pictorial* stated: 'The vast majority of people here have nothing but repugnance for the narrow-minded, uninformed prejudices expressed by the vicar's wife. There is – and will be – no persecution of coloured people in Britain.'[23]

However, another contemporary magazine, *John Bull*, detailed examples of the racist reactions that some Caribbean personnel had faced while deployed in the UK. 'Rudeness to colonial service girls in this country is surprisingly common,' it said, noting: 'A West Indian girl in the ATS was refused a new issue of shoes by her officer, who added: "At home you don't wear shoes anyway."[24] An Army Officer to a West Indian ATS: "If I can't get white women, I'll something-well do without."[25]

In recent years Ena has raised concerns about a damning account of war service and racism in the West by a black Guyanese author, which she feels does not acknowledge that other recruits from the British colonies had positive experiences. She has also made the case previously that, unlike the American military, Britain had mixed-race units in the RAF and some regiments of the British Army, although black troops from the Caribbean tended to be assigned to distinct regiments that were commanded by white officers.[26] Around a thousand volunteers formed the Caribbean Regiment, which was deployed overseas in 1944 to the Middle East and Italy. The Royal Navy did not accept any black crew members, though thousands of West Indian seamen served in the Merchant Navy.

Ena says she and her comrades were treated with respect. 'We didn't experience racism … I think they were keeping us together at first for safety and to [help us] feel at home, but after I wrote the letter [asking for a transfer], they started to move the others, and after a few months, others joined us [in the new unit] from Barbados and Trinidad,' she said in previously unpublished interview conducted in 2005.[27]

She made a number of close friendships with British women, including a Scotswoman named Jean. Ena introduced her to another friend called Alan, a serviceman who was also from Scotland, and the pair ended up marrying.

Ena also became good friends with Joan, an Englishwoman who later married a Parisian and moved to France. She kept in touch with and visited both in the decades after the war.

Ena recalls another instance of 'real kindness' from a stranger, which came about after she appeared in the press. 'A newspaper article came out, which included a photo of me with my name, and an English lady called Collymore saw it and got in touch with me via the War Office,' she explains. 'She invited me to stay with her for Christmas and said I could bring some friends.' Norma and Nellie joined her and the four women enjoyed a jolly Christmas together.

Ultimately, it was those friends who had travelled to England from Jamaica with Ena who remained her staunchest allies and confidantes. 'They became closer friends during the war, and they stayed friends after the war,' she says. To her surprise, one of her siblings, who had previously shown little interest in enlisting, also travelled to Britain. 'My brother, Roy, joined up after I left for England,' she says. He enrolled in the RAF.

Ena prioritised friendship over romantic relationships during the conflict. 'Romances didn't come up too early, because I didn't want to rush things too much. The romances came when I was a student after the war. Then I met different people from around the world,' she says.

Looking back, Ena is wistful about her wartime experiences. 'The most outstanding memories I have are the fellowship and the friendships,' she remarks. Stressing that she 'enjoyed the work' too, she adds: 'I have always viewed my time in the war in a positive light – as an experience and an adventure. I'm also very social; I interact well with people.'

Even small actions can make a difference to one's future, she believes, and credits her wartime service with instilling discipline and helping her learn to cope with hard times and challenges. It also bolstered her social confidence. 'I have always mixed with people from all classes, backgrounds and races. There were no boundaries in terms of gender, colour or class – as far as I was concerned,' she has reflected in a recent interview with the Women's Royal Army Corps Association.[28]

The contribution of female military personnel to the war effort helped pave the way for new educational and professional opportunities for all women in Jamaica, she believes. 'When I joined up, Jamaica wasn't independent yet; we were still a colony, so locals weren't given the top jobs. My generation of local women were determined to prove we were capable. I helped show what women could achieve, despite there being no female role models at a senior level of society at the time.'

After the war Ena lived in London on Gloucester Place, with four other women, including Norma. As soon as their weekly rations came in, they took great delight in using them up in one go in a big dinner for their friends. Norma soon married Flight Lieutenant Arthur Wint, an RAF pilot from Jamaica who was one of only a handful of Caribbean airmen who flew Spitfires during the conflict. He was later a noted athlete, doctor and diplomat, winning an Olympic gold medal for Jamaica in the 400 metres in 1948. The couple went on to have three daughters and in 1974 they returned to London, where he became Jamaican High Commissioner.

Focused on her career, Ena meanwhile became the first woman of colour to study at Gray's Inn, taking advantage of a further education and vocational training scheme for ex-servicemen and women after the war. After studying remotely via a correspondence course during the conflict, she was eventually released from the ATS to enrol full time. 'After the war, there was a programme for West Indians who had been involved in the war. So I think a lot of the men too, who were pilots and so on, went on to study law and then came back to the Caribbean and took up senior positions. Some became prime ministers,' she says.

Her 'driving spirit and competence' made her popular in London among her fellow students, according to a later article in *The Gleaner*, a Jamaican newspaper. She was active in student politics, becoming vice-president of the Inns of Court Students' Union and treasurer of the West Indies Students' Union. She recalls it being a time of great fun, and it was during this period that she enjoyed her first flirtations. She became particularly fond of a handsome Trinidadian named Eugene. He in turn appeared to be keen on Ena and duly invited her to a law ball. However, after she responded breezily that she was planning to go with the group, he took another woman instead. She would laugh about it afterwards as an episode that demonstrated just how much she enjoyed spending time with her friends – as well as the consequences of playing hard to get.

She seized the opportunity to travel throughout the UK and Europe, attending the World Federation of Democratic Youth conference in Prague in 1947. She also got to know other students from the Caribbean, with whom the issue of West Indian independence was the primary subject of intense debate. She also took on 'extramural' studies at the London Institute for the Scientific Treatment for Delinquency, designed for people who were not enrolled full-time at the establishment.

She is resolute that she would not have been able to become a barrister if she had not signed up to serve in the war and travelled to Britain. 'In those days, you know, you had to go to England to do law. I wouldn't have been able to afford it,' she has said in the past.[29] 'And if I hadn't gone to the war I might not have been able to go there. I might have got married and that would be the end of that, or something, so I thought it made a big difference.' Today she reflects: 'The war changed the course of my life. At first people didn't think much of women, but after a time, we were respected. In terms of the law, I was working in the court office as a clerk, and after the war I was able to study at Gray's Inn and qualify as a barrister.'

After receiving her qualifications in 1948, she went back to Jamaica, returning home on board the SS *Jamaica Producer*. Her arrival was noted in a Jamaican newspaper alongside a picture of her wearing a bonnet with the caption:

'Smiling barrister'. 'After the war there was a significant grouping of West Indians who studied [in Britain] and then came back to the West Indies,' she has remarked. 'They were part of a new generation that were supportive of independence, who were able to contribute to society. At the time I met people who went on to become the prime minister of Barbados [Errol Barrow], the prime minister of Guyana [Forbes Burnham]. We were separate at first but then all got to know each other.' Eugenia Charles, who went on to become prime minister of Dominica, was another friend.

Some of the West Indian women with whom Ena had travelled to the UK to enlist decided to stay, however. They were joined from 1948 onwards by new waves of migrants from the Caribbean. The first large group came on a ship named HMT *Empire Windrush*, which is how these Britons later came to be known as the 'Windrush generation'. For the next 25 years people from the West Indies continued to come to the UK to take up jobs in the nascent National Health Service and other industries hit by the post-war labour shortage.

Many of the male West Indian personnel who had enlisted in Western forces, including the Merchant Navy, never returned home. One estimate suggests that a third of Caribbean volunteers were killed in action during the Second World War.

Ena's legal career soared in the decades following the war. 'When I came back as a lawyer in Jamaica, I was the only woman. It was a novelty. People used to come to the court office to look at me ... It had to start somewhere and I don't like to take credit, but somebody had to do that. I wasn't the most brilliant schoolgirl, but I had different thoughts,' she remarked previously.[30]

She soon met, and in 1951 married, a civil servant named Victor Woodstock, who worked for the Jamaican Government in the agriculture ministry. The couple had three children: Careth, Robert and Marguerite. Ena now has four grandchildren.

The family travelled to Scotland on a number of occasions to see Jean and Alan Hamilton, the Scottish couple Ena had introduced during the war. Although they had passed away by the time Ena turned 100, she invited their son to her birthday party. She and Victor also visited Joan and her husband in France.

While she has become known as a woman who achieved many 'firsts' in Jamaica, Ena has always stressed the 'training and assistance from others' that she has received. Even during her school days she was fortunate that the teachers at her Anglican high school were kind and donated her books. Her family was poor and her brother fared worse at school, facing humiliation from a cruel headmaster who took pleasure in highlighting his inability to afford the required texts. One of her sisters had meanwhile been forced to give up a scholarship to a good school because she could not pay for the two bus rides required each way.

Throughout her adult life in Jamaica Ena has retained her links with the Girl Guides, becoming a Chief Commissioner, and receiving an MBE for her work with the group in 1967. She was active in the women's movement and was a charter member of Soroptimist International, a group that focuses on improving gender equality. She also helped change the law to give illegitimate children the same rights as legitimate children on the island. In law, she has been thrilled to watch the progress made by today's female lawyers in Jamaica, a cohort that includes one of her daughters and two of her female grandchildren. In recent years she declared in a speech to fellow lawyers: 'To see the amazing strides that women have taken in this illustrious field fills my heart with joy.'

A newspaper profile of her in the 1960s said she 'radiates charm' and 'in her quiet way leaves no doubt that she is a competent and devoted person'. It added: 'She has paved the way for women in the legal profession. She has brought hope to the juveniles of Jamaica and she has found time for the invaluable social work that she does.'

Her career took her overseas, and she lived for spells in Miami, Anguilla, and the Turks and Caicos Islands in the Atlantic Ocean, where a preparatory school has since been named after her. Today she lives between Jamaica, where her son Robert is based, and Barbados, where her daughter Marguerite lives.

School children in the West Indies have been taught about Ena's remarkable life, which she discovered upon arriving in the US on one occasion. Handing her passport to a border official, she was surprised to hear the Jamaican-born woman exclaim that she had written a school project on her.

When she was honoured by the Jamaican Bar Association some years ago, Ena gave a short speech looking back at her life up until that point. She said: 'At every stage of my career I have had tremendous support from family and colleagues. Without them my road would have not been so smooth. The great judge above has been kind to me and I give him thanks for his bountiful blessings.

'I would just conclude by encouraging persons – men and women – not to see barriers, but rather opportunities, and to reach up and grab them. There is no dream that you cannot achieve. Work hard, give back and be kind to everyone along the way.'

# Catherine Drummond

**DATE OF BIRTH:**

7 April 1922 (aged 17 at the outbreak of war)


**ROLE:**

Wireless operator in the Women's Auxiliary Air Force

'I was married when I was 21, and I was a war widow at 22 with an unborn child,' says Catherine Drummond. She had enjoyed just ten months of marriage to John Boyd, a dashing Northern Irish RAF gunner, before his plane crashed off the coast of Italy in 1944. It was a devastating shock for the young Scotswoman in the Women's Auxiliary Air Force, who was soon forced to bow out of the war effort as the birth of her daughter drew near.

Catherine had enlisted with enthusiasm at the age of 19 in 1941. Raised in an impoverished family in Coatbridge, a town to the east of Glasgow, she could not afford to stay on at school past 14. Work beckoned and she became a nanny in a children's hotel to help her parents make ends meet. Her mother was a 'very strict' woman and hard on her. Also called Catherine, her mother was employed as a cook at the same hotel, while her father Samuel, who had served in the Army during the First World War, worked for the local council on the 'bucket lorries' as a rubbish collector.

She was the eldest of three siblings; 18 months older than Charlie, who in turn was 18 months older than John. She had red hair, while her middle brother was fair and the youngest was strawberry blond. 'I was very jealous of Charlie's golden curls,' she says. 'I got the ginger-coloured hair and I hated it.' Their childhood was austere, with the family unable to afford activities or holidays. 'We were very poor,' Catherine says. The classroom and playground provided little respite; she did not enjoy her time at the local Episcopalian school. The only interval from the weekly routine of family life came from trips to her aunt's home in Stirling. 'I got on well with her. She had a huge garden, full of apples. I had a good feast,' she says, laughing.

In the months leading up to September 1939 and the formal declaration of war, the teenage Catherine was aware that conflict was brewing. 'We spoke about it at home. That was that. It was something that was happening,' she says. 'I didn't really understand what it meant,' she concedes. 'My father never spoke about the First World War. We were ignorant really.' She did not envisage events on the Continent affecting her life in Scotland.

Nonetheless, when recruitment drives for female personnel commenced, she was eager to be involved in the war effort and applied at the first opportunity. 'I saw an advert in the local daily paper advertising for women for the Air Force,' she recalls. The fact that this particular call-up appealed specifically for motor mechanics did not deter her. 'I just sent away for the particulars and that was me – I was chosen right away,' she says. The process was straightforward. 'I had to go and have an interview at the Labour Exchange at Stirling. I had to have a medical and answer all the questions. In no time at all I was on my way down to Gloucester to join the Women's Auxiliary Air Force,' she recalls.

The all-female auxiliary service had been created in June 1939, as war loomed, to help free up male RAF personnel for front line duties. However, it was born out of an earlier unit called the Women's Royal Air Force, which had existed between 1918 and 1920. Within four years of the Second World War the WAAF's ranks swelled to 182,000 members, with 2,000 women enlisting each week. Unlike the women's branch of the Army, the Auxiliary Territorial Service, where personnel served in separate female units, members of the WAAF came under the administration of the RAF. The organisation was never entirely independent from, nor entirely integrated with, the far larger all-male Air Force. Nor was it held in the same esteem: WAAF recruits were only paid two-thirds of the wage awarded to male counterparts of the same rank in the RAF.

At the start of the war, the majority of 'WAAFs' were drafted into commands as drivers, clerks, telephonists and cooks. However, as the conflict progressed, they became involved in telegraphy and intercepting codes and ciphers, as well as working as mechanics, engineers and fitters on aircraft. Others operated barrage balloon sites, raising and lowering the giant 65-foot-long inflatables that aimed to frustrate the accuracy of airborne enemy raids. This was one of the most physically gruelling jobs awarded to women during the war. Many other women in the WAAF were deployed in the Battle of Britain as reporters and plotters in radar stations, guiding British fighters against Nazi bombers – especially at night. Those based at Fighter Command airbases such as Biggin Hill and Manston in Kent were at great danger of Luftwaffe raids.

By 1945, a quarter of a million women had served in over 110 trades in the auxiliary force, including intelligence and producing weather reports. Aircrew duty was never approved for women in the service, although some 168 women became civilian pilots in the Air Transport Auxiliary during the war, ferrying military aircraft between sites.

Recalling how her entry to the WAAF began with training in southern England, Catherine says: 'I was all day on the train; we didn't arrive at Gloucester until 10 o'clock at night. We were bundled into a huge army lorry in the dark and taken to the base. There were the "biscuits" – that was the mattresses – and we were told, "Make your beds; you're going to have to get up early in the morning." At six o'clock

Ena Collymore-Woodstock in her Auxiliary
Territorial Service (ATS) uniform during the war.

Ena at her one-hundredth birthday party in 2017.

Ena when she first arrived in England from Jamaica to join the
war effort, talking to Private Marguerite Irving, 1943.

Recruits for the all-female ATS learning to march
during basic training, 1940.

Catherine Drummond in uniform, while working for the Women's Auxiliary Air Force (WAAF) during the war.

Catherine and her husband, Sergeant John Boyd, on their wedding day in Stirling, October 1943. He died ten months later in a plane crash while on active duty for the RAF in Italy.

A WAAF meteorologist releasing a weather balloon to ascertain flying conditions, 1941.

Betty Webb, a paraphraser in the Intelligence Corps of the ATS who worked at Bletchley Park, in Washington DC, June 1945. She was dispatched to the Pentagon to work in the Japanese division during the final months of the Second World War.

Betty now, residing at home.

Women in the Intelligence Corps of the ATS at work in the machine room in Hut 6 at Bletchley Park, the British Government's code-breaking headquarters in Buckinghamshire during the war.

Connie Hoe and her husband, Petty Officer Leslie Hoe, reunited briefly while he was on leave, 1942.

Connie with her daughter Christine (left), returning in 2014 to the house in Oxfordshire to which she fled to escape the Blitz in London's East End. Connie gave birth to Christine alone in her bedroom while waiting for help to arrive when she went into labour during a blizzard in November 1941.

Women working in a medal room, 1945.

Christian Lamb with her husband, Lieutenant John Lamb DSC, on their wedding day in London, December 1943. Engaged after ten days, they married in a brief window while his ship was docked in the capital for boiler maintenance.

Wrens sending and receiving morse code, 1944.

Cheers from a group of Wrens in Plymouth
after receiving the news that the war in
Europe was over, 8 May 1945.

they chucked us all out of bed. I thought, *What in the name of Jesus is happening here?* It really was frightening. I thought, *Have I done the right thing?*' The first day in camp was taken up with administration. Catherine was interviewed, then issued with a uniform, and sent along for another medical, which involved receiving vaccinations.

When she met with the camp authorities, she was told they were in greatest need of wireless operators. 'So I was asked to spell certain words and I did very well until I came to the word "cycle" and my mind went blank and I couldn't spell it,' she says, recalling her mortification. However, she passed the assessment and was assigned to the role, although it was not immediately clear to her what it would involve. When informed by an RAF officer, she says: 'I didn't know what he was talking about.'

A fortnight of marching and 'drill' followed at RAF Innsworth, the non-flying camp north of Gloucester, which was not a happy period. 'I had an inoculation and I had a very sore arm. I had my period, and I had a very sore tum. I had two beautiful, blistered heels. I was very, very miserable, wanting my mummy. I was homesick,' she says, laughing softly at her past self-pity. It was Catherine's first time away from home and she felt adrift – a sentiment shared by many of her young female comrades. 'We all wondered what was happening. We were in a long hut with a stove in the middle to heat the place and we were frozen. We had buttons to clean and shoes to polish. We wondered what had hit us,' she says.

Making friends was easy, however, and Catherine became particularly close for a short time to a fellow Scotswoman. 'I got on fine with everyone. I met a wee girl from Glasgow and we were together for about a fortnight before we were posted away. We were all in the same boat so we all stuck together.' She also recognises that there were upsides to military life. This included the uniform, which consisted of a blue, belted wool jacket and skirt. 'I liked it very much,' she says. 'It was very smart. I've got some nice photographs of it. I enjoyed wearing it.'

After Gloucester, she was posted north to a camp in Longbenton, just outside Newcastle. 'We were to go to "school",' she recalls, which entailed travelling daily by electric train from the camp to the General Post Office in the city centre. 'I was trained to learn Morse code; to send and receive messages to aircraft. I was there for six months among air raids. We worked from nine to five, then you came home at night-time in the dark. There was once an air raid and the electric train stopped dead in the dark, until it slowly moved towards the station, and you got out of the train and ran down the road to the air-raid shelter. It made me very claustrophobic.'

Her training was interrupted by a bout of ill health. 'While I was there in the middle of my training, I didn't feel very well. I had to report to the sick bay, where they told me I had vaccine fever,' she says. 'So I was kept in the sick bay and when there was an air raid, the bed would shake. They would tell me, "Get out of bed and underneath it." I said,

"Not on your life! I will stay on top of my bed."' She could not even muster the strength to seek shelter beneath the bed frame. 'I lost about a fortnight's training. The best thing was, someone said to me that if you've been in the sick bay, you'll get sent home on sick leave. That was a story. I didn't get that at all. I was very disappointed,' she says ruefully.

However, the man teaching the Morse-code course was kind and offered Catherine 'a little extra tuition to bring me up to date'. Learning the code did not come easily, however. 'I thought I'd never get it,' she admits. 'It was very difficult. Dash, dot, dash, de-da-de-da. Finally it comes to you. I enjoyed it. I can remember a wee bit now.' Explaining how it was used, she says: 'When the aircraft flew over, they would send a message in Morse and I would answer in Morse. It was very frightening to begin with, thinking of that aircraft flying up there; you sending messages. We didn't know what the messages meant because it was all sent to another room to be deciphered. We only took them down in Morse.'

Before being tasked with performing the job for real, she was posted to Blackpool for two more months of 'marching and learning', including drills up and down the promenade in the seaside town. Her billet in a boarding house was uncomfortable, her landlady's frosty reception matched by the freezing temperature of the house. 'The landlady was horrible. She didn't want us. I was cold; I asked her for an extra blanket. She told me to go and get one from the Air Force. It was terrible. It was eight weeks of misery,' she says. A low point was catching head lice. 'I had to go to the medical place where they put toxic lotion on the hair,' she recalls. 'They sent me out of the medical clinic with soaking-wet hair – they didn't even give me a dryer to dry it. So when I got back to the billet everybody knew that I'd had lice. I was absolutely stricken – I never got over that.'

A dozen other young women were posted to the same boarding house, but overall the resort was dominated by young men. 'There were more men than you've seen in your life, because they were all there waiting to go abroad,' she says, laughing. 'I went to dances in Blackpool Tower Ball-room. When we went dancing there you got in for eight pence in old money – that was cheap.' She adds: 'I never saw the dancefloor because there were so many men and women there dancing.'

After this stint on the northwest coast of England, she was posted to Scotland to work for Coastal Command in Oban, in Argyll and Bute, where she finally joined operations as a fully trained wireless operator. The coastal town was a key base for Short Sunderland 'flying boat' operations, since the bay and stretch of water between the mainland and Kerrera, a nearby island, offered ideal take-off and landing conditions. The 'huge aircraft' could carry up to 20 people, along with freight. 'They would go on long tours and they would keep in touch with you. So they would send messages in Morse code and I would answer them in Morse code, but I never knew what the messages were,' Catherine says. 'We were never told what they said when they were deciphered, because it was all secret.'

There were exceptional occasions when Morse code could be discarded, however. 'There were a lot of Canadians who came over to Oban and they used to practise flying and were allowed to send messages back and forward in English. It was more fun; you knew what they were talking about. We'd ask who you were and all that.' Norwegian units were also stationed in the coastal town, along with the RAF and Canadian units.

Catherine tended to work night shifts, starting at midnight and ending at eight o'clock in the morning. One evening, she and a friend named Margaret were on duty. The main task that evening was to monitor an RAF Sunderland Short that was transporting Prince George – the king's brother – and 14 others from Easter Ross, further north in Scotland, to Iceland. Shortly after take-off, however, frantic reports came in that the aircraft had crashed on Eagle's Rock, a hillside near Caithness. 'It was the most nerve-wracking thing – I'll never forget,' she says. Mayhem erupted in the office as her superiors struggled to gain clarity about the situation on the ground. 'There was great panic,' Catherine says. 'I had all the bigwigs standing behind my chair while I took down messages before the plane crashed. There I was – Margaret and I – sitting there taking down Morse code messages from the Duke of Kent's plane. Then it was over. We heard the plane had crashed and they walked out of the room.' It became evident quickly that there were multiple casualties. It was a traumatic episode and the failure of her bosses to recognise the role she and Margaret had played left Catherine feeling peeved. 'They never said, "Thank you for all your hard work," or anything – nobody did.' She adds quietly: 'It was very disappointing.'

There was a sole survivor amid the flight wreckage: Flight Sergeant Andrew Jack, the rear gunner. Prince George was killed, aged 39, alongside 13 others. The fourth son of King George V and Queen Mary, and the younger brother of Edward VIII and George VI, he had served in the Royal Navy in the 1920s, before joining the RAF in the late 1930s. His death marked the first time in more than four and a half centuries that a member of the royal family had died on active military duty.

Catherine lived in a large all-female boarding house called Burnbank House, which was populated with fellow wireless operators, military cooks and other women performing a variety of roles. She slept in the old drawing room, which had been converted into a dormitory for six. It was sparsely furnished. 'All we had was six beds, one chest of drawers and a mirror,' she remembers. Bursting into laughter at the memory of a mischievous trick she and her dormitory mates devised, she says: 'You had to clean underneath your bed. We had no dusters, no mops, no nothing. But we were supplied with sanitary towels free, so we just used those to polish the floor. We used them as dusters! We had a moment.'

Margaret, the wireless operator with whom she had been on duty the night of the military air crash, fast became her best friend. 'We played table tennis, we cycled when we were off duty and we went to dances,' she recalls. 'We were called "the terrible twins".' The pair also shared an appetite for pranks. Finishing their eight-hour shift one Sunday morning to find 'there wasn't a living soul to be seen' in the streets, they could not resist some fun as they wandered back to the boarding house. 'In pure devilment we rang doorbells,' she says, laughing. 'Isn't that awful?' While on duty the pair would use Morse code to 'send messages to one another in English' for practice and amusement, but only when the skies were quiet and their attention was not required elsewhere.

They took great pride in their work, taking down the coded messages from planes and passing them to the cipher room. 'It was very important. We were very lucky,' Catherine says. The focused application of her unit and thousands of other WAAF personnel vindicated those in government who had pushed to expand the roles open to female recruits amid doubts about their ability.

The RAF Museum today acknowledges that many WAAFs were greeted with 'scepticism and humour' in the early part of the war, a reception that gave way to 'respect and admiration' as women proved time and again their dedication and skill. Women in the Air Force won a glowing appraisal by the end. 'Day in, day out, they diligently did their duty. Great strength of character was required by many WAAFs in continuing to work despite the loss of friends and loved ones.'

Outside of work, dances and socials were a key source of entertainment, but Catherine and her friends also sought out other opportunities for respite. One such occasion arose when a unit of male RAF personnel stationed on the Inner Hebridean island of Colonsay, 40 miles southeast of Oban, invited them to visit. 'We were in touch with them, sending and receiving messages. One time they said they would like to meet us,' she recalls. 'So we said, "Right." We got titivated up in our best uniforms and got on an RAF Pinnace.' The 60-foot-long boat, part of the RAF Marine Craft fleet, was primarily used for lifting and laying marine and aircraft moorings, aircrew sea survival and towing duties. It was less suitable for ferrying women who wanted to look their most attractive.

'Once we were taken out of the bay, we were in the open sea and the rain came down in torrents. The water was rough and we were seasick,' she says with a loud guffaw. 'When we got off the boat at Colonsay, we were like drowned rats. They never asked us back again.' Their hopes were dashed. 'We had thought we'd probably get a boyfriend out of it.'

Although the WAAF personnel were keen to meet suitable young men, sometimes they found the male personnel deployed to the small town a little too eager. The starkest example of this arose when Oban was overrun by American GIs. 'A ship came in full of Americans and they hadn't seen a woman in six months – and, boy, did they chase us. They were typical Americans, you might say. Very self-confident! I've never felt so wanted in all my life.' It was not only the members of the female units who felt overwhelmed by the attention; the men of the RAF were also put out by the swaggering competition. Catherine recalls: 'The RAF police at that time had to chase [the Americans] out of the village. I'd never seen anything like that.' Pausing, she reflects: 'We had funny times and good times and laughter.' The moments of light relief provided by the Colonsay escapade and the advances of the GIs swiftly became inside jokes and were savoured. 'You had to see the funny side, because there was a sad side,' she says of the war.

The Luftwaffe was far from the only source of danger in Oban. Air accidents and crashes were relatively frequent and often distressing. Catherine recalls coming into close quarters with the aftermath of one such tragedy. 'There was a time when a Sunderland boat was out flying for so many hours and came back and crashed into the bay and sank,' she says. 'I remember my friend Margaret and I used to cycle to our work and we went to this big house, which is now a hotel in Oban. They had an outhouse and the guard on duty at the front door said, "Don't put your bikes in there." So, being nosy, we looked in the window and there were six dead bodies lying on the floor. They'd got them out of the bay. They were sad things [lying there] like that; you could even see they still had their watches on their wrists. I never forgot that. I can still see it in my mind today – these men, airmen, lying there on the floor, just after they had been taken out of the bay. We were sorry we looked in the window.'

At work Catherine began to get to know John Boyd, a wireless operator two years her senior, who worked 'in the same room, on the same shift' and was billeted in a nearby hotel in the town. He was 'very quiet – a shy person', but eventually he summoned the courage to ask her out. 'He just asked me to go to the pictures with him.' At first she herself felt shy and uncertain, but she soon relented. 'I said, "Hmmm," then I said, "Yes,"' she recalls. Hailing from Londonderry, John 'had a lovely Northern Irish accent,' she says. 'I liked that.' He also seemed a good, decent man and was trusting. 'He really was a nice person. He was too good to live in the land,' she says. Blond and, like her, blue-eyed, he had a slim physique and was just a shade taller than her at around 5 foot 5 inches. She ventures bashfully: 'I've been told by showing photographs of him that he was handsome.'

The pair felt at ease with one another from the start and the hours they spent together were filled with laughter. Reflecting on how their relationship developed, she says: 'I was just myself. I have a great sense of humour. We just seemed to hit it off very well.' Halting to take stock, she adds: 'I'm very, very sad and sorry that he didn't live long enough for us to have a life together.' The fledgling couple would spend time in Oban, walking around the town and going out when they could afford it. 'We didn't have much money. We were on about a shilling a day, and going to the pictures cost a few pence,' she says. 'We got on well. We started going out together and getting to know one another and it just carried on from there. Then when he went away.'

John's ambition to graduate from the operations room to the skies was the reason for their parting. 'After a while he wanted to fly, so he went on to be a sergeant air gunner. He was posted away down to various places in England,' she explains. He joined No. 114 Squadron, a light bomber unit. She was proud of his drive, although she maintained misgivings. 'When he was flying, he must have been like a bird in a cage in that turret he was in, being a gunner. It must have been terrible.'

Absence did not dim the couple's passion for each other and within a year they became engaged. The decision to get married was a joint one, influenced in part by the news that John was to deploy overseas. 'I think we just decided together, because he was posted abroad,' Catherine says. They wed on 15 October 1943. 'We were both on leave. He got in touch with the minister and he married us at six o'clock at night in church. I got coupons from my mum. I got this pink suit; I think it cost £4. It was a skirt and jacket and I wore a hat. John wore his uniform,' she recalls. 'It was just a spur-of-the-moment thing. You could get engaged and married very quickly in those days.'

It was a small wedding party, composed of Catherine's family, who approved of John and had given the couple their blessing. 'They thought there was no one like him,' she says. Her two younger brothers, both of whom had by this time enlisted, also happened to be able to request leave to attend. Charlie had joined the Army and John had signed up for the Royal Navy. It pleased the Coleman siblings that collectively 'we represented the three services'. Charlie acted as the bride's 'best man' in lieu of a maid of honour. Living so far away across the Irish Sea, John's family was absent. 'To tell you the truth Mr and Mrs Boyd didn't know we'd got married until afterwards. I think she thought we had to get married [due to an unplanned pregnancy], but we didn't,' she says, laughing.

The married couple enjoyed 'a wee reception in a hotel in Stirling – no wedding cake or anything like that'. She goes on: 'Then we just went and got on the bus and travelled to Edinburgh and that's where we spent the honeymoon, at a boarding house. It was a long walk when we got off the bus to get there. We stayed there for three days, then it was time to go. I went my way and he went his way. He went down to England and I was stationed up in Scotland.'

She is ambivalent today about the haste and lack of ceremony with which they wed. 'Everything was done in a hurry because you were in the services,' she says. 'Looking back now it was very romantic, but there were lots of things I wish I had done. I remember one of the girls, Betty, who was in our room when we were stationed in Oban. Betty got married and had a big white wedding. That's maybe what I wish now had been different.'

Margaret had not been granted leave to attend the wedding and, worse, had been redeployed further north to Wick in Caithness by the time Catherine returned to Oban from her short honeymoon. Catherine herself was then dispatched further north too, to Alness. Within a couple of months of marriage, she fell pregnant – a development that startled her. 'In those days you didn't know so much about the birds and the bees,' she admits.

Warm congratulations were not forthcoming from her superiors, however. When she visited the local hospital to be checked over, she was taken aback by the harsh reaction of the naval doctor who saw her. 'When he'd looked at me and confirmed that I was pregnant he gave me such a lecture. He had me in tears. To think that the government had spent all this money putting me through training and I go and get pregnant – and all the rest of it. I said to myself, "But I'm a married woman." I came home back to my billet in tears. I never forgot that,' she says. 'He gave me a letter to take back to the WAAF officer. Unbeknown to him I steamed it open. I'm very bad. However, it only said that I was pregnant. Do you think they would let me go? I fainted three times on duty before they would let me leave the services. I think I was needed – I don't know.' It was in April, when her uniform was 'getting a bit tight round the waist', that the WAAF finally discharged her.

Tragedy struck in the run-up to the birth. John had been deployed overseas, his whereabouts unknown to Catherine due to the protocols of secrecy surrounding personnel and foreign operations. She had striven to keep in check her anxiety about the dangers he faced while flying in a Boston bomber. 'There were so many planes being shot. It was a very nervous time,' she says. 'But you didn't complain.' Her worst fears were to be fulfilled, however, while he was taking part in a test flight. 'He was posted abroad. I'd no idea where,' she says. 'On 25 August [1944], I got a telegram to say he was missing, reported killed. His plane had come down in the sea somewhere off Italy. A month later my daughter was born. I was married for ten months.'

Before his posting John had been stationed in Melton Mowbray in Leicestershire, where the couple's last meeting took place. 'I went down to see him because they were going abroad. His pilot was Canadian and his navigator was Scottish. It was only the three of them on the plane,' she says. 'I'll always remember standing at the door of my digs there and they flew over and dipped, and that's the last I saw of them all. That was 25 May. It was exactly three months later that he was reported killed, aged 24.

'We were writing to each other. I didn't know where he was, though later I found out he was in Italy. My last letter asked, "What will we call the baby?" He never answered,' says Catherine. 'It was very heartbreaking at the time.' He did not even know that the baby they were expecting was a girl. 'That is another thing I regret,' she says. It took some time for the news that he was missing and feared dead to sink in. 'I just couldn't believe it. I always said, "Why me?" But there it was. That was my life.'

She continues: 'I never gave up hope until the end of the war, hoping against hope that my husband would be a prisoner of war. I never gave up hope until all the prisoners of war were home. Well, there was a chance that his plane had come down and maybe ...' She trails off. 'His plane came down in the sea in only so many fathoms of water. They can't understand why his body was not recovered because it wasn't very deep. But it wasn't to be,' she says. 'So when they had all the celebrations, it was no celebration to me. All these parties afterwards at the end of the war – that brought it all back to me,' she says. When Victory in Europe was finally announced on 8 May 1945, she eschewed the street parties and stayed indoors at home in Bridge of Allan. 'I didn't go out or see anyone or anything. I just kept to myself.'

Before John had deployed overseas, the couple had dreamed about their future life together after the war. 'We had a plan that when he came home from the Air Force, we would emigrate to Canada – because his pilot was a Canadian and he had got talking to him,' she recalls. 'But as I said, it wasn't to be.'

She came under pressure from John's parents to name the baby after him. While he was known in the RAF and by Catherine as Johnny, he was known by his family as Jack. 'They thought I should have called her Jacqueline – Jackie for short. I never gave it a thought, to tell you the truth,' she says. Nonetheless, she paid homage to his mother in the name she chose for the baby. 'I called her Catherine Mary – Catherine after my mum, and Mary after her other granny.'

To compound Catherine's emotional devastation, financial woes soon took hold. A single mother, unable to work while looking after her newborn, she was forced to live on the meagre provisions of state welfare. 'My pension from a grateful government was £4 a week; 22 shillings of that was to bring up my daughter. It wasn't a lot. I was a poor soul,' she says. 'Now it's all different,' she says of the current welfare system, which was forged in the crucible of the war. There was little choice but to move back in with her mother and father in Bridge of Allan in Stirling, returning to the house in which she had grown up on the edge of the estate of the children's hotel. One benefit was that her daughter could mix with the other infants at the institution, which was used principally to look after children whose parents worked and lived abroad.

In time Catherine also reprised her teenage job at the hotel, helping its owner teach table manners to the young wards. 'It was very difficult, because I got no help whatsoever [financially]. I just went out to work.' Employment was hard to come by, however, after the men who had served in the Armed Forces returned home and flooded the job market. The nationwide economy had been battered by the war and the local community floundered as a result. 'Things were very, very poor, because there was no work for people like my dad after the war. We had a struggle, I must admit, but as time went on, I started going out at night-time to hotels and waited on tables. I would get two and sixpence an hour. It was a lot of money to me,' she says.

Socially, life was difficult too. 'I don't think half the people knew that I'd been in the services and had been married. I think they took it for granted I was an unmarried mother. That's just the feeling I got. Nobody ever asked me and I never told anyone.' People in the community were either judgemental or uninterested in her. 'They just had their own lives and that was that,' she says. 'It was lonely when I was a young woman, working to bring up my daughter. I never broadcast the fact that John had died. I just took every day as it came.' As time went on she made a number of good friends, but felt that few of them understood the sacrifices of being a single parent. 'There were thousands like me. But that didn't help either,' she says softly.

The widows of the Second World War are often described as 'forgotten women', largely ignored by the government and wider society. A particular torment for many was the absence of any formal role in collective remembrance events, such as Armistice Day, in the years succeeding the conflict. They were left only with the comfort of personal remembrance. Another insult was the state's treatment of their war-widow pensions as unearned income and therefore subject to the highest rate of income tax. It made for a bleak existence in the decade of austerity that followed the war, during which many were forced to work to supplement these modest pensions, often juggling employment with children and other caring responsibilities. The final affront was that the pension was awarded on the condition that its recipient lived a respectable life. A war widow who cohabited with a new man, bore an illegitimate child or remarried would, bar limited exceptions, find her pension cut off.

Catherine found it tough spending time with and watching other contented couples interacting with each other and their children. 'I just felt sad when I saw other people getting on. I just got up and went to work every day and came back at night-time and listened to my mother moaning that my daughter hadn't behaved herself through the day. My mother was very strict, so she expected too much from Catherine [junior]. She grew up to be a nice lassy.'

Eventually a job came up in a newsagent. 'Funnily enough, I stayed there for 20 years,' she says. 'The wages were nothing. We had eight paper boys and when one didn't turn up, I'd deliver the papers.' The position meant she 'knew everyone and everybody' in the community and began to feel more integrated. A downside, however, was that early mornings were not her strong suit. Often she would get a 'ticking-off' for being late, since customers wanted to buy their newspapers to read over breakfast. Later she landed another office job pricing whisky bottles – a job she preferred because 'I got my fortnight's holiday, and weekends off, which I didn't in the paper shop, and Easter time and Christmas time. It made a great difference to me.'

Commemorating the war in the decades since it ended has been a bittersweet experience. The anniversaries are 'very sad for me at the time,' she reflects. 'Looking back, I think of all the women who lost their husbands and I know how they feel. I relate to all that goes on.' It is perhaps harder for others to understand Catherine's loss, however, or the cruel toll of the lingering hope that John could still be alive, a possibility that was hard to definitively rule out since his body was never found. While she has not kept their letters to each other, she has treasured his flying log book. 'The Air Force sent it to me five years later [following the end of the conflict], just out of the blue,' she says. 'It's precious.'

After the war she visited John's relatives in Londonderry and bonded with them over her daughter – their flesh and blood too. It cost a week's income to afford the boat trip to Ireland, but it was worth it. From that initial meeting onwards, she visited annually. Getting to know his family was a source of succour in her grief. 'That helped,' she says. Relations with John's mother, Mary, were strained, however. 'She was the "only one" who had lost a son. She wasn't interested in me. Of course, being a mother to her son, she didn't approve of the girl he married. I wasn't the girl that she wanted,' she says. It did not help that John's family were Presbyterian, while Catherine was Church of England. She got on better with other members of his family and a lifelong friendship flourished with his sister, who later emigrated to Australia. Catherine has since visited her there nine times in total.

She also joined the War Widows' Association, which was created in 1971 to campaign for fairer pensions for those women whose husbands had been killed in the line of duty, and continues to attend annual events in Edinburgh. 'You meet other people who have gone through similar life stories. They've all got their own sadness,' she says. In the past 20 years she has found it interesting to make friends with young women whose spouses were killed in Afghanistan and Iraq.

After retiring, Catherine chanced to meet Alistair Drummond, a fisherman, through a former WAAF comrade. The pair wed in 1984. 'I was a widow for 40 years and got married again,' she says. They had 17 years of happy marriage, before Alistair died of cancer.

Now Catherine resides with her daughter, through whom she has two grandchildren and three great-grandchildren. The pair are based in Dunfermline in Fife. 'We live together now. Catherine [junior] lost her husband 26 years ago, so we got together,' she remarks. 'She's a great help to me, because I am registered partly blind now, so I can't read and it's difficult to watch TV. I can't do what I'd like to do. I know I'm old, but I'm very agile. I do fine. The one thing I have is my health. I can't remember everything, but I do remember my war days.'

While casting back to memories of the war and thinking of John can be painful, Catherine draws positives from her experiences in the conflict, too. 'It gave me confidence. I grew up. I met lots of people. It was an education, actually,' she asserts. She is also grateful for the friends she made, particularly Margaret, whom she has now outlived. 'That was a long friendship, from when we were 19 till our 90s,' she says. Margaret was one of the few people in Catherine's life who knew her and John as a blithe young couple, providing a thread back to that brief, happy period.

While the two women kept in touch in the post-war decades, it was in later life that they became close again. Their war days were a favourite subject of reminiscence. 'When she was in care – and she had a better memory than I have – we spoke about it. People used to say, "You must have been very clever," but we never thought of ourselves [as] being clever, learning Morse code – sending and receiving messages. We never gave it a second thought. That was our job and that's what we did. But that cheered us up a bit.'

Beyond Margaret, there are few people Catherine has talked to about her wartime service. She did not even compare notes with her brothers – either at the time or afterwards. 'I knew John was somewhere on the open seas, and Charlie was somewhere on the earth, but that was all. You didn't really discuss it,' she says. 'My dad didn't talk about the First World War either. It wasn't until a few years ago we discovered my dad had a certain medal.'

The conflict elevated women's position in society, she believes, proving they were capable and worthy of respect. 'I think we had a wee bit more say in the world. After all, we were very much needed in the war,' she says. 'I know it changed me. It gave me more confidence in myself and it made me very independent. You were away from home and had to fend for yourself. You had to do as you were told. You were under strict military orders and you just obeyed. It just completely changed you.' Wistfully, she concludes with a nod to her strong belief in fate: 'Life is all mapped out for you, and mine was to be that. I've taken every day as it comes and I'm glad I'm still alive.'

# Betty Webb

**DATE OF BIRTH:**

13 May 1923 (aged 16 at the outbreak of war)

**ROLE:**

Paraphraser in the Intelligence Corps of the Auxiliary Territorial
Service, based at Bletchley Park

Betty Webb was a newly enlisted 18-year-old recruit to the
Intelligence Corps when she was thrust into the clandestine
world of Bletchley Park in 1941. 'It was something quite
unexpected and devious,' she says of her work at the top-
secret headquarters of the Allies' code-breaking efforts during
the war. 'It was certainly something I never anticipated.' Her
first duty upon arrival at the Buckinghamshire mansion was
to report to the commander's office to read and sign the Official Secrets Act. 'At my age and inexperience it was pretty
frightening because it's a very formidable document and of

course a very serious outcome if you break the rules,' she says. The presence of a senior officer, who casually laid his revolver on the desk before her, did little to assuage her unease. 'I couldn't even tell my parents where I was or what I was doing. I just had to be very strict with myself and promise myself I wouldn't break the rules.'

The Government Code and Cypher School, which had been set up as a peacetime 'cryptanalytic' unit after the end of the First World War, had acquired the Victorian manor house of Bletchley Park and its 60-acre site in 1938. Designated 'Station X' during the Second World War, its analysts broke into the enemy's strategic communications by cracking the codes of the famed German Enigma and Lorenz cypher machines. Bletchley drew a diverse array of personnel, ranging from mathematicians and linguists to chess champions. Their work handed Britain deep insights into the Axis powers' operations and movements, helping to shorten the war by years. Starting with a staff of 150, Bletchley employed almost 10,000 personnel at its height, of whom 80 per cent were women.

Home-schooled throughout her youth because her family lived in a remote part of rural Shropshire, Charlotte Elizabeth 'Betty' Vine-Stevens had been living with her family and completing the final parts of her correspondence course when war broke out in 1939. Her father, Leslie Vine-Stevens, had served with the Queen's Own Royal West Kent Regiment in Iraq and India during the First World War. As a decorated veteran, he enlisted as an officer in the local Home Guard when the Second World War erupted, but otherwise life continued for a time uninterrupted by the conflict. Intent upon their daughter gaining the best start to her adult life, Betty's parents encouraged her to enrol in a home economics course at a specialist college near Shrewsbury.

The plan collapsed within months. While Betty enjoyed learning how to cook and keep household accounts, such tasks felt increasingly futile as the war raged on the Continent and bombs ravaged vast swathes of the country. Daily reminders of the conflict were ubiquitous, from battle reports on the wireless, right down to the effect of rationing on the pared-down wartime recipes the young ladies were learning to cook. Many of her peers shared her discomfort, so a small group made a pact to quit together and enlist. 'There was a restlessness in the country at that time, with all the bombing that was going on,' Betty explains. 'There were four of us who decided we weren't really doing a very good job just learning to cook and so on, and the four of us left mid-term. It was the atmosphere at the time. We felt that was what we should do.' She adds: 'We'd had enough of making sausage rolls!'

Each of the four women opted for different services. Betty initially attempted to join the Women's Royal Naval Service, attracted by its smart uniform, but she was deterred by its lengthy waiting list. She then alighted upon the Auxiliary Territorial Service (ATS), the women's branch of the British Army. The force had signed up 65,000 female recruits by the time she joined in 1941, a total that had tripled by the time it reached its peak two years later as conscription swelled its ranks.

After passing the initial assessment, she underwent six weeks of basic training at Hightown Barracks, the home of the Royal Welch Fusiliers in Wrexham, north Wales. There she received her official kit: a khaki cap, shirts, collars, ties, a skirt, a tunic, underwear, pyjamas and 'beetle crusher' shoes. She took great pride in wearing the uniform. A great-coat, a raincoat, gas mask and shoulder bag were also handed over, along with a toothbrush, shoe brush and sanitary towels.

The gas masks issued by the ATS were heavier than civilian versions, making them a nuisance to lug around. The commanders of the camp devised an effective way of ensuring they were not left behind in the recruits' dormitories in the morning, however. 'We were taken to a small room while wearing our gas masks and a small amount of gas was released,' Betty wrote previously in a short account of her service.[31] 'We were then ordered to remove our gas masks and everyone was instantly convulsed by coughing and spluttering as the gas entered our lungs. It taught us the importance of carrying our gas masks at all times, taking gas warnings seriously and obeying procedure without question.'

After her isolated childhood and short spell studying home economics, Betty found the ATS camp 'a culture shock'. It was the first time she had met, let alone lived at close quarters with, women from tough inner-city communities. She was taken aback by the speech and manners of some of her contemporaries from poor areas of Liverpool and Cardiff. 'With respect to them, they were all serving well, but they were a very rough lot in the main,' she says. 'It was a total shock to see how some people behaved.' Pausing, she adds: 'The physical side of it was a shock, because one of the things I was asked to do was help look for hair nits. And a lot of them had them and we had to wrap their heads up in paraffin-soaked bandages. It was horrible.'

After a month and a half of training, positions were assigned. She had expected to become a cook or a driver. To her surprise, however, she caught the attention of the Army's Intelligence Corps. She is certain that it was her German language skills and perhaps even her experience of having visited Germany itself that cast her as a potential candidate for an intelligence unit.

Her mother, Charlotte, held a great affinity with Germany and as a result Betty had been raised in a Germanophile household. Charlotte, a music teacher, had unwittingly arrived in Leipzig to take up a school-mistress post in July 1914 – just as the First World War erupted. It took a year of diplomatic wrangling before she was granted an exit visa to leave the country again, but the experience did not dim her enthusiasm for Germany in the long term. Although as an 'enemy' she had been required to report daily to the local police station during that time, she was treated with courtesy.

Years later, married and with a family, Charlotte went on to employ successive German-speaking au pairs, from whom Betty and her sister learned the basics of the language. 'I was brought up to speak it – my mother in particular stressed the importance of learning another language, so we had helpers in the house who were either Swiss or German. We always spoke German, but it wasn't particularly good on the more technical side,' she says. In 1937 a private exchange between Betty and a German teenager named Elisabeth was arranged in a bid for both to improve their language skills.

Betty took the forbidding trip by ferry and train to Herrnhut, a small town near Dresden, to stay with the 14-year-old girl's family. They belonged to the Moravian Church, a Protestant denomination in which the women wore plain attire with bonnets and were segregated from men during worship. Unaccustomed to being away from her family or travelling overseas, she was racked with homesickness during the visit. In addition, her comprehension of German was too weak to allow her to participate in advanced conversation with the family.

Some of the sights she witnessed during the trip took on grim significance later. She attended the local school with Elisabeth and was required to partake in its rituals. 'In school we were obliged to stand to attention and give the Hitler salute at the beginning and end of every class,' she has written in the past.[32] 'I did not fully comprehend the German threat but felt it was diplomatic to join in with the class requirement to salute. I disguised my discomfort by waving my arms but not joining the verbal salute. I certainly felt an undercurrent of concern.'

Elisabeth's father, Gerhard, tried to convey to Betty the local anxiety about the political situation and Hitler's regime, but to her regret her German was not good enough to fully understand him. 'I kept in touch with the family in Herrnhut until World War Two broke out and did not hear from them again, which I regret,' she wrote.

Betty seemed to make German connections wherever she went. The following summer she became friends with Otto, a 17-year-old German, during a family holiday to the Welsh coast. Later that year a German refugee came to live with the family in Shropshire. Dorothea Schiffer was the daughter of a Jewish doctor and aristocratic mother, who had arrived in England as a refugee, aided by the Vine-Stevens' local church. She had fled from Breslau, one of the Nazi Party's strongest support bases in Germany in the 1930s, which later became the Polish city Wrocław under territorial changes made in the Potsdam Agreement in 1945. Dorothea spoke fluent English and ended up settling in the UK for good, where she went on to train as a children's nurse in London. She and Betty remained lifelong friends.

For her interview with the Intelligence Corps, Betty travelled overnight from Wales to London, sleeping on the corridor floor of the packed train. The purpose of her trip contrasted starkly with that of her only other previous visit to London. She reflected later that it was 'ironic that my first visit to the capital was as part of my journey to pre-war Germany, where I had received so much hospitality, and my second visit, as part of my duty in the fight against Germany'.

The capital appeared 'very grand' to her, despite the devastating bomb damage of the Blitz, as she made her way to Devonshire House in Piccadilly, an office complex occupied by the War Damage Commission during the conflict.

An army major led the interview, which was conducted in German. It went well and he needed no further time to consider her suitability. 'He gave me a railway warrant and said, "Get yourself to Bletchley,"' she recalls. 'I'd never heard of Bletchley and certainly didn't know what was going on there. It was a total secret, the whole thing.'

Arriving in Buckinghamshire, she was directed to civilian billets in the village of Loughton. Bletchley personnel attached to the ATS tended to be sent to individual homes, while those attached to the Women's Royal Naval Service were accommodated together at nearby grand houses such as Woburn Abbey. The abbey was also home to the Political Warfare Executive, a secretive body that produced foreign-directed propaganda to damage the Nazis' morale and bolster the spirits of overseas allies.

Betty's first posting was 'a rather unfortunate experience', she says. 'It was absolutely awful. Some of the places that were asked to take people from Bletchley were a little bit difficult to cope with and so cramped.' She continues: 'The loo was up the garden. Mind you, that wasn't a bother to me, because where we lived in the country we had a loo up the garden to begin with.'

She was put out, however, by the expectation that she should bunk up with another ATS recruit whom she had only just met on the train. In time, Wynn Angell, an English girl who had been living in Belgium at the time of the Nazi invasion in May 1940, became a firm friend, but at that juncture Betty was mortified at the prospect of 'having to share a bed with somebody I'd only just met!' She adds: 'That was very embarrassing.'

She was swiftly moved on to new accommodation, but this was also overcrowded. The family of six that lived in the small house were already struggling for space before the arrival of three ATS personnel. 'Not that I minded that,' she says, 'but there wasn't much room, as you can imagine, with that lot in it.' She was not demanding of luxury. After all, where she had grown up in Shropshire was 'very much in the country – no telephone, no water, no nothing. We had a very primitive life,' she says. However, she was used to plenty of space.

She requested another transfer and struck lucky the third time with the 'delightful' Foxley family, the owners of a large house who became lifelong friends. 'I was very happy there,' she recalls. 'They had a very good vegetable garden so it meant that our rations were rather better than most people's.' There was also an orchard. 'The woman was a very good cook,' she remembers happily. 'We lived next door to the old-fashioned bakery and by saving up the dried food ration, occasionally we had some rather nice cake. It was a huge house.'

Betty was 5 foot 4 inches tall, with dark-brown hair and blue eyes, and of medium build. 'Although I put on quite a bit of weight during the war,' she says, in part because there was a decent amount of food thanks to the bountiful vegetable patch at her billet. She adds that her working routine did not help: 'There was a lot of sitting around. I didn't have a great deal of time for exercise.' She lost weight when she fell ill, however. 'I had mumps at the time of the D-Day landings. I lost a stone,' she says, recalling being sent to a military hospital in Northampton. 'I learned some years later there was quite an epidemic at the time.'

She recalls vividly her arrival at Bletchley Park, a heavily guarded site with an 'ugly', sprawling house situated in the grounds, as well as the stern lecture she received about the Official Secrets Act, which she had signed. 'It was very, very strict and we had to abide by that until 1975,' she says. Even her parents knew nothing of the nature of her work. She could not tell them and they knew better than to ask. The only clue was the Intelligence Corps badge she wore.

A culture of discretion had developed in the country since the outbreak of the conflict, fostered by a government advertising campaign that warned: 'Careless talk costs lives'. One typical cartoon showed two women chatting on a bus, overheard in the rows behind by the prominent Nazi leaders Heinrich Himmler and Hermann Goering. The caption read: 'You never know who's listening!'

Betty and her fellow recruits rigidly adhered to the rules, which meant that she did not glean the significance of the work that was taking place at Bletchley until decades later, when wartime information was declassified in the 1970s.

'Under the Official Secrets Act, we were not allowed to say anything outside our own office. Anything we saw, heard or read was strictly within the four walls of your office. It wasn't until some years after the war, by reading books and going to reunions, we were all able to put the picture together. I was very surprised; I had no idea of the enormity of it,' she says.

Her role was to catalogue encrypted intelligence, which came in by dispatch rider or teleprinter, by date and call sign so that the messages could be drawn upon for reference by decoders and translators. 'We were registering the messages that came in from signalmen and women around the country and around the world. All that [had] to be catalogued, except there was nothing that was clear [in the coded messages], except the date,' she explains.

She recalls: 'There was a Major Ralph Tester – he was a brilliant German speaker. He needed to be able to call on certain dates of messages. So they all had to be very carefully catalogued, and we kept them neatly on cards on which the records were written in shoeboxes. We had very little equipment in those days. You couldn't read anything. The messages were in groups of five letters, or figures. There was nothing "in the clear" at that stage. But the decoders then had to make the best of it as they could.'

Once the messages were decoded, they were translated from German, Italian or Japanese into English, after which an initial analysis of their contents could take place. At that stage they would be assessed for urgency and importance, then forwarded to appropriate figures, including commanders in the field and even the prime minister. 'It was a very, very big operation,' she says. She worked hard and Major Tester valued her abilities. He even considered her for a promotion to the role of translator. However, after setting her a test, he had to inform her gently that her language skills were not at the required level of fluency.

It has only been in recent years that Betty has discovered that her unit handled intelligence between the Gestapo, the Nazi secret police, and the SS, the Nazi paramilitary group, about German activities on the Eastern Front. 'A lot of this traffic was to do with the Holocaust,' she says. 'I didn't know that at the time. We didn't know anything and we were not allowed to talk about everything outside our own room. We had no idea [of] the end product, and what the whole thing was about, absolutely no idea.'

She worked with three other men in a small, cold office above the ballroom in the mansion. While they were permitted to light the fire at night, the plan was often precluded by fuel shortages. Her wages were paid weekly in a formal pay parade ceremony, at which attendance was mandatory even on days off. She started as a private, for which the pay was modest, but was swiftly upgraded in rank. 'I think they gave me a lance corporal stripe just before I started helping look for nits,' she says, laughing. 'I ended up as a staff sergeant.'

In time she was also promoted from cataloguing coded messages to paraphrasing their contents. The task was undertaken as a precaution to prevent the enemy realising that their intelligence had been compromised if they intercepted Allied messages in the field.

Betty explains that her new role involved 'handling the messages which had been translated from Japanese into English, and then I had to reword them in such a way that when they were passed on – to our commanders in the field or perhaps direct to Churchill, I don't know – they would not necessarily have been recognised as having been picked up and decoded. Naturally we needed to camouflage that fact.' It was hoped that the information would appear instead as though it came from spies, stolen documents or aerial reconnaissance. The breaking of the German and Japanese military codes remained a closely guarded secret.

Maps of India and Burma adorned the wall of her new office, as she paraphrased messages about Kohima in north-eastern India, the site of a bloody battle in 1944 known as the Stalingrad of the East. It proved the turning point of the Japanese campaign in India. Betty marvels now that she took part in such a 'devious' and 'unexpected' task that was aimed at fooling the enemy. This work in F Block, which tended to involve intelligence relating to the Japanese Military Air Section, was 'more interesting' than her previous role, which she admits was at times 'tedious'. She enjoyed the chance to work with three other women rather than men, as well as finally reside in a building that boasted central heating.

It took Betty some time to adjust to life at Bletchley. She had been dismayed to learn upon arrival that she would be unable to receive telephone calls from her family, although she still continued to visit them on leave when the opportunity arose. However, after making friends and throwing herself into the social scene, she thrived. 'There was a jolly crowd of folks and the atmosphere was good. Having been brought up in the country – a very quiet life in the main – it was lovely for me socially,' she says.

Her childhood had been an isolated one. While she had a younger sister, Catherine, the seven-year age difference had rendered her unsuitable as a playfellow. 'It was difficult at times, because it was such a gap,' she recalls. A brother, David, was born in between the two girls, but he died around the age of three. She was never told why. 'I never really knew – these things weren't talked about in those days, but I know that he was very, very frail and nothing could be done to help,' she says.

Friends had also been tough to make in so rural a setting. She recalls only two companions from her younger years: one was the daughter of a family that owned a nearby holiday cottage, who was only in the area periodically, while the other was a farmer's daughter who also died young. 'That was about the extent of it, really,' she says. When she first enlisted in the ATS she felt awkward around the other women. 'I was rather shy and inexperienced,' she says. 'I think I felt a bit out of it, in a way, and I was very reluctant to tell anybody that I didn't go to a normal school for many years. It doesn't bother me now, but it did for quite a long time.' She soon 'got into the swing of things', however.

At Bletchley she experienced a social awakening. 'There was a general atmosphere of frivolity because people couldn't talk about their work outside their own offices. So outside it was much more relaxed and jovial,' she says. 'It was wonderful for me to meet all these people and it was an amazing mix, from aristocrats to people like me, and I found it extremely interesting,' she says. 'Everyone says there will never be a situation like that again. All walks of life were thrown together and had to work together.' To her delight, one of the four young women with whom she had walked out of the domestic sciences college also turned up at Bletchley, although she was assigned to the Women's Royal Naval Service rather than the ATS.

There was also a wealth of organised activities into which she threw herself. 'I joined the choir, which was run by a professional musician. I also joined a madrigal society, which met fairly frequently, and we had a gramophone group. There was plenty to take part in, work permitting,' she says. Lectures were hosted on a range of subjects, while a drama group and orchestra put on performances. When several hundred Americans arrived at the site, dances were also hosted. Betty took great pleasure in wandering around the estate parkland and walking by the lake, which was used for ice skating when it froze over during the winter. She had enjoyed cycling in the area too, until her bicycle was stolen.

The ability to socialise and enjoy the rich variety of activities on offer 'depended on the workload', however. She recalls: 'Ideally we could have a day off a week, but it didn't necessarily happen, and the shift system was from eight to four, four to midnight, or midnight to eight, which was a bit arduous. But it had to be done. I got very tired, especially on the night shift. The other difficult thing was having to start in the middle of the night. To begin with it was very upsetting to the system.'

When she first arrived at Bletchley, a fleet of buses transported personnel from their billets to the estate each day. The arrangement was expensive, however. 'Eventually they decided it was not practical from a financial point of view,' she says. 'So they built a camp, which was within walking distance of the park, and that was for the Army and the Air Force.' In 1944, therefore, she left her civilian home behind and moved on-site. There were 30 beds to a hut in the new camp, which was built from breeze blocks and bitumen. Coke-fuelled stoves were installed to provide heat, but they smoked to such a degree that they were deemed unusable. Instead, Betty and her comrades preferred to play vigorous rounds of table tennis last thing at night in order to get warm before rushing to their beds to tuck in. In balmier weather during the summer months, they slept outside under the stars.

Life at the camp had 'another atmosphere altogether', she recalls. 'We were a happy lot and the facilities were good. The only thing that was difficult, which was difficult for the whole country, is that we had to be very careful how much water we used. We were only allowed about four inches in the bath and that was not easy. But we just entered into the atmosphere as it was – and it was good.' Personnel would dine in the on-site canteen, which had the benefit of being state funded. This meant pay could be saved for toiletries, visits to the cinema or the occasional sweet treat. Betty's weekly luxury was a small bar of chocolate. In general the food served was 'adequate', but 'very limited, rationed, very uninteresting', she sniffs. One friend complained endlessly about how often beetroot sandwiches were served. 'I quite liked beetroot,' she says. 'But I quite understand. You can have enough of it.'

In the midst of a busy schedule at Bletchley, a nascent romance grew with a young intelligence officer who belonged to the Canadian Air Force. Stationed at an aerodrome on the southwest outskirts of London, John was the nephew of a couple who were friends with Betty's parents. The young pair were 'introduced in the formal way that one was in those days', she says.

They got along well, but after several months she decided they were better suited as friends than as anything more romantically serious. Looking back now, she says she simply resolved that there was insufficient spark to contemplate moving to Canada with him after the war. The break-up was not for want of effort on the young man's part, however. Eager to see her, he had turned up unannounced one day at the London address where he used to address his letters to her. Unfortunately, he had not realised that this was only a PO Box number for correspondence, and that she was miles away in Buckinghamshire. 'It was just not to be, you know,' she says, laughing. 'We were good friends, but that was just as far as it would go. It wasn't sufficiently good to carry on.'

Periodically she would take day trips to London, trying to time these excursions during quieter periods of bombing raids. It was 'tricky' to organise such visits, but the lure of an evening at the theatre or a restaurant was strong. During one visit she was startled at the end of her Tube journey. 'As I came out of the Underground, I saw everybody was lying on the floor. So I joined them and then realised that it was a doodlebug flying around,' she says. 'Actually, it went off – fortunately – enough miles away for us not to be hurt, but it was very much a nasty few moments. They were awful things.'

Although Bletchley itself was never a target, the Blitz still impacted on personnel there. 'One of our members had a family in London – a wife and son – and he asked for leave to go and see them because he hadn't been able to get through on the phone,' she recalls sadly. 'Believe me, I'll never forget that man's face when he came in next morning. We said, "How did you get on?" He said, "All I found was my boy's tie."'

When the announcement of Victory in Europe arrived on 8 May 1945, it was a source of joy, relief and surprise. 'Bearing in mind I was very junior, and in any event by that time I was working in the Japanese department, I wasn't aware of the imminent end of the war in Europe,' she says. There was 'a tremendous hurrah'.

'Once it came through, of course I joined in the general jollifications,' she says. Dashing for a train to London, she entered the city and headed for the River Thames. 'I joined in with the numerous crowds up there – who were dancing, singing and drinking – having a lovely time being jostled around by I can't tell you how many thousands of people. There were so many – you didn't have to consciously walk; you were just pushed along. I felt tremendous relief,' she says, adding with a laugh: 'Being me, I probably thought, *Perhaps we'll have some more food now.*' She recalls meeting on VE Day with Dorothea, her Jewish friend who was a refugee from Germany. 'We met up in London and were part of the milling crowds.'

The next day 'everybody had to get back to work. There was a lot of tidying up to be done,' she says. For Betty, the war was far from over. She learned that she was to be posted to Washington to carry on her work on Japanese intelligence from the Pentagon. She was surprised but excited. 'It was such a privilege,' she recalls. While a group of 20 female comrades were sent to Delhi, she believes she was the sole ATS recruit from Bletchley dispatched to the United States. A flurry of preparations commenced, including a round trip to Oxford to get a perm that would prevent the Washington humidity from playing havoc with her hair.

She then reported to the War Office Holding Unit near Hyde Park, where Winston Churchill's youngest daughter, Mary Spencer-Churchill, was stationed as junior commander of the ATS. It was the first port of call for all personnel waiting for deployment overseas. From there, Betty travelled to Poole and on 6 June she boarded a Sunderland flying boat to Baltimore.

It was her first time on board an aircraft. She was terrified and, to her mortification, was sick. The plane stopped in Ireland to refuel, then flew on to Newfoundland, the Canadian island off the eastern coast of the North American mainland. After sleeping on the floor of the aircraft during the flight, she enjoyed a breakfast of bacon and eggs there while surveying a vista of fir trees. Finally the plane arrived in Baltimore and she was accompanied to Washington by a male officer from Bletchley. She was overwhelmed by the openness of society there and the abundance of goods on offer. 'It was a different atmosphere in America. The situation there, from the point of view of food and clothing, was very much less strict than it was here. It was like a holiday, really,' she says.

The scale of the Pentagon also surprised her. Around 32,000 people worked at the site. She continued to work on paraphrasing Japanese messages, which had usually been intercepted in Burma, now Myanmar. On occasion she was also tasked with couriering secret documents between departments in Washington. She was given a warm reception by the British Embassy, where she was invited to sign the visitors' book. 'By way of acknowledgement we all received visiting cards from Her Majesty's Ambassador and the Countess of Halifax,' she recalls – a memento she has kept.

Life outside of work felt very different from that in the UK. Dairy and sugar were in bountiful supply, Betty was delighted to find. 'Coming from the ration situation in England to the richness of food in America was quite something,' she recalls. 'The thing that impressed me very much was having melon in my salad. I'd never had that before. I remember it clearly – it was lovely.' Other novelties that thrilled her were mint julep cocktails and jukeboxes. The military community in Washington was sociable and Betty received invitations to cocktail parties most nights. An aspect of American society that caused her unease, however, was witnessing racial segregation during her daily bus trips between the Pentagon and her hotel.

She made a number of good friends, including the daughter of Commander Alastair Denniston, who had been in charge at Bletchley. A young American servicewoman became another companion and invited Betty to stay with her parents in Rhode Island, affording her the chance to travel outside Washington. It was also a welcome opportunity to escape the dingy hotel in which she and another British recruit were billeted. It was hot and stuffy, with poor ventilation, but its worst affliction was a cockroach infestation. The warm climate of Washington rendered her ATS-issued, heavy wool uniform far too hot, so instead she borrowed a Canadian Women's Army Corps summer uniform, which was lighter.

On the day the first atomic bomb was dropped on Hiroshima, 6 August 1945, 'Washington went mad,' she recalls. 'Everybody who had cars fixed their horns and left them on for about 24 hours, and it was the most appalling cacophony.' The bombing, aimed at ending the war in the East, palpably boosted support for US President Harry Truman, who had taken office in April that year. 'Thousands of people were clinging to the railings of the White House, calling out, "We want Harry! We want Harry!"' Betty remembers.

After Japan surrendered on 15 August, she was deployed to a British Army staff office to take part in a 'tidying-up operation – destroying papers and packing up'. Then it was time to go home. 'It took a long time to wait for a boat to get back, but clearly once the [atomic] bombs had been dropped there was nothing else for me to do,' she says. Security remained stringent, even though the war was over. 'If I went shopping at lunchtime I had to show the guards everything I had bought, which could be embarrassing if it involved personal items,' she says. As she embarked on the journey home, an unexpected opportunity to spend several days in New York arose due to a porter strike at the docks. Visits to the ballet and theatre followed. In those final days, she filled four kit bags with gifts and clothes for her family.

The voyage to Southampton on RMS *Aquitania*, a British ocean liner used as a troop transport during the conflict, took five days. After arriving back in the UK, she was despatched once again to Bletchley, where 'they were shredding paper and dismantling machinery'. Dawdling ensued. 'I have no memory of how long I was there waiting for a new posting. I just remember the atmosphere one gets after everyone has gone home from a party or a feeling of emptiness after packing a house up before a move,' she has said previously.[33] Eventually, in February 1946, she was demobbed.

Looking back now, Betty reflects on how lucky she was not to have lost anyone close to her in the war. 'I had a cousin who was a regular army officer. He was out in lots of theatres and he came through unscathed,' she says. The years after the war were not easy, as rationing persisted and jobs were scarce. Employers 'didn't understand the conditions of the Official Secrets Act,' she says, which made it hard for those who had served at Bletchley to account for their war years and communicate the skills they had developed during that time.

'You couldn't tell a prospective employer what you'd been doing; that was absolutely out. And, understandably, they didn't accept that excuse. I lost a couple of jobs that way. It was difficult,' she says. 'I think it was even more difficult for men. Prospective employers would have thought, *Well, why isn't he in uniform?*' she adds.

Eventually she chanced upon a secretarial position at a grammar school near Ludlow, at which the headmaster had previously served in intelligence. 'Luckily he'd been employed in a fairly senior position at Bletchley so he didn't ask me any questions. I was very, very lucky,' she says. In later years another chance encounter linked to Bletchley resulted in a job. Betty had been visiting Chester when she bumped into June, with whom she had served in the ATS, and her husband, a senior officer in the Cheshire Territorial Army. The couple encouraged her to join the TA and she successfully took up a post as an adjutant in the permanent staff.

She remained with the service for more than a decade, then joined the Women's Royal Army Corps as a recruitment officer, a role she retained until her retirement in 1969. 'I was very lucky in being able to carry on with [military service]. I had a wonderful time in the West Midlands – quite near where I'm living now actually. My headquarters was Birmingham, and I had outstations at Hereford, Worcester, Shrewsbury, Coventry, Aberystwyth and Hanley – so I had rather a busy time travelling around.' She is a proud member of the WRAC Association today and remains president of its Birmingham branch.

Women who took part in the war effort should be proud of their contribution, she says. 'We formed the majority of the employees at Bletchley. There were 8,000 at the height of [the] activity, and we outnumbered the men three to one,' she says. 'It turned out that one or two of them were clever enough to be actual code-breakers and there were others who were linguists. We formed a major part of the workforce.' For her, Bletchley was 'the next best thing to a university'.

She is adamant that the war profoundly impacted on how women were valued afterwards. 'Because women had been so successful in the services, but also in the munitions factories and helping with the food distribution, it became recognised that women were up to it,' she says. 'Now, if you think about it, women can go into most things, can't they? Women did do things before the war, if you think of people like Florence Nightingale, but it was on a much bigger scale following the war,' she adds. The contribution of female recruits to the war effort is 'sometimes forgotten', she warns.

When she was in her late forties, Betty met Alfred Webb, and the pair went on to marry. The former veteran, who boasted dark hair and eyes, was head of a building firm. 'I was living fairly near where he was and we were introduced and that was that,' she says. He had been a drummer in the Royal Artillery during the war. 'He also had a nasty job – he had to help sort out the horrible conditions after the bombing of Coventry,' she adds. He did not divulge the horrifying details of those efforts. 'I think he had a pretty nasty time. He didn't talk about it a great deal.'

She was not able to tell him about her work at Bletchley Park because he died before the secrecy protocols were lifted in the mid-1970s. 'I didn't have the opportunity,' she says. 'I wasn't at liberty.' She was devastated by his premature death in his fifties. 'Having come through the war in Europe without a scratch, he contracted this wretched hardening of the arteries and having had to have both his legs amputated, his body couldn't take it and he died,' she says.

It is vitally important that children continue to learn about the conflict, she reflects. 'If everybody grew up knowing that they should steer everybody else against war, things might be better. I think it's good that the young know the sacrifices that were made by so many generations.'

She has remained in touch with members of the Foxley family, with whom she was billeted during the war. 'The youngest one, Donald, served in the tanks in Europe,' she notes. 'He was recently awarded the Légion d'honneur [the highest French order of merit]. He's blind and has never seen his medal – he can only feel it. Isn't it sad?'

She enjoys birdwatching through her window with binoculars. She is also currently thinking about writing her memoirs, which she downplays as 'a follow-up to my sort of showing off' – a reference to her book, recounting some of her recollections of Bletchley. 'I don't have any help in the house and I get quite tired physically,' she adds. 'I think, *Well, I'll just sit down for a minute.* Next thing I know, an hour has gone by.'

Today, as one of the last living veterans to have served at Bletchley Park, Betty receives torrents of letters from all around the world. She is friendly with other female veterans, including the code-breaking Owtram sisters. 'Pat was on signals, but not at Bletchley – sending things in. Jean was a FANY [a member of the First Aid Nursing Yeomanry],' she says. Pat, fluent in German, had been a special duties 'Y Service' linguist interceptor. Posted to secret listening stations along the British coastline, she intercepted enemy shipping radio traffic and fed the messages back to Bletchley. Jean, her sister, was a code and cypher officer who worked in the FANY for the Special Operations Executive. Betty says: 'We've met on occasion. Pat and I were at the Women of the Year lunch in London. I spoke to her the other day. We get on well, with our similar background.'

She believes popular notions of what happened at Bletchley in the war have become warped over time. 'There is too much focus on Alan Turing and his department. Everyone played an important role, however small,' she says. She has given more than 100 talks about her time there, a subject she only commented on for the first time in 1994. In 2015 she was awarded an MBE for her work remembering and promoting Bletchley Park.

# Connie Hoe

**DATE OF BIRTH:**

3 April 1922 (aged 17 at the outbreak of war)

**ROLE:**

Munitions factory worker

Connie Hoe survived the Blitz unscathed, but her home and neighbourhood did not. However hard she tried to press on with normal life in London's East End, she could not escape the Nazi bombs. The munitions wreaked destruction on her street, flattening her boyfriend's home and leaving her own building uninhabitable. Even her wedding night was marred by a Luftwaffe air raid that forced her to shelter in an Underground station with her groom. While some Londoners became inured over time to the nightly bombardment of their city, Connie's terror never waned. 'I was terrified,' she admits. Eventually she had to evacuate.

Born to an English mother and a Chinese father, Constance 'Connie' Margaret Lam was effectively orphaned at the age of eight and consequently taken in by a neighbour. Her parents, Constance and Fook, had not been an unusual couple in Limehouse, the district of east London that was home to Europe's first Chinatown. A small Chinese population had lived in the capital since the early nineteenth century, when sailors from the Far East brought tea, porcelain, silk and wallpaper to the city and began to settle near the port. By the mid-1880s, the poor and crowded streets around Limehouse – crammed with small terraces, canals, railways and workshops – had taken on Chinese names and hosted Chinese shops, restaurants and meeting places that were frequented by the local migrant community. It was a colourful and unusual quarter of the city, and one that captivated the imagination of writers as diverse as Charles Dickens, Oscar Wilde and Arthur Conan Doyle.

As the twentieth century wore on, the area became a byword for crime, sexual excess and mysticism. This was in large part down to Thomas Burke's collection of short stories about opium dens and the occult, entitled *Limehouse Nights: Tales of Chinatown*, which was published in 1916. In fact, by this time crime in the area had ebbed and most of the opium dens had gone. Gambling was still popular in the neighbourhood when Connie was born in 1922, however, and strife between rival gangs sometimes erupted into violent knife and gun fights. Throughout the Roaring Twenties it remained a popular destination for revellers seeking bohemian haunts. By the 1930s it was a calmer district, although sensational tales about drugs and crime still cropped up in the newspapers.

During Connie's childhood, Limehouse was a melting pot of English, Chinese and multiracial families who were on good terms with each other. Connie recalls friendly relations between all in the community and retains happy childhood memories of running carefree in and out of the homes of all her neighbours. She remembers no tensions or prejudice, although reports suggest that social attitudes towards marriages between English women and Chinese men were mixed, ranging from welcome acceptance to racist hostility.

The Chinese population, which numbered several thousand people, had split into two distinct neighbourhoods. A Cantonese community hailing from southern China had settled in the narrow Limehouse Causeway, while migrants from Shanghai and northern China had settled several streets to the east around Pennyfields. Each area boasted its own shops, restaurants, pubs and laundries as well as homes.

Connie stresses that it is a myth that all the Chinese in Limehouse were poor; to the contrary, many of the migrants who arrived on ships at the beginning of the twentieth century were affluent. Her father was among their number. He was highly educated, speaking and writing English fluently, and had attended the same college in Hong Kong as Sun Yat-sen, the statesman known as the father of modern China. Fook went on to study in the United States and it was at the end of this stint that he travelled to London. He soon took up a role organising bed and board for Chinese sailors arriving at the nearby docks during their stay in the city and was entrusted with handing them their pay on behalf of the shipping agencies.

While Connie was an infant, the death of Fook's father demanded his return to Hong Kong. As the eldest son, he was expected to take over the business and preside over a street of properties that his family owned. He decided that a change of location would be undesirable for his daughter and wife and so left them in London. Several years later, when she was eight, Connie was left without any family at all after her mother died of meningitis. She kept a photograph of Constance by her bed. 'I used to look at it and I used to think she was in heaven. Although I was only a child, I still realised I was on my own,' she has said previously.[34]

Before her death, Constance had made a solemn request of a friend named Katherine 'Kit' Wing, another Englishwoman who had married a Chinese man. Connie recalls the conversation between her mother and Kit, whom she referred to as her auntie. 'She said, "If anything happens to me, look after my Con." My auntie, who was her friend, said, "Yes," and she just took me in.' Kit, whose own daughter had died in infancy, had already taken in Dennis, a baby boy who had been abandoned at three weeks old. Kit and her husband, Chang, who had married at the Chinese Embassy, ran a general convenience store on Limehouse Causeway selling food and fuel for cookers. They were comfortably well off. Connie recalls that they owned a car and a piano, which distinguished them in the neighbourhood. However, before she joined their household, Chang, like Fook, left the country. Connie's adoption by Kit, whom she called Nannie Wing, did not involve the state. There was no legal process, nor any authority deployed to check on her wellbeing. It was only decades later that she recognised how fortunate she had been to end up with a safe and loving guardian.

She was a clever child, with a particular gift for mathematics, and won a place at a prestigious school nearby. She nurtured aspirations to become a mathematician, but was dissuaded from pursuing education past the age of 14. It was an irrelevant idea, Kit insisted, because she would be married by 18 and the 'time, cost and provision would be wasted'. Anxious not to defy Kit, Connie reluctantly agreed.

Leaving education so early meant that a prized office job as a shorthand typist or bookkeeper was beyond her reach. Such roles were reserved for young women who achieved their school certificate at 17. Instead she looked for shop and factory work. She and another friend accepted jobs at a press-cutting agency in Fleet Street.

Shortly before the war Kit moved from Limehouse to Canvey Island on the Essex coast to open a shop and Connie moved with her. However, when the conflict erupted, Kit was forced to leave the area, Connie recalls. 'We had to come back because she was married to an alien, and although by then [Chang] had died, because she married at the Chinese Embassy, that made her a Chinese national. And all aliens had to move away from the coast – they were not allowed to live on the coast, so we came back to London,' she remarked in the decade after the war.[35]

All foreign nationals were subject to a threat assessment during the war and placed into one of three groups: the most high risk were placed in category A and subject to internment; medium-risk nationals were placed in category B and subject to various restrictions, while low-risk individuals – including refugees – were put in category C and not subject to constraints. These labels extended to the British-born spouses of foreign nationals, too. The fear of invasion from the Continent fuelled the decision to bar category-B residents from living on the southeast coast, amid suspicion that they could collaborate with the enemy.

It was during the 'phoney war', the period between September 1939 and April 1940 when there was little fighting and no bombs dropped, that Connie met and fell in love with Leslie Hoe. He too had grown up in Chinatown, but since his father was from Shanghai, he lived in Pennyfields while Connie had been raised in Limehouse and their paths had never crossed.

Their introduction came at a friend's Christmas party and the chemistry was immediate. Leslie had recently completed his first overseas voyage, sailing to Australia and back, while seconded from the Royal Navy to the Merchant Navy. Two years her senior, he was 'a young, handsome sailor,' Connie recalls. A larger-than-life character and natural entertainer, he was strong-willed, sociable and kind. She, by turns, was 'a mixed-up girl' who was 'bowled over' by him.

Their courtship was complicated by Leslie taking a short job at Claridge's hotel while waiting for his next naval deployment. It entailed long hours and work in the evenings. Nevertheless, the couple carved out time to stroll in the park and catch a film. However, their great love was dancing and their favourite dates were spent on the ballroom floor at the Astoria Theatre in Charing Cross. Leslie was Connie's first proper boyfriend, while she was his first serious girlfriend.

In the early summer of 1940 Leslie left his West End job and nearby rented digs on Baker Street to volunteer for the war effort. He was enrolled as a Royal Navy gunner to defend merchant vessels and joined the treacherous Atlantic convoys, where the lines of communication were poor. Connie was left to ponder his whereabouts for months on end.

He was back in London, however, when the Blitz commenced, raining down destruction on London and other cities across Britain. In the very first raid of this new campaign on 7 September 1940, when 600 Nazi bombers targeted London, 840 sites were blasted. Chinatown was among the areas hit and Chinese names proliferated on the casualty lists thereafter.

Leslie's building on Pennyfields, which his family shared with a boarding house, was obliterated by a bomb. His parents and sister Rose had fortunately evacuated the dwelling before it was destroyed, but every single possession they owned was gone. Left only with the clothes in which they were standing, they moved into a neighbour's garden air-raid shelter. Connie's friend Alan witnessed the bomb attack on the building first-hand. Decades later he would take her to the vantage point from which he had watched in horror, and describe to her what he had seen as the building collapsed.

She and Kit were living in rooms on the opposite side of the same street and their building was also badly damaged. Connie recalls the day that Leslie's building was wrecked with vivid clarity. It was a Saturday afternoon and she had been working in Woolworths, a general store. 'The manager made us close the store and go into the shelter. It was about three or four in the afternoon and as we walked to the shelter we saw all these planes in the sky – German planes, though we didn't know that at the time. We stayed in the shelter till the all-clear went, then I had to walk home because there was no transport. As I approached where I lived I saw that a bomb had dropped and all the houses were blitzed,' she has said previously.[36]

Recalling the destruction of Leslie's building, she says now: 'The houses either side were also destroyed by the blast. Nobody was in the house at the time, but several neighbours were killed, including a friend. At the time, his parents and sister were elsewhere. The explosion so badly damaged other nearby properties, including 63 Pennyfields, where Kit and I were living, as to make them uninhabitable.' She concludes sadly: 'Leslie's house was bombed out, and so was mine.'

Nearby an explosive bomb on Dee Street ripped through 18 private houses and garages, a gas main, service pipe and the road, while in Venue Street 23 buildings were damaged and six people were severely injured. Enemy aircraft were indiscriminate in dropping incendiary, explosive and crude oil bombs all over east London, hitting wharfs, dumb barges, motor vehicles, roads and railway tracks. Contemporary records kept by the London Fire Brigade show that the roof of Poplar Town Hall was ruined and countless buildings, including many homes, were affected by fire damage and explosions. This included St Clements (a nearby mental observation hospital), the Port of London Authority offices, and warehouses and factories used by joiners, moulding manufacturers and wine and spirits merchants.

The East End, dubbed 'Target Area A' by the Germans, was an obvious mark for their bombers, with its busy docklands a crucial entry point for supplies to the capital and wider country. Even before the Blitz began, the British Nazi propagandist William Joyce, known as Lord Haw-Haw, forecast that the Luftwaffe would 'smash' Stepney, an area in east London. The area also bore the grim distinction of being the first target for a V-1 flying bomb, better known as a doodlebug, which carried a warhead of 850kg of high-grade explosive.

The biggest attack in that first raid, however, occurred further south in the city at the Royal Arsenal in Woolwich, a major armaments manufacturer for the British military. Explosive and incendiary bombs killed 49 men and injured a further 67 at the site on the south bank of the River Thames. The attack obliterated a plant in the complex that made detonator components, while factories making light guns and filling shells were damaged. After the raid, the workforce plunged by 8,000 to 15,000 staff.

In total 430 civilians were killed and 1,600 injured on the first night of the Blitz in London. Afterwards almost every family in Limehouse slept in air-raid shelters, as the capital withstood relentless attacks for 57 consecutive nights. Those whose homes still stood were encouraged to build Anderson shelters of semi-circular sheets of corrugated steel in their backyards. Those whose homes had been destroyed lived out of the shelters permanently, despite the lack of water, gas or electricity. Some people descended into London Underground stations, even though it was initially forbidden for these to be used as hide-outs during air raids.

On 13 September, King George VI and Queen Elizabeth, later known as the Queen Mother, visited West Ham in the East End to witness the destruction wrought by the Blitz. Hours earlier, at 11 a.m., the Luftwaffe had bombed Buckingham Palace. While not its first attack on the site, it had been its first hit on the building when the senior royals were in residence. In recognition of the heavy bombardment that east London was facing nightly, the Queen was famously said to have remarked: 'I am glad we have been bombed. Now we can look the East End in the eye.'

She was horrified at witnessing the bombed-out streets of West Ham, observing in an emotional private letter to her mother-in-law, Queen Mary: 'I felt as if I was walking in a dead city ... all the houses evacuated, and yet through the broken windows one saw all the poor little possessions, photographs, beds, just as they were left. It does affect me, seeing this terrible and senseless destruction – I think that really I mind it much more than being bombed myself. The people are marvellous, and full of fight. One could not imagine that life could become so terrible. We must win in the end.'

Connie remained 'terrified' throughout the Blitz, unable to get used to the unabating raids as some of her friends seemed to be able to do. After their building was rendered 'uninhabitable, although not directly hit', she and Kit moved into an air-raid shelter. They slept there at night and returned to their rooms during the day for some privacy and to prepare food. Leslie's family was also forced to live out of a shelter.

Two months after the start of the Blitz Connie's old school in Limehouse was evacuated to Wolvercote, a village to the north of Oxford. Many parents followed their children there and others in the community decided to flee the bombing as well. Leslie's mother and his sister, who quit her job as a finisher in a dressmaking factory, were among them. Terrorised by the Blitz, Connie needed little encouragement to follow. 'Leslie's family was evacuated to Oxford, so I joined them,' she explains. The local Woolworths where she worked gave her the option to transfer when she decided to leave the capital. 'We were given a list – any Woolworths, they would employ us. So I drifted down to Oxford with Leslie's family and got a job and digs.'

Since she was 17 and therefore regarded as an adult, Connie was not an official refugee and relied on the good will of the villagers. 'We knocked on every door in the village and asked, did they want to take in an evacuee, because they were in an area where they had to take in evacuees. Wolvercote was a typical little English village and it had all these Chinese children running about there,' she explained in the decade following the war.[37]

Not all of Limehouse emptied out into the countryside, however. Many older members of the neighbourhood – including Kit and Leslie's father – resolved to stay. A strong sense of community and solidarity persisted among them as the bombs continued to fall. 'Neighbours were unhesitatingly supportive in these awful circumstances. There were always benevolent families and people staying and helping those in adversity,' Connie reflects.

She took to her new rural environment with zeal, embracing the 'clean, breathable atmosphere' with 'daily fear largely dispelled'. She has said in the recent past: 'It could not have proved a nicer contrast to the horrors of the Blitz, destruction and deprivation. Of course we used to walk by the river – it was really lovely. The villagers were very kind to us. They accepted all these half-Chinese children with their "funny" names and just took them in. They liked us all. We became part of the village.'[38]

She was also able to grow vegetables and keep hens at her billet, so while 'everything was scarce', there was a little more to eat than there had been in the capital. However, 'there was no black market as in London,' she adds. The illicit trade of rationed goods – from clothes such as stockings to food items likes eggs – thrived in most cities. The sanctions levied on both those running black-market operations and their customers were tough, ranging from large fines to hard labour. This failed to deter a significant proportion of people from buying extra supplies when they could afford them, though.

The worst scourge that afflicted Connie was loneliness. She missed Leslie dreadfully and the long spells without contact made it worse. 'He sailed off to South America and I never heard from him for five months,' she recalls. 'That was in October, then at the end of March [1941], there was a knock at the door and there was Leslie. Because of the Atlantic war, no letters were coming through. There he was. But he had sent letters to say that when he came back to England to prepare to get married. Of course, I had no knowledge of this at all!'

The couple had hoped for a church wedding, since both were Christian. Connie was Church of England and Leslie was Catholic. However, their application to the Bishop of Oxford for a special licence was rebuffed on account of Connie's young age. She was told she required the approval of her guardian. 'We got married anyway,' she says, smiling, explaining that there had been little time to spare before Leslie was due to set sail again ten days later.

The marriage ceremony took place at Oxford Register Office on 2 March 1941. While Leslie's relatives were able to attend as they lived nearby, the wedding was arranged too hastily for Kit to be invited. With a note of regret, Connie concedes: 'My family was very upset about this, about how I never said anything about getting married. But of course I didn't know I was getting married.' Cheering, however, she describes their low-key celebrations. 'We came out of the registrar's and went to a café, just his family and my land-lady, and had a wedding breakfast.' Erupting into laughter, she says: 'On the menu was beans on toast, or beans on toast.' Leslie had been given some money from his father and had received his pay from the Navy, so he had the grand sum of £40 to spend on the day. The wedding breakfast did not make a significant dent in it.

The couple travelled to London on their wedding night in order to stay in a hotel, but were caught short by a heavy bombing raid before reaching it. Instead, they spent their first night together in an Underground shelter with an air-raid siren wailing overhead. Others hunkered down in the shelter and had little time for the newlyweds' excited chatter. 'They said, "Be quiet, because we've got to go to work tomorrow,"' Connie recalls. The honeymoon passed quickly and Leslie once again went to sea, working on a convoy transporting goods, fuel and armaments, during which one of his main tasks was training new crews to use the defensive equipment and weapons on board the ship.

By the time of his departure, Connie was pregnant. A difficult period ensued. She felt isolated and alone, anxious for her new husband's safety and aggrieved at her inability to contact him. Sick with fear and unable to eat, she shrunk to a perilous 6 stone. A snow storm was raging outside on 19 November 1941, when she went into labour two months early. The landlady of the house where she was billeted was mistrustful and, in part due to her slender figure, had refused to believe she was expecting a child. As a result there were no contingency plans in place for the birth.

When the contractions started, Oxfordshire was blanketed in thick snow, making it difficult for help to reach her. Still a teenager and unschooled in what to expect, Connie gave birth on her own and it was a traumatic experience. In an interview for an oral history project in the 1950s, she recalled her labour in detail. 'I woke up this night in pain and the person that I lived with thought that I had rheumatics or something like that. And it wasn't until it was obvious that the baby was being born that she went out in the blizzard to phone for the midwife. And it was dark and when she came back the baby was born. I had her alone … There was no central heating, no fires, no nothing. And nothing arranged for the birth or anything.' Her baby daughter was born on the floor of the bedroom. Connie scooped her up, swaddled her in blankets and got back into bed to await medical attention.

'And then, of course, the poor woman, when she came back she had to go out again to cancel the midwife and call the doctor out. But they couldn't come out because there was a blizzard on, you see. So I had to lie there until the doctor could come, which was the next morning. I forget what the odds were, but the fact that both of us were healthy and survived everything – one main thing being the cold, you see, and the baby being premature as well. But we survived, so that was a good thing.' Eventually the pair were collected and driven to the Radcliffe Infirmary in Oxford, where they were 'paraded around as survivors'. Her baby girl, whom she named Christine, had no fingernails, no eyebrows and translucent skin, but was otherwise healthy.

When Leslie arrived back at port on a tanker, he received word via telegram that his daughter had been born and was granted leave to meet her. It was a special reunion and hailed a happier spell for Connie. She managed to switch to new accommodation and moved into the large family house of Mrs Cherry, the friendly wife of an army major, and her two daughters.

Despite being a mother, and therefore exempt from conscription, Connie insisted on contributing to the war effort. 'I didn't have to go out to work because Christine was in the nursery,' she stresses, adding: 'I just got on with it – everybody did in wartime. I didn't have to go out to work, I just chose to.'

She took a job in the stores at the Morris motor works at Cowley, a major automotive plant that had switched its production to manufacturing tanks during the conflict. It was one of a series of factories owned by Lord Nuffield – better known as William Morris – that turned their output to armaments throughout the war. Collectively they made the Morris artillery tractor, which towed gun-howitzers and anti-tank guns, the 'Standard Tilly' utility vehicle, a range of armoured carriers and tanks such as the cruiser.

The Cowley plant manufactured a particularly wide array of materiel: vehicles including tanks and ambulances, munitions such as torpedoes and mines, and aircraft like the Tiger Moth trainer. It also made engines, frames and radiators for other planes. Major components of the Spitfire were manufactured there, as well as the Rolls-Royce Merlin engine, which was mounted on the Lancaster, Halifax and Mosquito bombers. Connie's primary role related to the assembly of gun coolers.

The plant was also an important aircraft base. Following the outbreak of war, the No. 1 Civilian Repair Unit, which fell under the control of the Air Ministry but was staffed by civilians, had been established there. It was supplemented by a metal-recovery depot, which was set up adjacent to the existing complex, as well as a maintenance unit that transported broken aircraft and parts for repair or scrap.

Between July and October 1940, damaged Hurricanes and Spitfires would land at the plant for immediate repairs before flying back into the fight. In total 150 fighters were returned to the skies during the Battle of Britain and by the end of the war 80,000 aircraft across all theatres had benefited from repairs at the plant.

At the height of the war, 3,000 people worked at the Cowley site, which operated both day and night shifts.

A Home Guard platoon was assigned to protect it. Men remained the foremen in the factories, but the vast majority of the workforce were women, drafted in when the male workers were called up to fight. Winston Churchill's cousin, Lady Sarah Spencer-Churchill, was among them, leaving behind high society for a year to take up a role fusing shells on an assembly line. It is said that she drove over from Blenheim Palace, her ancestral home in Oxfordshire, in an old Ford one day and reported for duty as 'Sally Churchill'. On one occasion she injured her hand in a jig so badly that she had to be rushed to the Radcliffe Infirmary for treatment.

Lunchtime shows were staged for the workers in a bid to boost morale. Well-known music-hall performers, comedians and orchestras came to perform in the factory canteen during tours of the country. The programme was organised by the Entertainments National Service Association, an outfit established in 1939 to organise performances for the Armed Forces.

The shifts at the plant started early and lasted between six and eight hours. It was hard work, but not physically overwhelming, Connie recalls, explaining the sense of pride she derived from it. It was also enjoyable. She liked the daily routine and valued the opportunity to make new female friends. Although it was a noisy environment, she and her colleagues could be heard sufficiently over the din to chat as they worked. Few other women from the Limehouse community in Wolvercote signed up at the factory, mainly because most were already skilled in dressmaking and drafted into wartime textile industries, so it was a chance for Connie to get to know more local women.

Her ability to take on a job was facilitated in large part by the creation of new state-funded nurseries, a move Connie emphatically supported. A crèche was set up specifically for parents who worked at the Cowley plant, with opening hours to match the shift patterns, which allowed Connie to deposit Christine there while she was on duty.

Before the war the government had played a far smaller role in childcare, as it was simply assumed that it was a woman's role to look after her children. Mothers forced by circumstance and poverty to go out to work had few childcare options beyond leaving their offspring with relatives or neighbours during the day. From 1940, however, Minister of Labour Ernest Bevin proposed to set up nurseries so that married women could be recruited to work in the factories. The day nurseries were set up and run by local authorities but remained few in number until 1941.

Eventually around 1,500 nurseries were created in England, financed by the Treasury, with women paying a shilling per child per day. Since the Ministry of Health regarded the idea of crèches in factories too dangerous due to the risk of bombing, they tended to be located some distance away. Nursery teachers came to be deemed essential to the war effort, and the profession was made a reserved occupation, a development that frustrated those who had wanted to take on other wartime jobs.

Priority was given to disadvantaged families, although there were reports of children being turned away if they appeared unclean. Many nurseries performed weekly de-lousing sessions with soap and combs to rid the children of head lice. Often the toddlers kept a towel and flannel at the nursery and were washed there, as well as being given iron and cod liver oil supplements. Day nursery provision declined from 1945 due to the withdrawal of state funding.

While Connie was living in Wolvercote and working at the factory, Leslie was away for a minimum of three months at a time, during which Connie would continue to fret about the dangers he faced. Whenever he could, he would send advance notice of his return. 'He just used to have the time that his ship was docked and, of course, it was a quick turnaround, so there wasn't much leave,' she recalls.

She would travel with Christine to meet him wherever his ship was due to dock. Once they received word of his imminent arrival, they would dash for a train to the port in question, visiting Liverpool, Cardiff and Edinburgh during the course of the war. On one occasion their suitcase, containing almost all their worldly possessions and Christine's christening certificate, was stolen from a luggage compartment. The trio would book into a boarding house until Leslie had to set sail again. Connie reflects that they did not come across many families doing the same. Laughing, she remembers how Christine, then a toddler, assumed that any sailor wandering down the plank from a ship was her father and would call out to them.

Leslie's voyages took him all over the world – to Russia, the Middle East and South America, as well as North America and North Africa. During an expedition to the latter, he spent time inland and afterwards regaled Connie and Christine with 'tall stories' about his experiences there. His favourite involved local tribesmen stealing the sailors' socks as they slept, then presenting the garments back to them for sale in the morning, stitched into a blanket.

During the lengthy periods that Leslie was away, Connie made occasional trips back to Limehouse to see friends. She and Christine slept in the crypt of a church to avoid air raids. The shelter was often packed to bursting; a bomb that had killed a large number of non-evacuated local children had encouraged more residents to make use of it. Christine began to think of it as her own home and would often ask why another child was sleeping in her wooden-plank bed.

When Leslie returned from the war, the Cherry family offered the Hoes the opportunity to buy their house in Oxfordshire at an affordable price. Connie, who had grown fond of the county, was tempted, but Leslie was adamant that he wanted to live in London again.

VE Day came as a surprise but a 'great relief' to Connie, with the reprieve from the air raids her greatest consolation. Nonetheless, she remained deeply concerned about the war still raging in the East. Leslie was in Aden, waiting to be demobbed, but she knew there was a significant chance of him being redeployed to join the ongoing war against Japan.

However, one of his superiors intervened to help dispatch him back to England to regroup with his young family.

He returned home safely, which could not be said of many of his naval comrades. Of the 12 classmates who also enlisted in the Navy, only six returned from the conflict. 'It was a safe bet at the beginning of the war that you'd lose half. The Navy wasn't a job that you were going to survive in easily,' he said.[39]

The reunited couple moved with their infant daughter into a single room in London, making meals on a gas cooker placed on a paving slab on the landing. It was cramped, but they felt fortunate to have been offered a place to live by a family friend. Still, Connie eventually decided to petition the local authority housing department for permanent accommodation. She explained that her husband had recently returned from the Navy. The officials told her to return with him in person, wearing his uniform. Leslie obliged and the couple were handed the keys to a new prefabricated home in the East End.

They were delighted. It was a modern, detached house, fully fitted with furniture, kitchen appliances and a bathroom suite. It also boasted a fireplace, a larder and a shed. In the garden, smells from the nearby docks, gas works and kipper smokehouse blew in, depending on the direction of the wind. They lived there for three decades.

Connie is unhesitating in her belief that the war altered women's place in society and the economy. 'Especially in the factories,' she says. 'Prior to the war, the women weren't employed in the factories. But when all the men got called up, the women replaced them.' She is equally certain of her opinion that her peers deserve the label the 'Greatest Generation' for the sacrifices they made during the conflict.

The ruins of the Blitz remained in stark evidence in the East End for more than a decade, with bombsites used as playgrounds by Christine and the other children of the neighbourhood. Employment was hard to come by, but Connie and Leslie both managed to secure jobs. She became a bookkeeper, working in Hatton Garden and other parts of London, while Leslie went on to become a professional chef, specialising in both French and Chinese cuisine.

Connie was an ardent supporter of Clement Attlee, the Labour MP for Limehouse who became prime minister in 1945. She saw Churchill as 'a supremely excellent wartime leader of the coalition government', but believed that Attlee's government might better recognise the acute deprivation in the East End and see that their needs were not overlooked.

In the years after the war Connie and Leslie reprised their passion for dancing and won gold medals in national competitions. They remained integral members of the local community and became custodians of the history of Limehouse Chinatown after most of the surviving buildings were demolished in the 1960s to make way for housing. Records, photos and memories were entrusted to the couple for safekeeping, and they also helped run a Chinese children's club in the area.

The couple eventually settled in Wanstead. They had no further children but had two grandchildren and five great-grandchildren. Leslie died in 2014 after suffering from Parkinson's disease for the last 13 years of his life. Connie was there holding his hand as he died. They had been married for 73 years.

# Christian Lamb

**DATE OF BIRTH:**

19 July 1920 (aged 19 at the outbreak of war)

**ROLE:**

Plotter in the Women's Royal Naval Service

'My war was really quite thrilling – on and off,' remarks 100-year-old Christian Lamb with a wry smile. She enlisted in the Women's Royal Naval Service at the outbreak of the conflict – the obvious option for the daughter of an admiral. Rising swiftly through the ranks to become an officer, she was appointed a plotter in the Battle of the Atlantic, the longest continuous military campaign of the Second World War. It was a high-pressure environment, in which the intensity of her work was offset by a lively social scene. During a posting to Belfast Christian met John, a dashing English naval officer, whose ship lurched into port needing repairs. Within ten days, on the eve of John setting sail again, the couple became engaged. She was then forced to watch aghast from the operations room as his ship sailed straight into a deadly Nazi submarine ambush.

Christian's wartime service profoundly altered the course of her life, but she also believes the conflict transformed society at large. 'People didn't have the same sort of restraint,' she says of the war years. 'They were probably more independent. They didn't do as their parents told them and did what they wanted to do instead.' She is adamant that the war bolstered the status of women, too: 'It made it much easier, definitely.' From the 1940s onwards, women were held in greater esteem and were able to take on a bigger role outside the home, she says.

Born in Edinburgh, Christian Mary Wolseley Oldham was the middle child of three. She was close to her sister Anne, who was only a year older, but a seven-year age gap with her younger brother Francis put distance between them. Her childhood unfolded across a variety of locations, with frequent moves necessitated by her father's flourishing career in the Royal Navy. The Highlands home of her maternal grandmother remained a constant, however.

The girls attended a private convent school in Kensington Square, a smart west London address distinguished by tall Georgian townhouses. The playful sisters conspired to route their daily bicycle ride to school by the local Post Office, where they would sign for sweets on their mother's account. Their mother was strict and unamused when she discovered the ruse. 'I don't think my mother ever liked me very much,' says Christian. 'She liked my sister much better. Anne was cleverer, prettier – everything was good about her.' Nonetheless, she gained succour from her sister's loyalty. 'She always took my side in everything.'

When Christian was ten, the family moved to Malta, where her father, Admiral Ronald Oldham, had been assigned to command a cruiser. Upon the family's return to Britain three years later, her parents separated. She describes their behaviour towards their offspring as 'very fair', but emotionally remote. 'I don't remember any particular affection,' she says. Her maternal grandmother was a warmer figure, she adds. 'She was my nicest relation, really.'

Christian and her sister were sent to a boarding school near Ramsgate in Kent. As a Catholic school, it was also popular with French and Spanish families, with many of the latter desperate to send their daughters away from the tensions at home, which in Spain spiralled into full-blown civil war in July 1936. For Christian, 'the extreme cold' of the institution was an unwelcome shock after the sunny climate of the Mediterranean. 'I raced from one radiator to the other. There was a wind from Siberia coming through the window,' she says. 'Awful! But I survived somehow.'

She achieved her school certificate and left education aged 17, yearning for adventure and romance. 'As girls we didn't know anything about love and sex. We were all full of romantic ideas,' she says. Fluency in a second European language was expected of young women of her background, so Christian followed custom and spent a year on the Continent perfecting her French. She decided to split her time between France and Belgium, staying with a series of families. 'My first object was to read all the books in French that had been banned by school,' she says. First on the list was the scandalising Stendhal's *Le rouge et le noir*, a tale in which the ambitious male protagonist uses seduction as a tool of advancement.

The carefree fun of her year in Western Europe was interrupted, however, by the outbreak of the Second World War. A telegram from her father arrived while she was staying with a family in the Vosges mountains near Strasbourg. He informed her of the deteriorating international situation and ordered her home at once. She was bemused by the contents and urgent tone of the missive. 'I hadn't read a paper for about six months. I had no idea what was going on. I was rather surprised,' she says, adding with a self-deprecating laugh: 'I was thoroughly idiotic.' She explains that she did not have any grasp of the profound changes that war would bring to the life of the nation.

She travelled to Dieppe, where she joined her mother and brother who had been on holiday on the French Riviera. Together the trio caught a ferry back to Britain and retreated to Scotland. At first, Christian supposed she would continue with her plan to go up to Oxford, where Anne was already enrolled reading philology, the study of the history of language. 'I passed the exams and then realised I couldn't do it,' she says. It would be unconscionable;

the right thing to do was to join the war effort. 'I was very patriotic,' she adds.

The next obstacle was deciding how best she could help. Since she knew some elementary first aid, she entertained thoughts of becoming a nurse. 'I practised bandaging my grandfather, whose bald head was very handy. He was long suffering, I thought,' she says with a grin. The proposal was quickly abandoned, however. A lecture on bandaging gruesome wounds precipitated the realisation that she did not have the stomach for nursing.

She had learned other skills in the meantime. The family chauffeur had taught her how to drive, while her grandmother tutored her to play bridge. It was ultimately through her grandmother's bridge set that Christian alighted upon the idea of joining the Women's Royal Naval Service.

The WRNS, or 'Wrens' as they become known, had been founded in 1917 but disbanded at the end of the First World War. The force was revived at the outbreak of the Second World War by Vera Laughton Mathews, the daughter of the pre-eminent naval historian Sir John Knox Laughton, who had been a leading member of the organisation the first time round. Highly educated and charismatic, she remained director of the service throughout the war and helped with staff training for the Free Dutch equivalent of the WRNS too. In 1946 she was made a dame of the British Empire in recognition of her service.

Christian's grandmother happened to play bridge with the WRNS chief's brother, Colonel Frank Laughton, and it was through him that Christian enlisted. Candid about the assistance she received, she says: 'I called [Laughton Mathews's] brother and asked him to give me a reference, which helped me to join, no problem.' Securing a place in the Wrens was not easy. It had swiftly amassed a lengthy waiting list of young women eager to join, in large part – Christian remains convinced – due to the flattering uniform. The outfits for the Army's sister force, the Auxiliary Territorial Service, and its Royal Air Force equivalent, the Women's Auxiliary Air Force, had wide waist bands that exaggerated the hips. The Wrens, meanwhile, enjoyed a navy-blue jacket and skirt that skimmed the figure to best effect. For Christian, however, it was the distinctive tricorn hat worn by officers that was the magnet. Throughout the war, she took to quipping that she only joined the Wrens for the coveted hat, a blue felt number with a white cover.

She was summoned to the capital for an interview and, despite having 'nil qualifications', was offered a job straight away. This was an illustrious role at the service's main offices in London. She was deflated, however, at the idea of working with mature women like her interviewer, Nancy Osborne, a senior Wren officer, and yearned for a chance to be placed alongside a younger cohort. 'I hadn't joined the Wrens to be working with a lot of stuffy old bags like her,' she recalls, laughing. 'Actually, I liked her very much, but I didn't sort of see her as a companion. She was a boss lady, and I didn't feel like working in the headquarters.'

Confronting the conundrum as delicately as possible, Christian asked if another position might be available. The gamble paid off and she was enrolled instead at a training school in Kensington, from which she would be able to volunteer for various roles alongside her peers. 'I thought coding sounded rather exciting and mysterious, so I volunteered for that,' she says. The director of the training establishment was Hilda Buckmaster, 'a very large lady with an enormous bosom on the desk, bluff and sea-going,' she says.

The training chief appeared to like her. 'She greeted me as a breath of fresh air, she said. I suppose she meant because of my father being an admiral, otherwise I can't imagine,' she reflects. It was a faltering start, however: 'I was never out of trouble there. I was always late for everything.' Touch-typing and squad drill did not come easily to Christian either. 'The whole thing was a disaster,' she admits. 'I spent a lot of time scrubbing the floor as a punishment. The boredom of it!' It was a rule-bound institution, but some furtive fun was shared with a school friend, who was attached to the First Aid Nursing Yeomanry and billeted at accommodation next door to hers. Her old classmate owned a motorbike, which the pair would sneak out to ride at night. They took great delight in roaring around Hyde Park.

A chance encounter allowed Christian to escape the drudgery of the training facility several months after arriving. While walking to lunch she found herself face to face with Nancy Osborne again. 'I said to her, "I suppose that job isn't still going at your headquarters?" And it was, so I was whisked away,' she says. The Wrens' headquarters were situated above Drummonds bank next to Admiralty Arch, just off Trafalgar Square.

Christian was content with the new placement – a highlight of which was occasionally spotting Winston Churchill on the stairs – and hoped that working at the heart of the service's operations would afford her the tricorn she coveted. It was not to be, however. 'I hadn't at that point realised there were officers and ratings. I thought you were just a Wren. So when I got there, I was very much shocked to find I wasn't going to have this hat after all that I'd been rather looking forward to. I was just an ordinary rating, and we had a really terrible hat,' she says.

The work was not interesting, but she got to know Diana Churchill, who worked in a nearby office. 'She so looked exactly like her father, Winston Churchill,' she recalls. 'She always kept her office in howls of laughter. They used to come out and make us laugh as well. She was a really nice girl. I remember, she had never got her tie tied – she'd always got a bit of it afloat somehow – but she was always good value.' Only five women had private offices in the building, which were allocated on the basis of their involvement in top-secret work. Christian was one of them. 'We none of us knew what the other ones were doing. We never asked – never had the faintest idea,' she says.

During her lunch break she would dash across the square to hear concerts at the National Gallery, some of which were performed by musicians who had escaped from the Third Reich. The gallery was sporting in accepting her lunch vouchers in return for sandwiches and coffee. Over Trafalgar Square itself she recalls the exhilaration of witnessing dog fights between the RAF's Spitfires and Hurricanes and the Nazi Luftwaffe bombers escorted by Messerschmitts. Such sites were not uncommon up until October 1940, when the Nazi regime abandoned daylight raids in favour of night-time bombing campaigns. The cover of darkness provided greater protection for their aircraft. 'Thus, the Blitz began,' she recalls.

While working at HQ, Christian lived at a 'Wrenery' boarding house near Finchley Road in north London. There she shared a dormitory with recruits from a range of backgrounds and for the first time made friends with women outside her own narrow social set. It was an experience that made her acutely aware of class divisions in British society.

The Wrens at the boarding house were determined to make the most of living in the city. It was money, rather than fear of the Blitz, that was the primary constraint on their activities. They were paid only 10 shillings a week after bed and board, an insufficient sum to fritter on hailing taxis back to the Wrenery after a night out. Christian did not allow scarce funds to check her enjoyment on such evenings, however: she walked or caught the bus home and simply accepted the castigation that followed a breach of the boarding house's strict curfew.

She and her friends were defiant in the face of danger, even as the nightly enemy bombing raids stepped up in autumn

1940. 'We didn't care about being safe,' Christian says. 'I remember being in the theatre when a bomb was coming too close and it whistled down. I remember the theatre, the whole audience, winced silently as they heard this whistling. And then it passed over and, okay, back to the stage, the show went on.' On her way to work on the Number 13 bus each morning she would gaze out of the window, noting the buildings that had been hit the night before. Often the bus route was diverted through the park when the roads became blocked with bomb debris. She and her friends survived a near miss after leaping off the bus spontaneously after work. 'We were passing Baker Street when we saw a cinema and it looked rather a good film, so we decided to go. So we got off the bus and went,' she recalls. The next morning, back on the bus to the office, the Wrens 'looked up and the cinema had completely disappeared'. She says: 'It had been bombed during the night. It must have missed us by about ten minutes. We were so lucky.'

Bombs wrought devastation near the Wrenery too. Christian slept in a semi-basement dormitory with five others on double bunk beds. One night they awoke upon hearing the impact of 'frightful bombs being dropped'. She recalls that 'the French window was blown open by a huge blast of evil-smelling cordite', but adds that she and her dormitory mates suffered only a 'good fright'. The other side of the street was not so fortunate: every other house was hit. A sombre operation commenced the next morning. 'Looking out the window at the other side, you could see wardens looking for bodies,' she recalls with a grimace. Vera Laughton Mathews visited later that day to check how the Wrens were coping. 'We were all right, but it was a nasty moment,' Christian says. After the initial shock wore off, life moved on. Even in the face of all the evidence that the bombs fell indiscriminately, she felt invincible. 'It never occurred to me that I could be hit by a bomb. Everybody else probably could be,' she says. Even when an 18-year-old school friend was tragically killed by a bomb that fell near Harrods in Knightsbridge, she recalls: 'I didn't, somehow, feel in danger.'

As the war intensified, however, a sense of uneasiness crept in. Around the time of the Dunkirk evacuation in June 1940, when British forces retreated from the Continent, she concedes: 'We imagined ourselves being taken prisoner or escaping to the hills in England or Scotland. The whole of the coast opposite us was now occupied by Germans. It was unbelievable to think of. Dover is so close to Calais. There were Germans there everywhere – the whole coast [of France].' She adds: 'We were quite frightened, really. We were rather put off by that. Hitler had said he was going to invade, so we were rather waiting for it to happen. Churchill turned it around – he was such a good leader, and everybody felt the same. It really was remarkable. I remember the feeling.'

She would occasionally catch a sleeper train from King's Cross to Scotland to spend the weekend with her grandmother. 'Two whole days of blissful linen sheets and comfort and food – and nice to see her again too,' she says, laughing. A distressing sight met her upon her return to the capital after one of these visits, though. While it was the dead of night, 'in fact, it was brilliant daylight because the whole of London was on fire. It was the East End dockyard that was being burned after they bombed it the night before,' she says.

From time to time Admiral Oldham would also drop by to take his daughter out to lunch at a fusty nearby hotel. On one occasion Christian pleaded with him to try a new venue. Laughing, she recalls: 'He said, "So where do you want to go, the Ritz?" And I said, "Yes!" We went – so that was good. It was just as grand as you can imagine – wonderful.' On the odd day off, she would also pay visits to another relation: her great-aunt, Christian Beaton, after whom she was named. The step-grandmother of society photographer Cecil Beaton, 'Aunt Tin' was a great character. Adorned in furs and bead-trimmed dresses, with a penchant for feathers in her hat, she was always accompanied by her yapping Pekinese dog 'who might bite,' Christian recalls.

After a year in London, Christian was reassigned to Coalhouse Fort in East Tilbury, Essex. Her primary task in the new role was to preside over degaussing, the process that neutralised the magnetic field of a ship by deploying an encircling conductor carrying electric currents. The purpose of this was to protect the vessel as it moved over a magnetic mine, hundreds of which had been laid by the Nazis at the mouth of the Thames.

'I just ran the office, aged 20,' she says, incredulous now at being handed so much responsibility when she was still so young. At the time, however, she simply took it in her stride. 'I just take things as they come,' she says. 'I thought it was an experiment. It was rather exciting and I learned as I went along, touching wood. You see, there weren't any courses for anything in those days. You were thrown into a job and just hoped you would be able to do it.'

Another part of her role was pastoral: looking after the Wrens assigned to her. The group were billeted to an old vicarage nearby, where 'we were always cold and never had enough to eat,' she recalls. The landlord was a 'nasty kind of character'. He and his wife 'didn't want to make anything nice for us; they didn't want to spend any money on keeping us warm or feeding us.'

Occasional day trips to London for a rare party or theatre performance continued, but there was no need to leave the fort in order to socialise or meet eligible male personnel. It teemed with young men – soldiers, sailors and marines of all ranks – who were eager to spend time with the small band of Wrens based there. Christian and her female comrades enjoyed the attention, she admits. They would visit the local pub, drinking first with the sailors in the public bar, before progressing to the saloon bar to chat to the officers. One Wren, a red-headed recruit named Ruth, became particularly popular with the sailors on account of her sewing skills. They pleaded with her to alter their bell bottoms, making them skin-tight at the top and ultra-flared at the bottom.

There were 'no serious love affairs', however. The primary reason was that the Wrens were gravely afraid of accidentally falling pregnant, Christian says. Bereft of any formal sex education, many believed a 'smoochy French kiss' could create a child. Even innocent clinches could spark waves of remorse the next day, and many recruits resorted to a range of cod therapies to prevent pregnancy, from steaming-hot baths, through drinking gin and quinine, to falling down stairs.

After 12 months at Coalhouse Fort, promotion beckoned again for Christian. She was sent up to Greenwich in south-east London for the officers' training course at the Royal Naval College. Lunch and dinner were served daily in the spectacular baroque surroundings of its famous Painted Hall. 'It was quite different,' she says. 'The food was so good. We had been used to this ghastly stuff.' She applied to switch specialisms. 'Because I had volunteered to be a coder, I was made to do the cypher course,' she says. 'But by this time I had learned that plotting was much more interesting.' She had initially been attracted to coding by the idea of reading encrypted messages containing classified intelligence. However, she soon discovered that a plotter was allowed to 'read all those laboriously decoded messages anyway', and on top of that had access to the coveted 'pink list', which contained the location of all the ships in the Royal Navy.

After passing the officers' exam, Christian was dispatched to Plymouth, where she learned she was to become the plotting officer in charge of a watch in the commander-in-chief's operations room. This would involve overseeing the plot for the whole of the Western Approaches, a rectangular area of the Atlantic directly to the west of the United Kingdom. 'I was in charge of the Wren operations role, which was quite alarming. I had no idea what I was supposed to be doing. Luckily I had all rather nice Wrens under me; they sort of initiated me into it,' she says.

An imposing cast of characters inhabited the same office. 'We had naval officers working at the back of the operations room, which was partitioned with glass so that they could see what was going on, but they weren't disturbed by it. All the bosses were in there,' she recalls. The operations room was split between the RAF, who oversaw a plot for their aircraft, and the Royal Navy, who oversaw a plot charting the location of their ships. 'These signals came through every day to give you the up-to-date positions [of vessels] and you had to keep the whole thing absolutely up to date,' Christian explains. 'The Wrens were on the telephone to radar stations around the coast. They would ring up and give positions of ships that they could see on the radar. They could tell if there were more than one or two or three ships, the speed they were going, the direction. We put them on the plot. If there was one that we didn't recognise, the Navy would send out a motor boat to find out if it was a U-boat creeping about or some other frightful enemy.'

The course charted by ships in the area was drawn in coloured wax crayon on a vast map of the Western Approaches, which was unfurled on a table and covered in powder. Small model ships, which represented convoys, were moved along the map as new information came in. A separate wall map, over which Christian also presided during her watches, showed the positions of any ship or convoy, as well as reported U-boats, in the whole of the North Atlantic. These ships were moved on the basis of intelligence communicated by signal, or else the known direction and speed of the ship at its last report. More sluggish convoys, which were constrained by the speed of their slowest vessels, travelled at 5 knots, while the fastest moved at 15 knots. All convoys followed zigzagged routes that were pre-arranged. An array of destroyers, corvettes, minesweepers, trawlers and other available ships accompanied the convoys. 'It was a really interesting job,' says Christian. 'The Atlantic was the most wonderful plot. It had all the convoys going. It was all very exciting.'

To her delight, the base was also highly sociable. The naval officers 'would invite us down for a drink on board, so we would go and make friends with them, and then go out dancing in the evening and have dinner in a place called Ginoni's in Plymouth,' she recalls. 'We had a good time. It was great fun.' On their days off, groups of male and female personnel would embark on local day trips. For Christian it was an opportunity to forge proper friendships with men for the first time. 'We used to go out with them all day, walking across Dartmoor, talking about everything under the sun,' she says. 'It was really rather an educational period of my life. There was never any question of going to bed with people in those days; you just didn't do it. I mean, I suppose lots of people did, but I didn't know anybody who did.'

She also became great friends with another Wren named Eve and the two conspired to share their wardrobes. 'She and I only had two evening dresses each, I think, which we used to always wear at the weekends. So we used to wear each other's, and change them around.' Their clothes switches became an in-joke among the group, prompting some of the male naval officers to quip: 'Why don't you change into our dinner jackets? That would make a change for you.' Christian recalls finding it complicated to do up a bow tie.

Other exploits took place outside of Plymouth, including in Bath, where she was dispatched for a residential training programme. At the end of the course she discovered to her dismay that she had missed the final train back to the coast for the day. A Polish officer whom she had met the night before at a cocktail party offered to help. 'I was astonished when he asked, "Shall I take you back in the old crate?". I replied: 'An old crate?". I responded with complete astonishment as he explained he meant by air. I just about managed to indicate my joyful acceptance.' She was thrilled to fly south in a Miles Magister two-seater training aircraft, with the pilot staging mock dives into cattle fields.

Around a year after she arrived in Plymouth, the Western Approaches headquarters was moved to Liverpool. However, Christian received orders to relocate to the maritime headquarters at Belfast. 'Although it wasn't as grand as the operations [hub], we were the nearer place to where the convoys joined up, north of Belfast,' she says. This was the granite islet known as Rockall. 'All these ships would assemble there. That's 30 or 40 ships in a convoy, and then the escorts would be destroyers, corvettes, trawlers – anything that was available. They would all join from Belfast.'

Life in Belfast was good. The most striking change from England was the better food, she recalls. Although rationing was introduced in Northern Ireland in 1941, some goods remained easier to procure than in the rest of the United Kingdom. Smuggling was also rife across the border with the Republic of Ireland, where there was no rationing regime in place. Christian and her female friends made several visits to Dublin to buy clothes and edible treats. There was an obstacle to bringing the fruits of these spending sprees back into Belfast, though: the strict customs regime enforced by the rail officials. A variety of techniques were deployed to evade suspicion. Newly purchased garments could be worn, deliberately creased to appear old or else left in a bag suspended outside the train window.

Christian's arrival in Belfast coincided with the intensification of the Battle of the Atlantic. British moves to improve the protection of their cargo ships had been matched by the Nazi U-boat commanders developing more sophisticated 'wolf pack' tactics to attack them. The Northern Irish port city received a high proportion of ships that had suffered damage during skirmishes or been impaired during storms.

Christian remembers with vivid clarity the arrival of an O-class fleet destroyer on 30 March 1943. The ship had been providing rapid defence to threatened convoys when rough seas had cracked its 'iron deck', a toughened steel deck over the engine room, forcing it to berth at Belfast port for repairs. 'This particular ship, HMS *Oribi*, arrived and their first immediate operation was to ring up the Wrenery and ask us down for a drink. So half a dozen of us went down there,' she says. The decision to meet the officers in the wardroom on their first evening in harbour had profound consequences. 'It took me ten days and I got engaged to the First Lieutenant John Bruce Lamb,' she says, laughing. It was a bolt-from-the-blue romance with the naval officer, who had won a Distinguished Service Cross after his light cruiser, HMS *Glasgow*, was torpedoed by Italian bombers off Crete in 1940. He had singled out Christian as soon as she walked through the door, swooping in to hand her a drink and engage her in conversation. They talked for most of the first evening, oblivious to all around them. In the days that followed they spent every free hour together, resulting in the swift betrothal. 'No time was wasted,' John wrote in his diary. Christian did not wait to ask her parents' permission to wed, casting off the etiquette of old. She later wrote: 'I didn't feel pressured to get engaged. It just happened.'[40]

Black-tie celebrations to mark the whirlwind engagement ensued and lasted almost all night. Christian recalls: 'When we got engaged, they had the most tremendous party.' Pink gins, white ladies, gimlets and dry martinis were drunk, fuelling the high jinks that followed. This included a round of 'wardroom polo', which involved riding chairs and using a potato for a ball and spoons for sticks, and an obstacle course that demanded participants traverse the cabins without touching the deck. As the night wore on, one of the officers was selected to play the part of a torpedo in an imaginary battle, and was 'fired' down the polished dining table, shooting off the end onto a sofa.

The spiralling romance sparked much amusement among the junior Wrens under Christian's care, who awarded themselves the tongue-in-cheek sobriquet the 'Hags' Watch'. They could not resist sending John a stamped reference for his new fiancée. 'We have known her for five months, and find her honest, sober, kind and cheerful at all times,' the group stated. 'She is quite approachable in the mornings, though rather dopey for the first few moments after waking. There has been a slight tendency to madness during the past fortnight, but otherwise she is considered normal, healthy and clean.'

In the aftermath of the engagement party, John was forced to set sail again on the treacherous seas. He had already endured great danger. Earlier in the war his ship had completed seven crossings of the Arctic Circle while escorting Soviet convoys, protecting vessels ferrying vital supplies to Murmansk and Archangel. For Allied escorts, it was a 2,000-mile voyage, conducted in pitch black in the 24-hour winter-darkness zone and within range of German air, surface vessel and submarine attack for three-quarters of the route. However, it was the weather that induced the greatest terror in the sailors.

John recorded a description of the voyage. 'It was rarely safe to venture on deck, where you were liable to be washed or slip overboard into the Arctic Sea,' he said. 'Spraying the exposed working areas with scalding water fed from the boiler room froze on impact and made things worse; the rigging, right up to the crow's nest and guard rails, became ice blocks as thick as a man's arm, and could only be cleared with picks and hammers; the weight of this, if allowed to grow, would cause the ship to heel over to a most dangerous degree. Guns and torpedo tubes were kept operable with electric heating coils, fitted to blank cartridges in their breeches.'

After the betrothal, John's ship was dispatched to join a support fleet of 15 other warships in the Atlantic, which were tasked with providing ad hoc protection wherever it was required. Christian waved him farewell from the ramparts of Belfast Castle, wondering when she would next see him. She watched in the operations room as his ship was added to the plot. Soon HMS *Oribi* was assigned to shield a slow convoy of 43 merchant ships that had left Liverpool bound for North America. Turbulent winds and choppy seas reduced the convoy, known as ONS 5, to travelling at 1 knot. It was while creaking along at this pace that the convoy was ambushed by more than 30 German U-boat submarines in a confrontation that erupted into one of the most seismic maritime battles of the war. The skirmishes ebbed and flowed over the space of the week, with heavy losses sustained by both sides.

In all, 13 Allied ships were sunk, while seven U-boats were destroyed and another seven were damaged. The epic confrontation proved a turning point in the Battle of the Atlantic. The losses to the U-boat arm of the German navy were ultimately more significant, ushering in the period known as 'Black May', during which the Nazis suffered grave casualties in the North Atlantic. The toll led to the Germans' withdrawal from the arena, handing the strategic advantage to the Allies.

John's ship, HMS *Oribi*, was engaged at the centre of the struggle, driving off three U-boats and helping to sink a fourth, U-boat 125. Christian surveyed the incoming signals in the operations room in Belfast, gripped with fear. 'This happened to be the biggest Battle of the Atlantic, and I was plotting it,' she marvels now. 'We had air support as far as halfway across the Atlantic, but there was a huge gap in the middle. The Canadians would come over from the other side to help as far as they could. So, it was always there that the battle took place – between the two escorts.'

Her anxiety about John's fate grew as the clashes intensified, but her comrades' pleas for her to stay away went unheeded. 'They tried to keep me away from the plotting room, but I obviously had to stick to it and find out all the signals,' she says. 'There was no television or anything like that, but you had signals coming in, in progress. They say it was the most terrible weather it had ever been and the whole convoy scattered. I was very, very anxious, as you can imagine. I was on duty a lot of the time. Watching the battle and, of course, if I had to go home, I would immediately be told by everybody else what was going on. I thought I was going to lose this man I had just captured ...' She trails off. Her fear was that he would 'disappear' in the middle of an attack. To her immense relief, however, he escaped tragedy.

'John's ship edge ... rammed a U-boat. He described what it was like – the U-boat was half onboard the ship,' she says breathlessly. 'They rammed [the U-boat] and it was very exciting. They lost their bow, but most ships are luckily built with airtight compartments. So they only lost about two of those, but the rest of the ship was still there. They proceeded to go much more slowly until they got to America, where they were provided with a new bow.'

John later set out his own recollections of the episode. He had been getting some rest in a vacant cot when he was 'abruptly awakened by a terrific crash and a frightful bump,' he recalled. 'My first thought was that we had been torpedoed, then that the ship had gone aground, as we seemed to ride up over something; I soon realised that this was impossible as we were many miles from land,' he wrote. 'These thoughts flashed through my head as I scrambled out of the cot but was quite unable to find the deck. The ship had heeled over so far that what I was trying to stand on turned out to be the normally vertical bulkhead, with the racks of medicine bottles and sick-bay utensils.

'All this only took seconds, and by the time the alarm gongs began clanging I had scaled the two flights of ladders to the bridge. There, I watched incredulously as the ship tried to ride over the submarine we had rammed, and whose conning tower was clinging crazily to our port side. We were in the very centre of the action, and all around, occasionally lit up by a star shell, were corvettes attacking deadly and daring U-boats, still on the surface, who in turn were trying to get a few more of the convoy before they had to dive. Every now and again would come a "crump", another explosion, and in the background the incessant "ping, ping, ping" of the ASDIC [an early form of sonar used to detect submarines] with frequent "ping-go" as it picked up its target.'

Christian also recalls how events unfolded: 'From the early report of the impending battle over ONS 5 [John's convoy], the Operations Room at Belfast Castle received signal after signal, and the teleprinter buzzed on endlessly. The build-up was slow to begin with, and of course we did not realise the drama ahead. The tension grew as Oribi was obviously heading for the "wolf pack" and the plot displayed a vivid picture of the action. As we couldn't get instant communication it made the progress all the more worrying. My plotters tried various excuses to persuade me to change watch and be spared the view of what was unfolding before our eyes. But I would not leave the scene – the time dragged on heavily, but soon the Canadian Air Force was within range and the residue of the bitterly defended convoy sailed safely on.'

At this juncture Christian could finally relax. 'Having watched the battle go on, I knew he was on his way; he was safe,' she says. 'Twelve knots they were able to do to get back to America. Then he was able to send a telegram to say he was alive.' The ship lurched on with a chunk of its bow missing and stopped first at St John's, Newfoundland, to be patched up with reinforced concrete before sailing on to Boston for permanent repairs. She says: 'Afterwards the papers reported it as the biggest battle in the Atlantic and Hitler was absolutely furious. He sacked his general. And so, after that the battles in the Atlantic were never as bad again.'

The couple, who wrote to each other weekly, were more determined than ever to wed and pressed on with their plans. 'We managed to make our parents meet somehow, but it wasn't a great success,' she says, recalling that her own parents did not warm to John's. 'They didn't like either [his mother or father] much. I just remember that sort of atmosphere that wasn't a hundred per cent.' It was the only time Christian and John met in person between their engagement and their wedding.

Her mother and father's aloofness towards John's family did not deter Christian; nor did the concern of her sister, Anne, who queried her haste to get married. 'My sister came over to stay with me for a bit. She was a sergeant in the Women's Auxiliary Air Force and came to stay in my Wrenery, which was an officers' quarters. She really wanted to make sure, as I had only known him for ten days.' Laughing, she adds: 'Anne was no example; she got engaged to people by the dozens. She kept on finding someone she liked better!'

Attempts to plan for the wedding were complicated by her fiancé's uncertain movements, which were dictated by the Navy and liable to change at short notice. Christian recalls: 'John said that his ship was likely to be having its boiler cleaned about the middle of December. So my mother said, "Okay," and she arranged the wedding for 15 December. It worked out; it was very lucky – the bridegroom appeared.'

Christian's mother was resourceful when it came to mitigating the impact of rationing on the wedding. 'My mother bought my wedding dress second-hand,' she says, laughing. Clothes were rationed from 1941, but used items were exempt. 'You couldn't buy clothes, really, but we used to have a magazine and it had a wedding dress for sale – a white velvet dress – which was quite suitable for December. I think she bought it for £7 and she sold it on again for the same after the wedding, which was quite good.' She adds: 'It hadn't been tried on, of course. You just had to hope it fitted, which it did, more or less.'

They wed at St James's Church, Spanish Place, a Catholic church in central London, with a congregation that included the officers of HMS *Oribi*. A reception at Dartmouth House in Mayfair followed, replete with a giant wedding cake from Searcys of Sloane Street.

The married couple spent their wedding night at the Savoy, the grand hotel based on the Strand in central London. A week's honeymoon in Oxford followed, after which Christian returned to Belfast and John set sail again with the Navy. He was soon appointed to a role in Stornoway, the capital of Lewis and Harris in the Western Isles of Scotland.

Christian came to visit at the first opportunity. 'John's job was to train other trawler captains and other ships how to escort convoys,' she explains of his posting. Her own attempts to set up a homestead were less successful. 'I had never so much as boiled an egg, so you could imagine, we had some digs to live in. We lived on kippers and gin,' she says. A cookbook lent to her by the Navy was little help, containing mass recipes for feeding 240 sailors at a time.

She returned to Belfast, where she was discharged from the Wrens midway through her pregnancy. John arrived in time for the arrival of their first child, a daughter, whom they named Felicity. Christian remarks: 'Luckily you didn't have husbands at the birth in my day. Thank God. I wouldn't have liked that at all – most undignified.' John was then sent to Hong Kong – 'collecting people who'd been incarcerated by the Japanese,' she says.

Having had a child, Christian could no longer work in the services. She went to stay with her mother for a spell, and then her new mother-in-law, but quickly grew bored. 'I got tired of this and decided to take a job. So I answered an advertisement in *The Times*, which said "Companion/help required". So I said, "Well, I wouldn't be much help with a full-time baby, but I'll be a companion and [accept bed and board, but] I don't want to be paid because I won't be "help".' I went up to the Lake District and we made great friends. She was a really amusing girl; we had a lot of fun. She was young. She didn't have any children, luckily. But she taught me how to do housework, which I'd never been taught by anyone. Frightfully valuable, really. I'd only had to clean my room.'

After the war Christian took care of her daughter, while John remained in the Navy. 'I didn't really take a job of any kind. I didn't really feel able to take a job with a baby,' she says. The couple went on to have three children in total and moved around the world, following John's work. He retired from the Navy around 15 years later, at which point the family moved to Cornwall. The couple went on to have seven grandchildren and 15 great-grandchildren.

One thing Christian remains wistful about is missing out on studying at Oxford University. 'It is a regret, of course,' she says. The lack of further education jarred in the years after the war 'because I was so uneducated,' she says, laughing. 'I had these children; I had to educate them.' Some years later friends persuaded her to re-enter education and she enrolled in a course at the Open University.

Today she lives by the Thames in southwest London. She took up writing at the age of 80 and painting in her nineties. She has just finished writing a new book. 'I just wrote it because I like having something to do,' she says. 'Writing gives me a certain amount of satisfaction.'

Looking back on the war now, she muses: 'I imagine that women were spared a great deal of boredom.' Had she not enlisted, a lengthy residential course in domestic skills likely awaited her between her return from France and university. 'I probably would have had to go to some sort of place where they taught you how to keep a household. I was terribly bored with that idea, so it suited me very well to join the Wrens,' she says.

She developed a greater sense of self-esteem and autonomy through her wartime service than she might have otherwise. 'I became very much more independent for the whole war,' she says, adding that the same held true for all her sex. 'When I left [the Wrens], women were more independent.' She concludes: 'There was a certain amount of freedom one had. It gave you choice and opportunities for doing what you wanted to do.'

# ENDNOTES

1. Lucy Noakes, *Women in the British Army: War and the Gentle Sex, 1907–1948*, p.117.
2. WO 373/55/347, The National Archives; republished online by Pegasus Archives.
3. The Slab, Issue 14, Autumn 2016, p.8.
4. Tim Clark and Nick Cook, *Monopoli Blues* (Unbound Digital, 2018), p.76 (ebook edition).
5. *Ibid.*, p.59.
6. *Ibid.*, p.51.
7. Giles Whittell, *Spitfire Women of World War II* (Harper Perennial, 2008), p.11.
8. Interview in *Legion* magazine by Stephen J Thorne, 5 December 2018.
9. Howman & Cetintas with Gavin Clarke, *Secret Spitfires: Britain's Hidden Civilian Army* (The History Press, 2020), p.119, p.126.
10. Interview, February 2019, for the Juno Beach Centre Association.
11. C.G. Grey, quoted in *A Spitfire Girl: One of the World's Greatest Female ATA Ferry Pilots Tells Her Story* (Frontline Books, 2016), by Mary Ellis and Melody Foreman, p.46.

12. Interview in the *Daily Mirror*, 27 July 2018.

13. Giles Whittell, *Spitfire Women of World War II* (Harper Perennial, 2008), p.10.

14. Interview, February 2019, for the Juno Beach Centre Association.

15. Joy Hunter, *Joy's Journey: A Memoir* (Umbria Press, 2014), p.63.

16. *Ibid.*, p.89.

17. Kenneth Little, LCP Newsletter, 1943.

18. Ben Bousquet and Colin Douglas, *West Indian Women at War: British Racism in World War II* (Lawrence & Wishart Ltd, 1991), p.103.

19. Dalea Bean, *Jamaican Women & the World Wars: On the Front Lines of Change* (Palgrave Macmillan, 2017), p.199.

20. Previously unpublished extracts from an interview conducted in 2005 by Dalea Bean.

21. Dalea Bean, *Jamaican Women & the World Wars: On the Front Lines of Change* (Palgrave Macmillan, 2017), p.204.

22. *Ibid.*, p.195.

23. 'Vicar's wife insults our allies', *Sunday Pictorial*, No 1,343 (6 September 1942), 3. Quoted in Peter Fryer's *Staying Power: The History of Black People in Britain* (Pluto Press, 2018), p.359.

24. David Olusoga, *Black and British: A Forgotten History* (Pan, 2017), p.486.

25. Jeremy A. Crang, *Sisters in Arms: Women in the British Armed Forces during the Second World War* (Cambridge University Press, 2020), p.181.

26. Previously unpublished extracts from an interview conducted in 2005 by Dalea Bean.

27. *Ibid.*

28. Interview conducted in October 2020 with the WRAC Association.

29. Dalea Bean, *Jamaican Women & the World Wars: On the Front Lines of Change* (Palgrave Macmillan, 2017), p.204.

30. Previously unpublished extracts from an interview conducted in 2005 by Dalea Bean.

31. Charlotte Webb, *Secret Postings: Bletchley Park to the Pentagon* (BookTower Publishing, 2014), p.29.

32. *Ibid.*, p.23

33. *Ibid.*, p.59.

34. Interview for the BBC documentary *Britain's Greatest Generation* (2015), directed and produced by Steve Humphries.

35. Taped interview from the 1950s, stored in the Museum of London's oral history archive and transcribed in the book *The War on Our Doorstep: London's East End and How the Blitz Changed it Forever* (Ebury Press, 2012) by Harriet Salisbury, p.253.

36. Sue Elliott and Steve Humphries, *Voices of World War Two: Memories of the Last Survivors* (Cornerstone Digital, 2016), p.117.

37. Taped interview from the 1950s, stored in the Museum of London's oral history archive and transcribed in the book

*The War on Our Doorstep: London's East End and How the Blitz Changed it Forever* (Ebury Press, 2012) by Harriet Salisbury, p.304.

38. Interview for the BBC documentary *Britain's Greatest Generation* (2015), directed and produced by Steve Humphries.

39. Taped interview from the 1950s, stored in the Museum of London's oral history archive and transcribed in the book *The War on Our Doorstep: London's East End and How the Blitz Changed it Forever* (Ebury Press, 2012) by Harriet Salisbury, p.374.

40. Simon Parkin, *A Game of Birds and Wolves: The Secret Game that Won the War* (Sceptre, 2019), p.201

# A NOTE ON THE TEXT

The interviews in this book were conducted primarily by telephone and video call, owing to the constraints of the coronavirus pandemic on travel and physical meetings during the period in which it was researched and written.

The events described, which for the most part took place more than 75 years ago, have been fact-checked where possible. Allowances must be made for minor discrepancies that have crept into recollections during the intervening decades.

The transcripts have been edited in a small number of places to aid clarity.

# PICTURE CREDITS

All photos from contributors' personal collections, with the following exceptions:

## Section 1
Page 1: Photo by Ian Jones/AFP via Getty Images
Page 3 top: Photo by Fox Photos/Getty Images
Page 4 top right: Everett Collection/Bridgeman Images
Page 6 bottom: Universal History Archive/UIG/Bridgeman Images
Page 7 bottom: Trinity Mirror/Mirrorpix/Alamy Stock Photo
Page 8 bottom: The Print Collector/Alamy Stock Photo

## Section 2
Page 2 bottom: PA Images/Alamy Stock Photo
Page 3 bottom: Daily Mirror/Mirrorpix
Page 5 bottom: Photo by SSPL/Getty Images
Page 6 bottom: © Royal Mint Museum/Bridgeman Images
Page 7 bottom: Mirrorpix
Page 8: Mirrorpix

# ACKNOWLEDGEMENTS

I am profoundly indebted to Betty, Catherine, Christian, Connie, Ena, Hilda, Jaye, Joy, Marguerite and Marjorie for their trust and many hours of fascinating conversation. This book has been a pleasure to research and write, and I only hope it does justice to their stories. I am also deeply grateful to Baroness Boothroyd for writing the foreword.

My sincere thanks goes to my agent Max Edwards at Aevitas Creative and to the marvellous team at HarperNon-Fiction: publishing director Kelly Ellis, editor Holly Blood, copyeditor Holly Kyte, publicity director Isabel Prodger, project editor Sarah Hammond, cover designer Caroline Young, and production controller Sarah Burke.

A very special thank you goes to Simon Robinson, whose help, interest and kind encouragement have been invaluable to this project.

Thank you also to all those family members, friends and helpers of the women featured herein, who helped set up interviews, sought out information, and retrieved wartime records, letters, diaries and photographs for me. They are David Warr, Adrian Warr, Ann Cooper, Tim Clark, Will Clark, Dr Lauraine Vivian, Lady Rollo, Catherine Johnstone,

Christine Smith, John Smith, Marguerite Woodstock-Riley QC, Careth Flash and Neil Edwards.

I would also like to acknowledge my gratitude to those who came up with good suggestions for interviewees and helped to connect me, including Hannah Kapff, Timothy Pleydell-Bouverie, Steve Humphries, David Findlay, Cherish Watton, Valentine Low and Brent Richter.

Thanks to Mark Hickman for providing archival material, and to Stephen Bourne for his time and advice.

I am grateful to *The Times* for initially granting me permission to write this book and since moving to *The Daily Telegraph* I am grateful to my new colleagues for their support while finishing it.

A huge thanks goes to my family – my mother Anne, father Angus and brother Jack, as well as Deborah, Neil, Uncle John, Johnny and Georgie – for their encouragement and enthusiasm.

Finally, my deepest thanks goes to my husband Theo, who is my ultimate champion and backed this project from the start. He has talked through countless ideas, read every draft, made myriad improving suggestions and been a source of humour and good cheer throughout.

All errors are my own.

# INDEX